Praise for *Letting Go of the Words*

"Short of having Ginny sitting at your desk helping you think about your site, I can think of nothing better than having this book. The table of contents alone offers detailed guidance for readers, making this book an active resource for day-to-day use – one of my key criteria for a 'usable' book. The wealth of examples makes it easy to see how to apply concepts to your particular situation."

Duane Degler
Principal, Design for Context

"I have been using Ginny's book to teach my Writing for the Web course for the past three years. Students love it because the guidelines in each chapter are straightforward and are well supported by skillfully selected examples. With the addition of various cases and new and updated visual aids in the most recent edition, the book is a valuable teaching resource that helps me organize productive classroom discussions and develop individual and collaborative projects."

Natalia Matveeva, Ph.D.
Assistant Professor, Professional Writing, University of Houston – Downtown

"Ginny's first edition has been right at the top of my 'most valuable books about web sites' list, and I refer to it constantly. It's an excellent resource for anyone planning to create, revise, critique, or contribute to a web site. It looks at all aspects of what makes web sites clear and easy to use. The book itself is a model of good writing and presentation – clear and concise, beautifully formatted, showing as well as telling how to write for the Web. I look forward eagerly to the second edition."

Penny Lane
the Center for Health Literacy at MAXIMUS

"People come to my online writing teams from many different backgrounds. *Letting Go of the Words* has been an indispensible resource for making sure everyone is level set with the basic principles and best practices for online communication. Whether you are writing for a web site, portal, app, blog, or online learning course, you will find tips here that will help you reach your target audience with just the right number of compelling, useful words."

Chris Frederick Willis
CEO, Media 1

"As an experienced technical writer and trainer, I have relied on Ginny's expertise for years. She is an outstanding and pertinent instructor and mentor who shines above all others. I refer other writers to this book and to Ginny's classes. Without fail, she gets rave reviews. I highly recommend *Letting Go of the Words*, which continues to be a most valuable resource in my professional library."

Katey Simetra
Technical writer and trainer for 25 years with Washington state government

My grad students and I love this book. It has given us the key that unlocks the mystery of how to write content for the web: engage in *conversation* with your user. And with an engaging, conversational style, Ginny Redish makes this not only a must-read but an easy, delightful read. A great book for getting started in web writing or for rethinking how to do it from the user's point of view.

Carol Barnum, Ph.D.
Director of Graduate Studies, Information Design and Communication programs
and Director of the Usability Center, Southern Polytechnic State University,
Author of Usability Testing Essentials: Ready, Set . . . Test!

If you want to take your web content to the next level, you need this book. If you're an experienced writer, you'll find tips, hints, and ideas that will help you refocus and improve your writing, and convince your colleagues and clients. If you're new to writing for the web, Ginny will teach you, guide you, and give you confidence that you can create great user experiences by improving your web content. Invaluable.

Caroline Jarrett
Effortmark Ltd, Co-author of *Forms that Work: Designing Web Forms for Usability*

Letting Go of the Words

Letting Go of the Words

2nd Edition

Janice (Ginny) Redish

AMSTERDAM • BOSTON • HEIDELBERG • LONDON
NEW YORK • OXFORD • PARIS • SAN DIEGO
SAN FRANCISCO • SINGAPORE • SYDNEY • TOKYO
Morgan Kaufmann Publishers is an imprint of Elsevier.

Acquisitions Editor: Meg Dunkerley
Editorial Project Manager: Heather Scherer
Production Project Manager: Jessica Vaughan
Designer: Eric DeCicco

Morgan Kaufmann is an imprint of Elsevier
225 Wyman Street, Waltham, MA 02451, USA

Library of Congress Cataloging-in-Publication Data
Redish, Janice.
   Letting go of the words : writing web content that works / Janice (Ginny) Redish. – 2nd ed.
     p. cm.
   Summary: "Learn how to have great conversations through your site or app. Meet your business goals while satisfying your site visitors' needs. Learn how to create useful and usable content from the master – Ginny Redish. Ginny's easy-to-read style will teach you how to plan, organize, write, design, and test your content"– Provided by publisher.
   Includes bibliographical references and indexes.
   ISBN 978-0-12-385930-3 (pbk.)
   1. Web site development. 2. Web sites – Design. 3. Online authorship. I. Title.
   TK5105.888.R427 2012
   006.7–dc23
                                                    2012010668

British Library Cataloguing-in-Publication Data
A catalogue record for this book is available from the British Library.

For information on all MK publications visit our
website at *www.mkp.com*

ISBN: 978-0-12-385930-3

Printed in China

14 15 16   10 9 8 7 6 5 4 3 2

Working together to grow
libraries in developing countries

www.elsevier.com | www.bookaid.org | www.sabre.org

ELSEVIER   BOOK AID International   Sabre Foundation

For Edward F. Redish,
who has always been called "Joe,"
with love and deep appreciation

Contents

Interlude 1: Content Strategy   37

7 Focusing on Conversations and Key Messages 125

Interlude 2: Finding Marketing Moments 151

10 Tuning up Your Sentences   **197**

Foreword

For the past five years, every time I've given a talk about usability I've had a slide near the end to remind me to recommend *Letting Go of the Words*.

Here's what I say when I get to it:

> "This is probably one of the best pieces of advice I can give you:
>
> If you know *anyone* who writes or edits for the Web, they *have to* have a copy of this book."

When I say it, I always see some people nodding their heads in agreement (more with each passing year). To drive the point home, I pick one of them and ask,

> "I'm right, aren't I? It really is a *great* book, isn't it?"

The response is always some very enthusiastic variation of "Yes!"

Personally, I think the first edition was so good that it could have stayed just the way it was for many more years.

And I can tell you from experience that there are two things that strike fear in the heart of any author facing the prospect of writing a second edition:

1. **New topics.** There are always things worth adding – things you've figured out since you wrote it, and things that have suddenly become important to your readers. The problem is working them in. Since it usually feels like a miracle that you got the whole thing to hold together and make sense in the first place, if you do more than just drop a paragraph in here and there, you know there's a good chance you might end up feeling like a kid who's taken a clock apart. Not good.

2. **New examples.** People who haven't written a book full of examples have no idea how hard it is to come up with them. It takes a ridiculous amount of work, so they're precious. Letting an old one go, and finding a new one to replace it, can be a terrifying prospect.

Just thinking about these makes me want to reach for the TV remote.

But not Ginny.

She didn't just throw in a paragraph here and there about SEO, content strategy, accessibility, mobile sites, or social media. She figured out what we really need to know about them, and made them play nicely with all the other concepts she'd already explained so well. She embedded them, like war correspondents.

In fact, she didn't just update the book. She rethought and rewrote the whole darned thing.

Knowing her as I do, I'm afraid it's just a case of too much integrity: She couldn't not do the right thing.[1]

And then there's her pesky passion for wanting the written word to be clear and understandable and accessible for everyone.

Oh, well. Leave it to Ginny to take something so useful and make it even better.

So here's my revised recommendation when I give talks from now on:

> "If you know someone who writes or edits words that appear on a screen, buy them a copy of this book. They'll be your friend for life.
>
> If you own the first edition, give it to a friend and buy this one for yourself. Like *Godfather II*, it's that rarest of creatures: a sequel to something great that's even better than the original."

Steve Krug
Brookline, Massachusetts, April, 2012

------

[1] No, I didn't throw in a double negative just to make Ginny crazy. Even Ginny would acknowledge that saying things clearly sometimes involves bending the rules.

Acknowledgments

Once again, with gratitude to all who helped me bring this book to you:

- Steve Krug for updating the Foreword with his wonderful, kind words
- Kristina Halvorson and Jared Spool for the kind quotes on the back cover
- Duane Degler, Natalia Matveeva, Penny Lane, Chris Frederick Willis, Katey Simetra, Carol Barnum, and Caroline Jarrett for adding their praise
- Kristina Halvorson, Caroline Jarrett, Ahava Leibtag, and Natalia Matveeva for reviewing drafts and offering excellent suggestions
- Jeff Rum for helping with Chapter 3
- Elaine Brofford for once again pointing me to so many great examples (examples desperately in need of letting go of the words and examples that shine by already applying the principles in this book)
- Caroline Jarrett for sharing so much – a detailed review of every page of the book, ideas, examples, case studies, and her time and shoulder when it all got to be too much
- Many others who graciously allowed me to use their material or their photograph, including Carolyn Boccella Bagin, Sarah Bauer, Tom Brinck, Robert Ciconte, Ken Davis, Sarah Horton, Allan Frewin Jones, Dian Lawhon, Mike Lee, Staci Lewis, Cullen McCarty, Suranjan Mukherjee, Jakob Nielsen, Yuna Park, Gina Pearson, Judi Pfancuff, Whitney Quesenbery, Ian Roddis, Jared Spool, and Kathryn Summers.
- The team at Morgan Kaufmann/Elsevier who shepherded the book from proposal to what you hold in your hands:
  - Steve Elliot, Publisher
  - Meg Dunkerley, Acquisitions Editor
  - Heather Scherer, Editorial Project Manager
  - Jessica Vaughan, Associate Project Manager (Production)

- All my clients, colleagues, conference attendees, and workshop participants who have helped me hone my key messages so I can share them with you clearly and concisely
- And, as always, Joe Redish for being there for me

Thanks to all of you (and myriad others who have helped me grow throughout my career) for your encouragement, examples, and support.

Letting Go of the Words is about creating great content for web sites, mobile sites and apps, and social media by thinking of content as conversation.

My goal is to help you give people a successful, engaging experience that satisfies both their needs and yours.

Together, through *Letting Go of the Words*, we'll plan, design, select, organize, write, illustrate, review, and test content.

What's new?

In this second edition, I've emphasized the theme of **content as conversation** even more than I did in the first edition.

- **Content** – Whatever you write, this book is for you. Copywriter? Technical writer? Subject matter expert who contributes content? Author or consultant creating your own web site? Editor? Content curator? Other team members working with content contributors? *Letting Go* is for all of you.

- **Conversation** – Every use of every web site and mobile app is a conversation started by your site visitor. In addition, today, we're all involved in conversations through social media, blogs and news with comments, and recommender sites where people post reviews. We use our smart phones for conversations (whether through text, voice, apps, or web sites).

In the new *Letting Go of the Words*, you'll find lots of guidelines for having great online conversations.

Lots has happened in the digital world since the first edition of *Letting Go of the Words*. In this new edition, you'll find tips and examples for content strategy, mobile, search engine optimization, and social media.

I found room for a chapter on usability testing and other evaluation techniques. Throughout, I didn't just add; I revised. I read every word and checked every example from the first edition. And I have lots of new examples to share with you.

In *Letting Go*, I call the people you are conversing with your "site visitors." I realize they may be "app users" or "people who read my blog" or "people who converse with me in social media." Please allow me to wrap all those phrases into "site visitors." Thanks.

What's the book like?

Let's talk about what this book is and what it is not, as well as about how you might work with it.

Letting Go is about writing and design, not technology

Letting Go of the Words is about strategy and tactics, not about tools. Technology changes too fast to be a major part of the book – and the principles of good writing transcend the technology you use.

Letting Go includes many examples

You'll find many screen shots – often with call-outs to show what works well and what I recommend changing. For many of the examples, I show how I might revise the content. In consulting projects, I work closely with the client to be sure that what I suggest is accurate and consistent with the web site's personality and style. But I haven't worked with all the groups whose sites I show in the book. So, sometimes, my revision is my best guess at what might work well.

Sites and apps change quickly. If you look for an example from the book, it may already differ from what I show. That does not invalidate my example. Even old examples can make excellent learning opportunities.

Letting Go reflects user-experience design

User-experience design (UX) is a philosophy, an approach, and a process for creating products that work well for their users. When you practice UX, you focus on the people who will use what you create: their goals, their needs, their ways of working, and their environments.

When you talk to others, you may hear terms like "reader-focused writing," "usability," and "plain language." To me, those are all names for what we are striving for. They are all part of the same idea; they are all aspects of UX.

You can jump around in the book

A book has to be linear, but you don't have to use it that way. The path I've set is a logical way to move through the book:

* planning (including content strategy), overall design, home pages, pathway pages, and destination pages

- organizing, headlines, headings, writing, lists and tables, links, and illustrations
- getting from first draft to final content, starting an organic style guide, and evaluating your site or app or social media strategy

But that may not be the most logical path for you or your project. Feel free to jump around in the book.

For example, if you are revising a web site, you might want to start with the first two chapters and the first interlude and then jump to the end of the book, doing a usability test of your current site and developing an organic style guide.

Many people tell me they use the book as an ongoing reference. They went all the way through it when they first got it. They come back to it over and over when they have a specific question or need. Some use the table of contents as a checklist. Find your own path through the book. Keep it nearby and use it often.

Let's continue to converse

Questions? Comments?

Write to me through my web site, the Elsevier web site, Twitter, LinkedIn, or other social media – or join me at a conference or webinar.

www.redish.net – includes my blog, a list of events where I'm speaking, and lots more.

http://booksite.mkp.com/redish/lettinggo – includes a link to a site for instructors (sample syllabi and suggestions for exercises)

Twitter: @GinnyRedish

LinkedIn and other social media: Ginny Redish

Content!
Content!
Content!

The theme of this book is content = conversation. My goal is to help you have great conversations through your web site, mobile app, social media, and whatever future innovations encourage interactions between you and others.

People come for the content

People don't come to web sites or mobile apps or social media for the joy of navigating or searching. They don't usually come to admire the design. They don't focus on the technology. They come for the content that they think (or hope) is there.

People come for information that answers their question or helps them complete their task. They want that information to be easy to find, easy to understand, accurate, up to date, and credible.

Effective navigation and search are critical.

Clear and usable design is critical.

Technology that works well is critical.

But these three legs of the stool don't stand by themselves.

Navigation, search, design, and technology support the content. The stool needs a seat to be useful and usable.

Content = conversation

Every use of your web site or mobile app is a conversation started by your site visitor.

That's true whether your site or app is for e-commerce; a nonprofit organization; a government agency; a university; a city, county, state, or country; a recommender system; or your personal blog or site.

Yesterday, I

- looked up the same health question on three different sites to build confidence that I was getting an answer I could trust
- bought a book for my daughter
- compared prices for a new printer for the office
- skimmed hotel reviews for a trip my husband and I are planning
- sent a huge file through an online service

In each case, the most productive way to think about what I was doing is as a conversation.

We converse both by talking and by writing. You may text others more often than you call them. You're still conversing with them.

I need to send a large file.

No problem. Just do it here on my home page.

Send a File *Try it now*

From:
Your email address

To:
Separate multiple emails with commas

SELECT FILE

⊙ **Subject** *(Optional)*
⊙ **Message** *(Optional)*

Pay-per-use options:
☐ Premium Delivery ($9.99)
⊙ More

Preview what your recipient will see.

SEND IT

By clicking on the 'SEND IT' button, you agree to YouSendIt's Terms of Service.

www.yousendit.com

Yesterday, I also

- tweeted about my next workshop
- checked my Twitter stream to see what others were saying
- caught up with a former colleague through LinkedIn
- participated in a global committee meeting on Skype
- read a few of my favorite blogs

Isn't social media all about conversations?

Do you react well when web sites and mobile apps converse with you? I do. Figure 1-1 is the message I get when I leave my Twitter stream open but get caught up in my work.

Figure 1-1 A conversational message from the site I use to read and send tweets
www.hootsuite.com

Web = phone, not file cabinet

Too many sites still seem to be virtual file cabinets, saying to site visitors, "We'll let you rummage around in our file cabinets because we assume you are looking for documents." "File cabinet" is the wrong metaphor for most web sites.

Web = phone (whether you use it for voice or for texting). Web = asking people to serve themselves instead of calling or writing.

File cabinets house documents. We use phones to converse. People seldom come to web sites for documents. They come for information. They come because they have questions. And they are happiest when the web site answers those questions.

To create great web content, you must

- understand the conversations your site visitors want to have with your web site or your app
- satisfy those conversations

- engage your site visitors enough to make them want to continue in the site or app and come back again
- meet your business goals (whether your goal is to sell stuff, to be the major source of information on your topic, or to get more members for your organization)

Online, people skim and scan

Most site visitors are very busy people who want to read only as much as they need to satisfy the goal that brought them to your web site.

We hurry from the home page through pathway (landing, gallery, navigation) pages, reading as little as possible. We jump at the first item in a search results page. Even on an information page, we often skim and scan first to find just what we came for.

Nielsen and Loranger, *Prioritizing Web Usability*, 2006: On average, people in their study left the home page within 30 seconds.

Why? Because we are focused on our own conversation – on the goal that brought us to the site. Navigation and search may be necessary to get there, but that's not where we want to spend time reading.

Home pages – Chapter 4
Pathway pages – Chapter 5

People do read online – sometimes

Do people ever read on web sites and in apps? Of course we do. We read when we find what we came for – the answer to our question, information for the task we came to complete, sometimes labels on the form we are filling out.

On forms as conversations – and everything else about how to create great web forms: Jarrett and Gaffney, *Forms that Work*, 2008

We read social media messages, blog articles, news that interests us. We read to do. We read to learn. We read for fun.

Note, however, how much of this reading is "functional." In this book, I'm not talking about novels, poetry, or games on the web. I'm not talking about the entertainment part of entertainment sites. I am primarily talking about being able to quickly find and understand when the local movie theater is showing the film we want to see or how much it will cost to see a favorite band's next concert.

I'm talking about e-commerce sites, information-rich sites, nonprofit sites, blogs and social media, e-learning, and the information parts of web and mobile applications.

People don't read more because ...

- We are too busy.
- What we find is not relevant to what we need.
- We are bombarded with information and are sinking under information overload.

Writing well = having successful conversations

Good web writing

- answers your site visitors' questions
- lets your site visitors "grab and go" when that's what they want to do
- encourages further use – now or on a return visit
- markets successfully to your site visitors
- improves search engine optimization (SEO)

- improves internal search
- is accessible to all

All those aspects of good web writing are critical because that's the way that you meet your business goals. In this book, I show you how to do all of this. For now, let's just look briefly at each aspect.

Answer your site visitors' questions

On many sites, people come with questions. Answer those questions and you'll have a successful web site.

I'm not advocating making your entire site one large set of frequently asked questions (FAQs). That would be disaster. No one would find what they need.

What I am advocating: For every topic on your site, think about what people come wanting to know about that topic. And then think about how to give them that information as clearly and concisely as possible.

Questions as good headlines – Chapter 8

And as good headings – Chapter 9

Let your site visitors "grab and go"

Site visitors often want to just *grab* what they need and *go* on to look up their next question, do their next task, make a decision, get back to work, or do whatever comes next for them. You can help site visitors grab and go by

- breaking your text into short sections with clear headings
- starting with your key messages
- writing short sentences and short paragraphs
- using lists and tables
- writing meaningful links
- illustrating your content

Breaking up text – Chapter 6

Key messages – Chapter 7

Writing – Chapter 10

Lists and tables – Chapter 11

Meaningful links – Chapter 12

Illustrations – Chapter 13

Encourage further use

 Do you want people to stay on your site? Read other blog articles you've written? Buy more? Come back often?

Clear, concise content that answers people's questions doesn't have to be boring. Tone and style can help you engage site visitors. Making it easy to find related information can keep site visitors on your site. But the most important element of engagement is satisfying the need that brought the customer to your site. Successful experiences make people return.

Market successfully to your site visitors

Whether you are marketing goods, services, information, or memberships, think about the difference between direct mail or email advertising and the web.

- With mail (paper or online), you start the conversation.
- For your web site or app, your site visitor starts the conversation.
- Despite the time and money spent to build it, your site or app "exists" only when someone chooses to go to it. And that changes everything. You have to satisfy what your site visitor came for first. Then you can cross-sell or up-sell.

Marketing on the web – Interlude 2 after Chapter 7

Improve search engine optimization (SEO)

SEO |

Search engine optimization (SEO) means making sure your web site comes up high in the list of nonpaid ("organic") results at Bing, Google, Yahoo, and other search engines. Much of what I am helping you with in *Letting Go of the Words* will also improve SEO for your site.

For tips on SEO, look for the SEO icon throughout the book.

A note about SEO

The SEO advice that you'll find throughout the book is true now at the time I'm writing it. But search engines change their algorithms frequently, so check for the latest specifics at each search engine and in the major blogs about SEO.

Also, I touch only on points about SEO that are relevant to writing the content. SEO covers more than that – another reason for checking other sources about SEO.

What isn't going to change is that the most important key to good SEO is having great content – content that people want; content that includes the words people use when they search; content that people want to share and that other sites want to link to. Every search engine starts its SEO guidelines with this point: Write for people, not for the search engine.

A useful blog to follow for changes in SEO:
www.searchengineland.com

Improve internal search

Getting people to your site is only part of a successful experience. Having them find what they need easily on the site is also critical. Writing clearly *with the words that your site visitors use* is the key to internal search success as well as to success at external search engines.

On how to analyze and learn from what your site visitors search for: Rosenfeld, *Search Analytics for Your Site*, 2011

Be accessible to all

In the United States, somewhere between 36 million and 54 million people have a disability. About 7 million people have vision problems – and this number is growing as the population ages.

Is yours an e-commerce site? These people have money to spend. Are you missing out on having them as customers?

Is yours an information-rich site? Don't you want everyone to benefit from your information?

In the United States, all federal government web sites and any site paid for with federal government money must be accessible to all. Many other countries also require that web sites work for everyone. Think of all your potential site visitors as you design, develop, and write your web site or app.

For advice on how to make your site or app universally usable, look for the accessibility icon throughout the book.

U.S. statistics:
www.disabilitystatistics.org
www.aahd.us

U.K. statistics:
http://odi.dwp.gov.uk/disability-statistics-and-research/

Information about many countries:
www.w3.org/WAI/policy

Information about U.S. law:
www.section508.gov

Universal guidelines:
www.w3.org/WAI

Book on why and how to make sites accessible: Shawn Lawton Henry, *Just Ask*,
http://uiaccess.com/

Three case studies

Content as conversation is a useful mantra for all types of sites. Let's close the chapter with three cases:

- Mint.com where the writers anticipate site visitors' questions at every step of the conversation
- eBags.com where each product page holds great conversations with almost no text
- A city's site where the text is not at all conversational when it should be – and I'll show you how I would rewrite it

Case Study 1-1 | **Conversing well with words**

Mint.com allows you to keep all your financial information in one place and helps you budget and plan – all for free.

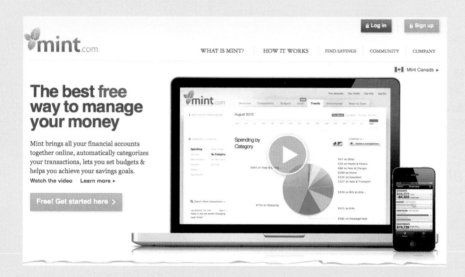

The home page looks clean and fresh (like mint candy – the name is a wonderful double entendre of mint for where money is made, and mint, a refreshing plant). The tag line is vibrant and compelling – the best way to manage your money (and by the way, it's free). Notice how conversational all the writing is on this page: lets you set budgets; helps you achieve your savings goals.

But remember that it's always the site visitor who starts the conversation.

The writers at Mint.com anticipated this conversation from Lisa and Bob. The very first link after the name is What is Mint?

When Lisa clicks on What is Mint? she gets a short, quick answer. (In Chapter 7, you'll see this as a "bite" or "snack" – key message right up front.) And she gets the answers to her follow-on question: Why should I sign up?

Your financial life, all in one place

Free! Get started here >

Mint pulls all your financial accounts into one place. Set a budget, track your goals and do more with your money, for free! **Watch the short video** ▸

Lisa and Bob are intrigued, so they skim down the page. But when they see that Mint is going to automatically capture all their financial data, they become worried.

The Mint.com writers "heard" that question. They acknowledge Lisa and Bob's worry with a section on safe and secure further down the page.

Bank-level security

Mint uses the same 128-bit encryption and physical security that banks use. Our practices are monitored and verified by TRUSTe, VeriSign and Hackersafe, and supported by RSA Security.

No one can move any money

Mint is a "read-only" service. You can organize and analyze your finances, but you can't move funds between—or out of—any account using Mint. And neither can anyone else.

And that makes Lisa and Bob feel good about Mint.com.

This conversational approach – anticipating and answering site visitors' questions – has worked well for Mint.com. Within two years of launch, the site had more than 1.5 million users, managed $50 billion in assets, and helped people track nearly $200 billion in purchases (numbers from http://www.mint.com/history/). And now Mint is part of the Intuit family. Intuit (maker of Quicken, Quickbooks, TurboTax, etc.) has always followed the mantra of product as conversation.

Case Study 1-2   **Conversing well with few words**

eBags.com wants you to buy from them. But site visitors probably have a number of questions about each bag they look at.

No problem. eBags.com has anticipated what site visitors might ask. The site answers all of Paula's questions and more on each product page.

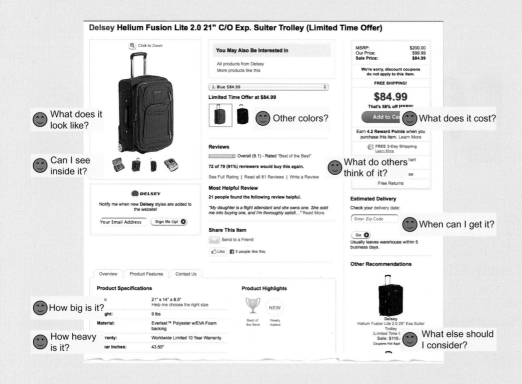

Wow! So much conversation – in so few words! Great customer support in the content. No need to call and ask. The web page is conversing well with eBags' customers. The catalog writers and designers might not have thought of their content as conversation, but that's exactly what it is and why it works so well.

And it works. eBags.com has been the #1 online bag retailer since 1999 (claim at www.ebags.com home page).

Case Study 1-3	Revising web words

Not all sites are as good at conversation as Mint and eBags. If yours is not yet, you may find this example helpful about what not to do and how to fix it.

The situation

Many cities and counties allow residents to participate at meetings of the city or county council or the local school board.

The current site

This city puts the agenda for its meetings online with these instructions.

> ▼ 14. COMMENTS FROM THE FLOOR
>
> a. COMMENTS FROM THE FLOOR: 3-minute time limit per individual; 20-minute time limit per topic
>
> **ITEMS <u>NOT</u> ON THE AGENDA** - Persons wishing to speak to items **not on the agenda** are asked to complete a "Request to Speak" card and present it to the President prior to the meeting. Persons submitting a "Request to Speak" card will be given an opportunity to speak **at this time**.
>
> **ITEMS ON THE AGENDA** - Persons wishing to speak to items **on the agenda** are asked to complete a "Request to Speak" card and present it to the President prior to the meeting. Persons submitting a "Request to Speak" card will be given an opportunity to speak **at the time the item is discussed** by the Board.

What's your reaction to the writing in these paragraphs? Is it inviting? Engaging? As clear as it could be?

What's wrong with this version?

- The information comes too late. (It's Item #14, but you have to have turned in a Request to Speak card before the meeting starts. How many people study all the items on the agenda before a meeting?)
- Instructions are buried in paragraphs.
- It doesn't talk *to* people.
- Information about how long you have comes before information on what this is all about and what you have to do.
- It does not answer a critical question: Where do I get a Request to Speak card?

How can we do better?

1. Get the answer for the missing information.
2. Rewrite it all as lists and as conversation.
3. Move the information so people see it before the meeting and so it is also at the top of a handout people get when they first enter the meeting room.

What might a revision look like?

The title connects to what the site visitor wants to do.

To converse well, we must tell people where to get the card to fill out.

This version makes it clear *when* someone must act.

Instructions are in separate steps.

Bulleted items are easy to grasp quickly.

The information answers people's questions.

If you want to speak at the meeting

Before the meeting starts
1. Get a Request to Speak card from *need to find out where*
2. Fill it out.
3. Give it to the President **before** the meeting starts.

Notes
- Time limit for each speaker: 3 minutes
- Time limit per topic: 20 minutes
- **Item on the agenda**? Your turn to speak will come when the Board is discussing that item.
- **Item not on the agenda**? Your turn to speak will come under Item 14 "Comments from the Floor."

Summarizing Chapter 1

Key messages from Chapter 1:

- People come to web sites to satisfy goals, to do tasks, to get answers to questions.
- Navigation, search, design, and technology support the content that people come for.
- The best metaphor for the web is phone, not filing cabinet.
- Every use of your web site is a conversation started by your site visitor.
- Social media is pushing the web to be even more conversational.
- To have good conversations through your web site:
  - Answer your site visitors' questions throughout your web content, not only in sections called frequently asked questions.
  - Let your site visitors "grab and go."
  - Engage your site visitors.
  - Market successfully to your site visitors by first satisfying the conversation they came to have.
  - Improve search engine optimization (SEO) and internal site search.
  - Be accessible to all.

Planning: Purposes, Personas, Conversations

2

Successful writers don't start by writing. They plan before they write (and they plan while they write and through all their revisions).

At every level and for every piece of content (entire site, web page, mobile app or site, social media message, blog article), start by asking yourself:

- Why?
- Who?
- What's the conversation?

Your site = you = one side of the conversation. You have to know what you want that conversation to accomplish.

Your site visitor = the other side of the conversation. To have successful conversations with your site visitors, you must understand them and what they need and want.

Why? Know what you want to achieve

You may want to make money, reduce phone calls, increase phone calls, have people be able to access the site wherever they are and whenever they want, or have people come to your site before any others for your topic.

Planning is part of developing a content strategy. See Interlude 1 right after this chapter.

You might call what I'm covering here your creative brief.

As you state your goals,

- focus on what you want your site visitors to do
- be specific

Focus on what you want your site visitors to do

To meet your goals for the site, you must help site visitors have successful experiences. Put your goals in terms of what your site visitors should do. A few examples of what I mean:

 We want to sell a lot of shoes.

 We want people to buy shoes from us.

 We want to give out a lot of information on this topic.

 We want to answer people's questions about this topic.

 We want to increase subscriptions.

 We want site visitors to feel so engaged with us that they subscribe.

The differences here may seem subtle. But the shift of focus will help you change from only thinking about what you have to say to thinking about how to have successful conversations with your site visitors.

Be specific

When asked to explain why they are putting up a web site or specific web content, most people speak in generalities: to inform, to persuade, to educate. That's fine as a start. But it's not enough to help you select the right content or to organize and write that content so it engages and satisfies your site visitors.

Be specific. Fill in this sentence: I'm writing this so that (who?) (can do what?).

Kenneth W. Davis gives us a good example in the blog post I've included as Figure 2-1.

> **THIS WEEK: START WITH PURPOSE**
>
> If a coworker interrupts us while we're writing a letter and asks, "What are you doing?" most of us will answer "Writing a letter."
>
> That answer reveals a focus on the written product, not on its purpose. Such product-focused thinking keeps our writing from being as effective as it could be.
>
> This week, when you start each writing job, take a few seconds to think about your purpose—about what effect you want to have on your reader. This week, if a coworker interrupts your writing and asks what you're doing, be prepared to answer (for example), "I'm trying to get this customer to forgive us for a shipping mistake we made."

Figure 2-1 Being specific about your purpose helps you write well. www.manageyourwriting.com (Nov. 21, 2011)

Think of SEO

SEO | For most sites, coming up high in search engine results is very important. You probably want to have it on your list of purposes: We want people to find us easily in organic (not paid for) search results.

Think of universal usability

 Making your site work for all site visitors is good business. It should always be one of your purposes: We want everyone to be able to use our site easily.

Know your purposes for everything you write

You will have overall purposes for your site or app or blog. You will have even more specific purposes for each part of the site, for each piece of content, for each blog article, for each part of a mobile app, for each social media message. Always ask: What do I want to happen because I wrote this?

Who? What's the conversation?

A web site needs visitors. If no one comes to your site, all the effort you took to design and write it is for naught.

A web site is successful only if site visitors can

- find what they need
- understand what they find
- act appropriately on that understanding
- do all that in the time and effort that they are willing to spend

Understanding your site visitors and their needs is critical to deciding what to write, how much to write, the vocabulary to use, and how to organize the content on your web site.

And you must remember the first law of creating successful user experiences:

We are not our users!

You may be an early adopter of new technology, eager and engaged in all manner of social media. But your typical site visitors may not be. You have to know about and understand how to meet their needs because the only way to meet your business goals is to satisfy your site visitors.

> **This is my definition of both usability and plain language. See** www.usability.gov, www.plainlanguage.gov, **and** www.centerforplainlanguage.org.

We all interpret as we read

People aren't just passive receptacles into which writers can pour information. Even when we think that we share the same language, it isn't entirely the same. We may not know the same words. We may have different meanings for the same words.

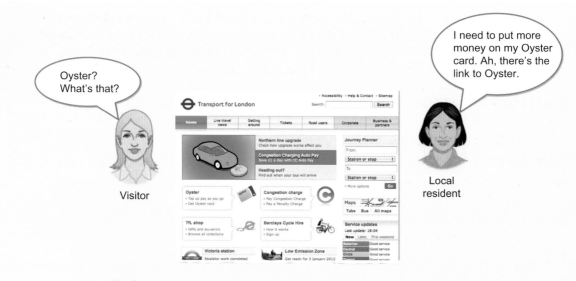

All of us interpret what we read in light of our own knowledge and experiences. (In case you don't live in London: An Oyster card is a prepaid travel card for public transportation.)

You can find out lots about your site visitors

Later in this chapter, I'll show how to turn data about your site visitors into personas and scenarios. First, let's talk about how to get that data.

To understand your site visitors, start with these four steps, which you'll probably cycle through a few times.

1. Gather information about your site visitors.

2. List groups of site visitors.

3. List major characteristics for each group.

4. Understand the conversations they want to start.

1. Gather information about your site visitors

You can start to understand your site visitors by thinking about them. But that's not enough. To really understand who they are, why they come to your site, what they need, and how to write web content for them, you have to know them and their realities.

If you write your web content based only on what you *think* your site visitors are like, you will be writing from *assumptions*. If your assumptions are wrong, your content won't work.

Here are several suggestions for finding out about your site visitors. They are all valuable, but best is actually watching, listening to, and talking with current or potential site visitors. That gives you a truer picture than any of the just thinking techniques or information filtered through other people.

For many techniques for understanding your users: Courage and Baxter, *Understanding Your Users*, 2004

- **Think about your mission.** Whom are you supposed to serve? What are you supposed to help them accomplish?

- **Read the emails** that come through Contact Us and other feedback links. Who is writing? What are they asking?

- **Read feedback** from your web pages. (Give people an easy way to send feedback on your web pages.)

- **Read reviews, recommendations, blogs** that mention your site, your topics, or where your site visitors are likely to express themselves.

- **Talk to colleagues in Customer Service.** Who is calling with questions? What are those questions?

- **Talk to colleagues in Marketing.** Whom are they targeting?

- **Talk to colleagues in Usability and User Experience.** What have they already learned in their user research?

- **Analyze your site search logs.** See what site visitors are trying to find through your site's Search box. See the words they are using to find what they need.

- **Use web analytics.** Learn where people are coming from, where they go on your site, how long they stay, when and where they leave, and the words they search with at Google and other search engines. Web analytics give you interesting facts. However, they don't explain "why?" Did people leave a page quickly because it was wonderful and gave them just what they needed? Or did they leave quickly because their first glance told them it would not help them?

- **Use social media.** Participate in relevant online discussion groups and communities where you can raise questions to people like your site visitors.

- **Track social media conversations** that mention you, your brand, your company, your site.

- **Get people who come to the site to fill out a short questionnaire**. Ask people a few questions about themselves, why they came to the site, and whether they were successful in finding what they came for.

- **Interview people** who use or might use your web site. Use these techniques:
  - **Contextual interviewing** (watch and listen as people work)
  - **Critical incident interviewing** (ask people to tell you their stories of specific times when they used the site)

- **Watch and listen to people in other places.**
  - If your web site mirrors a brick-and-mortar business, observe and listen to customers in the physical location.
  - If yours is a government site, realize that government agencies often have "brick-and-mortar" equivalents. Spend time in a local office of the agency, watching and listening for whatever is relevant to your web content.
  - If your site is for a nonprofit with projects, programs, and grants, go see what your grantees' lives are really like. You may see that they have technology challenges and very hectic days. You may hear what topics are most important to them, what they value, what words they use. If you can't go out in the field yourself, talk to people who spend time with your grantees.

- **Do usability testing of the current content**. Watch and listen to people as they work with your site. You can have them show you tasks they

On analyzing site search logs: Rosenfeld, *Search Analytics for Your Site*, 2011

On using web analytics: Kaushik, *Web Analytics, 2.0*, 2009

On designing surveys: Dillman, Smyth, and Christian, *Internet, Mail, and Mixed-Mode Surveys*, 2008

On contextual interviewing: Holtzblatt, Wendell, and Wood, *Rapid Contextual Design*, 2005; also http://www.usabilitybok.org/methods/contextual-inquiry

On critical incident interviewing: http://en.wikipedia.org/wiki/Critical_Incident_Technique; also http://www.usabilitybok.org/methods/p2052

On watching, listening to, and talking with people at their work or home: Hackos and Redish, *User and Task Analysis for Interface Design*, 1998

Usability testing – Chapter 15

commonly do. You can give them tasks to try. Don't only test the navigation. Watch them work with information pages and application pages. Also ask them about themselves, their needs, and their ways of using content.

2. List groups of site visitors

One way is to ask: "How do people identify themselves with regard to my web content?" For example:

- patients, health care professionals, researchers
- parents, teachers, students
- passengers, pilots, mechanics, airport operators

Another way is to ask: "What about my site visitors will help me know what content the web site needs and how to write that content?" This may lead to listing

- experienced travelers, occasional travelers
- local residents, tourists
- lookers, bookers
- shoppers, browsers

Notice that when I list these user groups, I'm always referring to people – to human beings. Don't get caught up in naming departments, institutions, or buildings as users of your site.

 Don't say that you are writing for "Finance." Finance may be a department with many people who have different jobs, different knowledge, and different needs from your web site.

3. List major characteristics for each group

As you find out about the people who come (or should come) to your web site, list relevant characteristics for each of your user groups. Here are some categories to cover:

- key phrases or quotes
- experience, expertise
- emotions
- values
- technology

- social and cultural environments; language
- demographics (age, ability, and so on)

Key phrases or quotes

If you asked your site visitors what they want you to keep in mind about them as you write to them, what would they say?

Experience, expertise

What do your site visitors know about the subject matter? How technical should your vocabulary be?

For example, travel sites (like Travelocity, Figure 2-2) have been hugely successful partly because they don't force travelers to know airline jargon.

You may have groups with vastly different experience and expertise. You may have a range of expertise even within one type of site visitor. If you do, it's critical to know about those differences so you can decide how to meet the needs of all your site visitors. For example, the U.S. National Cancer Institute has two sets of information about every type of cancer: for patients, for health professionals (Figure 2-3).

Even for experts, conversational style and simple words work best. See the research by Summers and Summers, 2005. I show data from that research in Chapter 10.

"Search for flights" connects to what the site visitor wants to do

Form = conversation. Each step is a question.

You can type in the airport name. No need to know a code.

If you drive part way, you just type the new airport name. No need to know this is an "open jaw" ticket.

Not sure who count as a "minor" or a "senior"? The site explains with just a few numbers.

Search for flights

1 What type of trip are you planning?
○ Round-trip   ○ One-way   ⊙ **Multi-destination**

2 Where would you like to go?
Flight #1
From: _find airport_   To: _find airport_   Depart:
Washington Dulles   Miami, Florida   mm/dd/yyyy [ ] [Anytime ⇕]

Flight #2
From: _find airport_   To: _find air_
Orlando, Florida   Washington Dulles

Select a Date: [Close]
          previous month
August 2012		September 2012
Su Mo Tu We Th Fr Sa		Su Mo Tu We Th Fr Sa
1 2 3 4		1
5 6 7 8 9 10 11		2 3 4 5 6 7 8
12 13 14 15 16 17 18		9 10 11 12 13 14 15
19 20 21 22 23 24 25		16 17 18 19 20 21 22
26 27 28 29 30 31		23 24 25 26 27 28 29
		30
          next month

Flight #3
From: _find airport_   To: _find airport_

Flight #4
From: _find airport_   To: _find air_
          mm/dd/yyyy [ ] [Anytime ⇕]

3 How many travelers? (up to 6)
Adults (18-64) [1 ⇕]   Minors (2-17) [0 ⇕] ⍰   Seniors (65+) [0 ⇕]

4 Do you have travel preferences?
Class: [Economy ⇕] ⍰   Fare Type: [All Types ⇕] ⍰
Airline: [Search all airlines ⇕] ⍰   ☐ Only show non-stops ⍰

Figure 2-2 To converse well, you must understand your site visitors' expertise (and lack of expertise).
www.travelocity.com

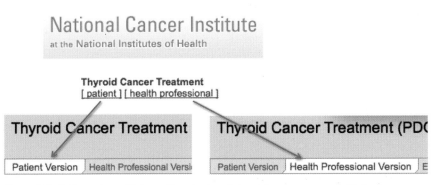

Figure 2-3 Both versions of information about each type of cancer are available to everyone, but they have different levels of detail and use different words.
www.cancer.gov

Emotions

In many situations, people's emotions are important characteristics for you to keep in mind. Your site visitors might be

- fun-loving
- passionate
- intrigued

- curious
- impatient
- angry
- deadline-driven
- nervous
- anxious
- frustrated
- skeptical
- stressed
- pressured

 In Chapter 7, we'll consider writing for injured workers who are checking on their worker's compensation claims. What would you say about their emotional state?

Did you say: Anxious, nervous, skeptical about whether the agency really wants to help them?

If reporters are a major group of site visitors for you, what would you put down for them? Did you say: Deadline-driven, impatient?

What about people seeking help with a product problem (like a paper jam in the printer)? Did you say: Angry, frustrated, anxious?

If the web site focuses so strongly on marketing messages that information about customer service is hard to find, will that only frustrate these site visitors more? If your content about the problem is in convoluted, technical language, will that only make them angrier?

And what will they do if the web content doesn't help? Call up – and cost the company more money? Buy someone else's product next time? Write a scathing review on social media sites?

Web content for people who are angry, frustrated, anxious, or stressed has to be particularly clear and simple.

Values

Knowing what matters to your site visitors may help you decide what content to include and what to focus on or emphasize in the content. Knowing their values may help you understand why they don't want to read much, why letting go of the words and writing in clear, conversational style matches their needs.

When I have a customer on the phone, and I can't understand what I find on our policy web site, I'm frustrated.

Price is important to me. When I shop online, I need to know shipping costs early.

I hope I can trust what I'm reading on this health site. I'm going to be making some pretty important decisions based on this.

Technology

What resolutions are your site visitors working at? What speeds are they connecting with? How steady is their connection? Do they pay for every minute they are on? Are most site visitors coming to your site on a smart phone? Answers to those questions will affect your web content.

Despite the tremendous growth of broadband, it is not universal. In many places, people pay for each minute of connection – they don't have unlimited access for a monthly charge.

And, of course, today you must design for screen sizes from large monitors down to small phones.

Also, of course, you can use web analytics to find information for your specific site, including what browsers your site visitors are using.

Technology changes so fast that any statistics I put here would soon be out of date. So instead of numbers, here are some web sites you can check to track technology issues like broadband, typical resolutions, and more: http://www. websiteoptimization.com/bw, http://www.w3schools.com/ browser/browsers_display.asp

Social and cultural environments and language ("context of use")

You should also understand where and when people come to your content.

Are your typical site visitors likely to be

- alone or with someone else?
- in an office cubicle or at home or at the public library or walking down the street looking at their smart phone?
- in a different country or from a culture that is different from yours (even within the same country)? How well do they know the language of your site?

Are your typical site visitors likely to be

- coming directly to your site or coming through a search engine like Google? (If so, search engine optimization (SEO) will be a very important consideration.)
- very interested in participating in social media, user-generated content, and interactivity? Or would they rather just find static information or complete a task?

Are your typical site visitors likely to be

- interrupted as they work with your information? (This might be true for most office workers. It's also likely to be true for a parent shopping from home while the kids are playing.)
- on your site for a long time every day? (This would be the case for some applications.)
- answering questions for someone else, so they might have someone on the phone waiting for the answer while they try to get that answer from your content? (This would be the case with the customer service group in an e-commerce environment, for example.)

Demographics

Age may matter for your site. If you are writing content for a particular age group – for example, for young children or for teens – that will likely affect your writing style as well as the design of your site.

But age isn't all there is to demographics. Recent studies of older adults have shown how diverse the audience of 50+ or even 65+ is. Even within the older adult audience, you have to think about differences in computer and web expertise (aptitude), in feelings about the web (attitude), and in ability (vision and other problems).

On designing mobile sites for children: Druin, *Mobile Technology for Children*, 2009

On understanding older adults and the web, see the resources listed on my web site at http://redish.net/articles-slides/articles-slides-older-adults

Also remember that if you see a statistic such as 75% of 16- to 24-year-olds are active on social media sites, that means that 25% are not!

4. Understand the conversations they want to start

All of the ways I listed earlier for finding out about your site visitors give you information about both *who* they are and *why* they come to your web site. Let me add two more guidelines for helping you get your site visitors' stories.

Don't translate

As you gather people's questions, tasks, and stories, note *their* words. Don't rewrite what they say into your jargon.

Finding out the words site visitors use to describe what they want and need is critical. Then you'll have their vocabulary to use in your content.

Analyze site searches

One way to see site visitors' words is to analyze the words they use to search at your site. Site search analysis does not tell you *who* but does tell you *what* site visitors are trying to find – in their words.

Breathing life into your data with personas

When you've done the user research we've talked about so far in this chapter, you'll have a lot of facts about your site visitors. But it may be hard to imagine real people in the facts you've gathered. Do the facts seem dry? Do they lack "human interest" – a real sense of the people your content is for?

A great way to bring your web or app users "alive" for yourself and your team is to create personas.

What is a persona?

A persona is an individual with a name, a picture, specific demographics, and other characteristics. A persona is, however, not usually based on one actual individual. Rather, each persona is a composite of characteristics of real people in the group the persona represents.

A very important point: As you create your personas, you must be true to the data you have so that the personas represent your site visitors – not you.

Alan Cooper popularized personas in design. Cooper, Reimann, and Cronin, *About Face 3*, 2007

On personas: Adlin and Pruitt, *The Essential Persona Lifecycle*, 2010; Mulder, *The User Is Always Right*, 2007; Pruitt and Adlin, *The Persona Lifecycle*, 2006; http://www.usability.gov/methods/analyze_current/personas.html

Figure 2-4 introduces you to Win, one of nine personas that The Open University in the United Kingdom (OU) has for potential students whom they want to serve.

More OU personas at http://www8.open.ac.uk/about/ebusiness/strategies/accessibility-and-usability/personas

Win, turn my job into a career

The Open University

Tell us a bit about yourself	I'm 32, I'm married with two children: Lewis, 10 and Florence, 7. We live in Cardiff. Since Lewis was a baby, I've been working as a registered childminder but my current kids are going to school next year so I'm really looking for a job now.
Have you got any qualifications?	National Childminding Association - Diploma for the Children and Young People's Workforce
What is your ambition?	I love working with children, but being a childminder at home doesn't pay well. I want to turn that into a career.
Why didn't you go to university?	Where I lived, you were pleased to survive school and we didn't come out with anything. It was hard enough to get any type of job, never mind uni.
What do you want to know?	How many hours per week? How long will it take? How will it help my career?
How did you find out about the OU?	I searched for 'early years distance learning'

Segment: Not Employed Adults (C2)
- 24-49
- Not employed
- Considering HE
- No OU experience
- No degree
- Progress career

Figure 2-4 The OU team developed these personas from interviews with more than 140 potential students.
(Photo ©Ronald Summers/Shutterstock.com. Persona used with permission of Ian Roddis, Head of Online Services, The Open University, and the rest of the team that did the user research and developed the personas: Sarah Allen, Caroline Jarrett, Whitney Quesenbery, and Viki Stirling.)

Figure 2-5 on page 31 introduces you to Edith, one of eight personas from AARP (the U.S. organization that invites everyone 50 and older to join).

What makes up a persona?

To make the abstract information into a persona, add a picture and name. Then, extract the key points from the data you collected.

Picture and name

You know you have a good picture and a good name when they resonate with your web team. Be sure to select a picture and name that make the team respect the persona. Funny or cute names are signs of disrespect. You must have good conversations with your personas to write web content that will make good conversations with your actual site visitors.

Edith

- 73 years old
- retired restaurant owner
- now lives in Miami
- married almost 50 years to Doug
- limited income
- four children, ten grandchildren

"I love getting pictures of the grandkids in email, but I don't understand how the kids make that happen."

"My son, Jerry, showed me how to print out the pictures. I always follow just what he said to do."

Typical web tasks:

- email
- find health information for herself and Doug and sometimes for friends
- get information for travel — she hasn't yet actually bought online, even though the kids do it all the time and say it's very safe

Edith didn't even know there was an AARP web site until she saw something about it in the AARP magazine. The magazine said there was more travel information on the web site, and Edith likes to plan trips that include visiting grandchildren and also doing some sightseeing.

Edith and Doug get by on Social Security and what they got when they sold the restaurant.

They put down a lot of cash for their small retirement house to keep the payments low.

Edith and Doug are enjoying retirement. They like the slow pace (especially after all those hectic years in the restaurant). They like the sunshine and the social life.

Edith is a cautious web user.

She checks her email regularly because the children are so busy that they don't come to visit or call as often as she would like — but they do send email.

Edith uses hearing aids and glasses. She took off the glasses for the picture, but she needs them to read or look at the computer. She has slight arthritis in her hands, so sometimes using the mouse is a problem.

Figure 2-5 Edith represents the older (but not oldest) retired part of AARP's site visitors. (Used with permission)

You can buy or license stock photography, but many teams find that casual, personal photos are better than photos of models. You may find appropriate pictures at photo sharing sites like Flickr. Just be sure the picture is being shared under the Creative Commons license that gives permissions for the way you will use the photo.

Photos of friends or family often work well, but don't use a picture of someone the team knows. They'll find it too hard to talk about "Jack" if they know it's really a picture of Lisa's brother Mike. Also, be sure to have the person's permission to use the photo.

Demographics

Demographics (age, family status, education level, and so on) are important, both to identify which groups of site visitors the persona represents and to make the persona "real" to everyone.

Quotes, values, stories, tasks, and more

Use the data you gathered. Include whatever is going to be important to the team as they design and write. In this chapter, you see just a few of many ways to present personas:

- Win's persona has questions and answers.
- Edith's persona has a quote, a bulleted list, and a short narrative.
- The posters for Ari, Valerie, and Susan (Figure 2-6 on page 33) have different colored backgrounds to help distinguish them.

How many personas?

Most of the web sites I have helped have several primary site visitor groups and, therefore, find they need more than one major persona.

- As you just saw, the OU has nine personas for potential students. AARP has eight personas for its members and potential members.
- Gina Pearson's group at the U.S. Energy Information Administration has six personas, including one for Data Hound, a software robot.
- Ahava Leibtag helped Sharath Cherian and his team develop six personas for HipHopDX, a site for new hip hop music, news, and all things rap and hip hop.

 You may want to have a persona who uses assistive technology, such as a screen-reader or screen magnifier. Although the persona's special need will be only one of many special needs among all your potential site visitors, your persona (for example, someone with vision problems) will remind the web team to always make sure that everything on the site is accessible to everyone.

How do personas work with a web team?

For your home page, you probably need to keep all your personas in mind. For a specific web page, you may be conversing with only one or a few of the site's personas.

Personas become members of your web team. Figure 2-6 shows how one team keeps their persona in clear view as they work.

Figure 2-6 Gina Pearson, Staci Lewis, and Robert Ciconte keep their personas with them as they plan and design.
(U.S. Energy Information Administration; Used with permission)

Instead of talking generically about "users" for your web content, you start talking about your personas by name.

- What questions will Kristin ask about these shoes we want her to buy?

- When Sanjay comes to this web site, will he search or navigate? What search terms will he use to get to the content I am writing?

These are just a few of the ways that personas have become members of web teams:

- Personas come to team meetings as life-size cardboard cutouts.

- Personas' pictures and information hang on the wall in the team's work space. The social media strategist for HipHopDX has done that, and Ahava Leibtag (their content strategy consultant) says that contributed to their 47% increase in traffic in the past year.

- Personas' pictures and information are printed on place mats or mouse pads so that they are on the table at meetings and in team members' work spaces.

- Emails from personas and about them circulate in the team.

Breathing life into your data with scenarios

Your persona descriptions should include the persona's most common reasons for coming to your web site. (Look back at Win and Edith.)

As you plan your web content, however, you should move from simple lists of goals, tasks, and questions to scenarios (stories, conversations). Scenarios give life to these lists in the same way that personas give life to other data about your site visitors.

On storytelling for designing great user experiences: Quesenbery and Brooks, *Storytelling for User Experience*, 2010

How long? How many?

Scenarios can be as short as the two sentences in each bubble below or as long as the stories about Mark and Mariella on the next pages.

If you have developed one or more major personas for your site, you should have several scenarios for each of them.

Scenarios for whom?

You may also want to have scenarios for a few secondary personas. For example, if your main personas are frequent shoppers and casual shoppers but you also have investors and reporters coming to the site, you may want to do "mini-personas" for them along with their scenarios.

 Do the mini-personas with scenarios in Figures 2-7 and 2-8 give you a sense of these people and their lives? Would they be helpful to you in creating web sites for people like them?

How do scenarios relate to content?

Everything on your web site should relate to at least one scenario, one conversation that a site visitor would want to start. If no one needs or wants the information – if there is no plausible site visitor's conversation

Mark Williams is a sales coordinator for one of the divisions of FGH Corporation. His job, like that of most of his friends, includes many different responsibilities. He often feels as if he's juggling tasks all day long.

Today he's trying to put together some projections that his boss wants "immediately." But Mark also has to deal with questions that his staff can't handle on their own, and that often involves looking up policies on the company's intranet.

The telephone just interrupted Mark's work on the projections for his boss. It's Anu Pati out in the field negotiating a deal with a client. Anu needs to know whether company policy allows her to offer volume discounts to this client and what those discounts can be.

Mark needs to find the right policy quickly both to keep Anu and her potential client happy and because he wants to get back to the job for the boss. He also hopes the policy is clearly stated so he and Anu are both confident they are giving the client correct information.

Figure 2-7 A scenario for developing an intranet site

Don and Mariella Garcia just had their second baby so they need a bigger car. Don's construction work is going well, but Mariella is staying home for a while, so they're worried about money. They're going to need a loan to buy the new car and they want a good deal.

Mariella knows about computers and the web from the job she was doing before she got married. But she can only go look on the web in spurts – when the children are napping or late at night when Don can look with her. And then they are both very tired.

They're not financial experts; they don't know all the banking terms that some of these sites use. They're trying to find a site with good loans that talks to them with words they understand.

Figure 2-8 A scenario for developing a banking or credit union site

for the content – why have it on the site? It's only taking up server space and perhaps showing up in search results where it distracts people from what they really need.

Scenarios can help you

- realize how goal-oriented most site visitors are
- focus on what is important to your site visitors
- write your content as conversation
- write with your site visitors' words

Summarizing Chapter 2

Key messages from Chapter 2:

- Planning your content is critical for apps, web sites, individual web topics, blogs, social media messages – everything you write.

- Planning means asking: Why? Who? What conversations?

- To have successful conversations, you have to know
  - what you want to achieve through your content
  - who you are conversing with
  - what they want from your app, your site, your topic, your message; what task they want to accomplish

- List all your purposes. Try to make them measurable.

- Understand that your readers are not blank slates. We all interpret as we read, bringing the baggage of our past experience and our own understanding of what words mean.

- Know your readers.
  - You have many ways to learn about your site visitors.
  - Gathering data from real sources from analytics to social media to site visits and usability testing is much better than making assumptions about your site visitors.

- List major characteristics for each group of site visitors, including:
  - key phrases or quotes
  - experience, expertise
  - emotions
  - values
  - technology
  - social and cultural environments and language
  - demographics

- Gather site visitors' questions, tasks, and stories.

- Use your information to create personas.

- Use your information to write scenarios.
  - Scenarios tell you the conversations people want to start.
  - Everything on your site should fulfill a scenario.
  - Scenarios can help you write good content.

Between the first edition of *Letting Go of the Words* and this one, the words "content strategy" exploded into the web development world. The first conference devoted to content strategy was in 2010 in Paris. Now there are several around the world each year. Content strategy "meetups" gather every month in many cities. The phrase "content strategy" yields 1.5 million results in a Google search.

Of course, content strategy isn't entirely new. It's been a growing practice for at least a decade. And many people who now call themselves "content strategists" had been doing that work for even longer with other job titles.

Why is content strategy so important?

Content strategy

- provides your site visitors with consistent messages
- builds credibility through that consistency
- strengthens the brand
- keeps writers on purpose, on message
- keeps the web site from being cluttered with outdated and inaccurate information

What is content strategy?

Following good practice in clear writing, let's turn the two nouns into a verb phrase:

Content strategy = thinking strategically about your content

Thinking strategically means that instead of letting everyone post whatever content they want when they want with whatever messages they want, all the content on your web site is part of your overall business plan. Content strategy also means:

Aligning your content with your business goals

More on content strategy:
Halvorson and Rach, *Content Strategy*, 2nd edition, 2012

Bloomstein, *Content Strategy at Work*, 2012

Rockley, *Managing Enterprise Content*, 2nd edition, 2012

Kissane, *The Elements of Content Strategy*, 2011

Handley and Chapman, *Content Rules*, 2011

Find a Content Strategy MeetUp near you, www.meetup.com

Content strategy brings what we talked about in Chapters 1 and 2 – focusing on the people who are conversing with you – together with a deeper look into your company or organization or yourself.

Content strategy is about governance

Content strategy means that all the content is not only created (or repurposed or revised); it is also

- planned
- coordinated
- reviewed regularly
- managed and maintained with someone in charge
- removed when it becomes outdated

Content strategy is about messages, media, style, and tone

To have a content strategy, you must answer questions like these:

- What are the organization's key messages?
- What are the key messages of each piece of content, and how does that piece fit into the overall strategy?
- What mix of media will you use?
- What style guide will you use or create?
  - How formal or informal will the writing style be? (It can all be the same, but it does not have to be. You can have different styles and tones for different groups of site visitors. You can change style and tone among your regular site, your mobile apps, your social media. Content strategy means that you plan those differences, so writers know which style to use in each case.)
  - What guidelines will you have about illustrations and other visuals? About use of video? Use of music and other audio?

Content as conversation is a strategic choice for messages, style, and tone.

Content strategy is about people, processes, and technology

Part of planning for your content is understanding roles and skills:

- Who will write? Edit? Illustrate? Produce? Publish?

- Who will be in charge of social media? How active will you be in social media groups or in engaging with people who comment on your blogs?
- Who will decide on future content and keep up the strategy?
- What skills do these people need?

It is also about how you will make the strategy work.

- How will these different people work together?
- What systems will you use?
- What training will you give people in the strategies, processes, and technology you expect them to use?

Content strategy is about purposes, personas, and scenarios

Everything in Chapters 1 and 2 goes into your content strategy.

AAA
ACCESS   As you develop your content strategy remember the needs of all your site visitors. Plan for both usability and accessibility.

Content strategy supports and carries out business strategy

Your content strategy must be part of an organization-wide business strategy that links all the ways you touch the people you care about (e-commerce customers, nonprofit or professional society members, citizens and visitors, etc.). That means brand strategists, business strategists, documentation strategists, marketing strategists, social media strategists, web content strategists (and probably more) all have to work together.

What does content strategy cover?

Content is everything you have on your web site:

- text (copy)
- illustrations
- charts
- graphs
- tables
- forms

- PDFs
- videos
- podcasts
- blogs
- forums
- other social media

Develop your content strategy first, and let that drive your system choices – not the other way around! A content management system (CMS) should support and facilitate your content strategy. The CMS should not drive and constrain the strategy.

Content strategy includes all communication channels

Content is also everything you have in print, emails, social media outside of your web site (for example, Twitter, LinkedIn, Facebook, Google+, recommender systems), and more. Your web site is only one of the ways you converse with your customers. Developing a content strategy for your web site may be all you can manage at first. But to be truly successful, a content strategy should include all your communication channels.

Web, print, direct-mail marketing, digital advertising, email that people sign up for, blogs, and messages through social media should all support each other and support the organization's brand values and message architecture. You may use a different mix of copy, pictures, and video in these different channels. You may use different styles and tones. But those choices should be deliberate – that's what "strategy" is all about. And "content = conversation" always applies.

"Message architecture" is Margot Bloomstein's term for your communication goals in priority order (Bloomstein, *Content Strategy at Work*, 2012).

Social media strategy is part of content strategy

As part of your content strategy, you'll want to think strategically about how you use blogs and social media:

- Who will blog? Will you take comments? Will you moderate comments? Will someone respond to comments?
- Will you invite or allow others as guests on your blogs?
- Will you place guest content on other blogs? In other places that accept user-generated content?
- What social media will you use? How will you use each?
- Will you form groups within social media? How will you use them?
- Where will the resources come from to write for, monitor, and moderate the social media that the organization participates in?
- What rules or guidelines will you give people within the organization who are responsible for or have permission to participate in these social media? For example, you might want guidelines for
  - how frequently people within the organization should post to each blog or other social media

- what topics are desired, what topics writers should avoid
- how colloquial the style can or should be in different social media

 Search engine optimization is part of content strategy

Your content strategy should include:

- guidelines for achieving the best SEO you can
- what you know at this point about relevant keywords for different parts of your content
- how you will continue to monitor how you are doing and how you will update your SEO strategy

Who does content strategy?

As with so many aspects of creating great web sites, many different backgrounds can be starting points for content strategists. People doing content strategy today have expanded their skills from being copy writers, information architects, journalists, marketing communicators, technical communicators, user experience specialists, web designers, and more.

Seven steps to carry out a content strategy

Follow these seven steps to understand the content you now have and how to get to the content you should have. These steps work at all levels. You can use them for an entire web site or suite of sites, mobile and more, for a specific part of a site, and for going beyond web and app to have a consistent content strategy for all the ways you converse with people.

I'm concentrating here on the content itself. But don't forget that content strategy is also about governance, roles, and technology.

1. Inventory the current content.
2. Decide on messages, media, style, and tone.
3. Start an organic style guide – and use it.
4. Create workable designs that focus on content.
5. Audit the current content – and act on the audit.

6. Test the strategy.

7. Plan for the future.

The first four steps don't have to be sequential. You may be working on Steps 2, 3, and 4 while you are doing Steps 1 and 5. And all of this is built on your knowledge and understanding of your purposes, your site visitors, and your site visitors' conversations.

1. Inventory the current content

You have to know what's there to know what to do with it.

One useful way to keep track of and show the inventory is a spreadsheet with columns like the following.

Columns to use for inventory

- URL
- Page title
- Short description
- URLs that link to this page
- URLs of links from this page
- Date created (if known)
- Date last updated (if known)
- Current owner (person or part of the organization)

Columns to use for auditing

- Fate (delete, move, combine, separate, edit)
- Importance (high, middle, low – to set priorities for dealing with its fate)
- Comments related to fate and importance
- Person responsible for making changes (and possibly more columns related to "who" for owner, writer, editor)
- Due date for changes
- Status (not started, in process, in review, published – or whatever stages you have set for the process)

2. Decide on messages, media, style, and tone

How do you want to converse with your site visitors?

Messages, media, style, and tone – Chapters 7–12

3. Start an organic style guide – and use it

How are you going to stay consistent on the web site – and beyond? An organic style guide starts small – with whatever decisions you have now – and grows as needed to answer questions from content contributors and editors.

Organic style guide – Interlude just after Chapter 14

4. Create workable designs that focus on content

Content is a critical part of every web page. Include real content from the earliest designs.

Design – Chapter 3

5. Audit the current content – and act on the audit

Your audit will help you answer these questions:

- How well does your current content meet your strategic goals?
- Is it on target with the messages you want to feature?
- Is it organized well for site visitors?
- Does it answer site visitors' questions?

To act on your audit, you'll decide what content to

- delete because it is not needed, is outdated, or duplicates other content
- move because it fits better into a different part of the information architecture
- combine with other pages
- separate what is now together into shorter pages
- edit because it is good information but needs better organization and clearer writing to

- meet site visitors' needs
- achieve better SEO
- engage site visitors more

You'll also identify gaps for which you need new content.

To make those decisions, you'll use your business goals, personas, and their conversations. You'll also use information that you glean from

- usability testing
- web analytics
- SEO analysis, site search analytics, and possibly conversion optimization analysis (figuring out how best to get people to convert from lookers to bookers, browsers to shoppers, readers to subscribers)

Once you know what needs to be done with the content, you have to arrange logistics – people, schedules, budgets, technology – so that you get from the content you have to the content you need.

As you move from inventory through audit, create a content map (the information architecture of the site). And, of course, you must then use, revise, and create the content based on your audit.

6. Test the strategy

When you do usability testing of your site, you are in fact testing your content strategy – or your lack of a content strategy.

7. Plan for the future

Business goals may change. New messages may become critical. You may want to reach new groups. Information may become outdated. Media will continue to evolve. For all these reasons, you'll want a regular review schedule for your content strategy.

More on information architecture: Morville and Rosenfeld, *Information Architecture for the World Wide Web*, 3rd edition, 2006

Usability testing – Chapter 15

A final note: Be realistic. Consider resources – time and people. Will you really be able to write a blog article every day? Every week? How often will you really post to social media sites?

Designing for Easy Use

Your site visitors react to the look of your web site or mobile screen before they've read anything. If the initial appearance turns them off, you may never get to converse with them.

Design continues to be important throughout the conversation. Information design – layout, spacing, fonts, color combinations – can help or hinder your site visitors.

A study on how people's judgment of the visual appeal of sites within the first 50 milliseconds holds up on longer looks: Lindgaard, Fernandes, Dudek, and Brown, 2006

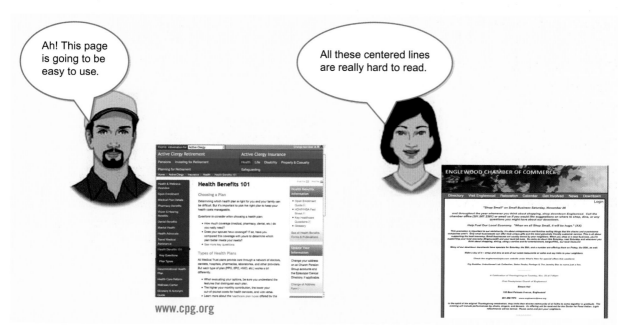

Ah! This page is going to be easy to use.

All these centered lines are really hard to read.

www.cpg.org

For successful conversations, you must develop design and content together. Waiting until the end and just pouring content into a design that was created without real content is a recipe for disaster.

Who should read this chapter – and why?

Content and design are deeply intertwined. That's why I think it is critical to have a chapter on design in a book about content – and why I think that every book about web design should have a chapter on writing web content.

- If you are a designer, read at least up to the section on color on page 51. Involving content strategists and content writers early and continuously will greatly reduce last-minute frustration for all of you and greatly increase the probability of launching a successful product.

- If you are a content specialist, my goal is to give you an overview of some important points about information design so you can collaborate well with designers. This whole chapter is for you. I hope you are working with visual designers to be certain that decisions on color, space, fonts, and so on allow site visitors to easily see and read the content.

- If you wear both hats, this chapter gives you ways of talking about content and design that should help you when you're collaborating with people who don't have your skills.

My two first broad guidelines:

- Integrate content and design from the beginning.
- Build in flexibility for universal usability.

Then, I have just a few guidelines for you in each of three categories:

- Color
- Space
- Typography

(I realize that each of these three specific topics could – and does – fill entire books. For each, I have just a few points I want to be sure that you are thinking about as you – designers and content folk – work together.)

Integrate content and design from the beginning

I hope that all of you – content strategists, content writers, and designers – are working together with a list of all the content types the site will have, as well as how, when, and where the different types of content will appear on your site or in your app.

I also hope that you are working closely with other team members – brand, business, documentation, marketing, and social media strategists, as well as information architects and user experience specialists.

Look back at the list of content types in Interlude 1 on content strategy. Note that content includes much more than text – illustrations of all types, video, audio, interactive elements, and so on.

Answer content and design questions together

Content specialists and designers must work together to answer large questions like these:

- What types of content will appear on each type of page (home page, pathway pages, catalog pages, information pages)?
- How will the content and the presentation of that content differ for large screens and for small screens (classic web, tablet, mobile)?
- How will what you do for web and app work well with what you do for social media?

And more detailed questions like these:

- For catalog pages: What specific pieces of information will each item in the catalog have? How much space (character count) will you allow for descriptions? Will you have videos? Interactive elements?
- For articles: How long will typical headlines and headings be in the content? How many levels of headings will typical articles need? Will information pages have same-page links? Where will you put them? Will you have a photo, a video, or other nontext elements with the text?

Design decisions that constrain what writers can do come up at every stage as design progresses. Content specialists must, therefore, be part of all those decisions.

Use real content throughout the process

The tradition in design has been to use dummy text that starts with the words *lorem ipsum dolor* as content during design. Using this text is called "greeking" even though the words are Latin and not Greek. (Greek would be in a different alphabet.)

More about the history and use of *lorem ipsum*: www.lipsum.com

The reason I've typically heard for using dummy text is that it lets people concentrate on design features without being distracted by the content. But why do that? The design has to support meaningful content, so we should evaluate design and content together.

At a recent talk in a room full of designers, I declared, "No more *lorem ipsum*!" The designers applauded loudly. Many designers want content early. But they tell me that clients often push them to design without content. They have trouble getting content early enough. So we need to educate clients, too, to understand the importance of content strategy and how critical real content is for successful design.

Build in flexibility for universal usability

 As you design, keep all your site visitors in mind. Meeting everyone's needs is much easier if you plan for accessibility and flexibility from the beginning.

I've been making this point for a long time. See the proposal at the end of my paper on the needs of low-vision web users: Theofanos and Redish, 2005.

Make adjusting text size obvious

Make it easy for people to adjust the type size by giving them controls on the web page (Figure 3-1).

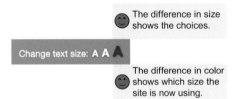

Figure 3-1 Every site should allow people to change text size — and give them an easy widget to do that.
www.cpg.org

Most people do not know that they can change the text size through browser menus. Even for those who do know, controls on each page make the option obvious. They send the message that the site cares about them. They increase trust.

Make all the text adjust

All the text on your web pages should get larger or smaller as people adjust the type size. On some sites, unfortunately, only the main content area adjusts with these changes. The side columns of navigation and other elements don't change.

All the content is important. Don't make people squint — or leave your site — because they can't read your menus or the sides of your pages.

Also, make sure that your pages are still usable at larger type sizes. For example, make sure that people can still get to the control of a dropdown box and that they can still use the fields in your online forms.

Allow other changes – contrast, keyboard, voice, and more

People's needs vary widely. Some people must use certain colors to see contrast between text and background. Others can only use the keyboard. Some need captioning for videos. Others need to hear everything.

Ford Mobility (Figure 3-2) and Ability.net (Figure 3-3) both provide lots of help to site visitors with special needs. You can, too.

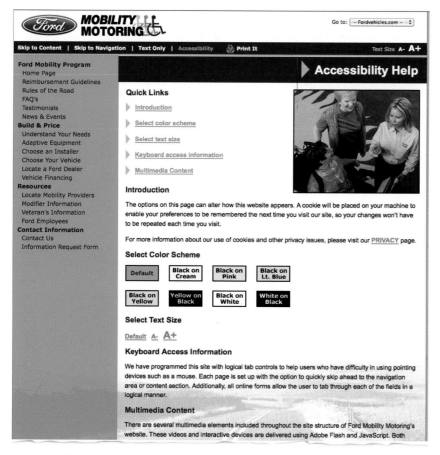

Figure 3-2 Your site visitors may need these changes to use your site successfully.
http://www.fordmobilitymotoring.com/accessibility.mob

The BBC also has an excellent page for both web users and web designers at www.bbc .co.uk/accessibility

Figure 3-3 This site helps people customize for their special needs.
http://www.abilitynet.org.uk/myway

Check the colors for color-blind site visitors

Never let color be the only indicator of a feature, function, or information.

About 5% to 8% of males have some form of color deficiency. Most often, they cannot distinguish red or green. Some women are color-blind, too, but the percentage is very small.

Consider what would happen on your site if someone cannot tell that the items on the page are in red or in green (or in other specific colors). Figure 3-4 shows what a row of hats looks like to different people. If it is important that people see hats with five different colors, these colors won't work for people with deuteranopia, a form of red/green color-blindness.

Some colorful hats

As seen by a person
with deuteranopia,
a form of red/green
color-blindness

Figure 3-4 What you see as bright and different colors may not appear that way to everyone else. www.vischeck.com

Selecting colors that work for people with different variants of color-blindness is not simple. It isn't as easy as just avoiding all reds or all greens. The shade of red or green matters. And other colors can be problematic in combination with certain reds and greens.

Think about the cultural meaning of colors

Universal usability also means being sensitive to differences in language and culture both within your own country and across borders. Some graphics and colors are pretty much universal. You can drive almost anywhere and assume that a traffic light has red, amber, and green; that red means stop and green means go.

Colors also evoke connotations like aggressive, soothing, cheerful, luxurious – and those connotations differ across cultures. Colors are sometimes associated with political parties, which, of course, are country-specific. Rather than spout a few factoids about specific colors in specific cultures, the best advice I can give you is to test your site with people from the different cultures that you want to reach.

Color

In the early days of the web, we often saw an exuberance of design with wildly colorful – but not usable – web pages. Design exuberance can be wonderful – if it matches the personality of your site. But it also has to work with and not against the content. If you want people to read what you are putting on your site, you must make the text and illustrations legible.

The best way to know if your web page is going to work is to have people who are color-blind test it. You can use sites like www.vischeck.com and www.checkmycolors.com to get a preliminary view of how your web pages will look to people with different types of vision problems.

Be wary of factoids you read on web sites. Many are old or urban legends.

The rest of this chapter focuses on color, space, and typography for text. Although words are not the only part of your content, they are a vital part – and the part that I know best. Illustrations – Chapter 13. As I say in Chapter 13, you'll have to look beyond this book for best practices in creating great videos.

As you plan colors, consider these four guidelines:

1. Work with your brand colors.
2. Use light on dark sparingly.
3. Keep the background clear.
4. Keep the contrast high.

1. Work with your brand colors

If you are working with an established organization, the brand will almost certainly dictate the color palette to work with. Unless you have serious problems, with it, work within that color scheme.

2. Use light on dark sparingly

Light text on a dark background is called "reverse type." Most people find reverse text difficult to read for sustained periods, so don't use it for your main content.

If you want to change the contrast from dark on light (the best) to light on dark, use reverse type only for small bits and make the type bold so it stands out. For example, many designers make reverse type work well on tabs, as Staples does in Figure 3-5.

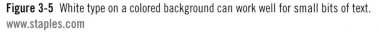

Figure 3-5 White type on a colored background can work well for small bits of text.
www.staples.com

3. Keep the background clear

Patterned backgrounds obscure the text, as in Figure 3-6. Don't do it. You defeat your goals if you make the page hard to see and the text hard to read.

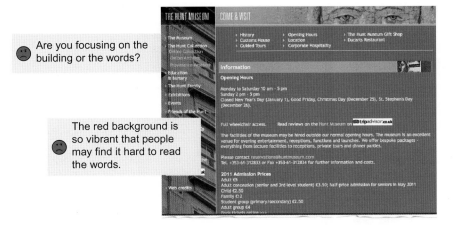

Are you focusing on the building or the words?

The red background is so vibrant that people may find it hard to read the words.

Figure 3-6 When the foreground (the words) and the background compete for attention, it's hard to read the words.
www.huntmuseum.com

4. Keep the contrast high

Legibility requires high contrast between text and background. Many color combinations make text difficult to read because they don't provide enough contrast between text and background (Figure 3-7).

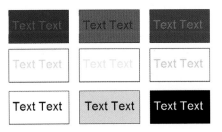

Figure 3-7 Some color combinations make text very hard to read.

Dark on dark (top row) or light on light (middle row) isn't as clear as dark on light or light on dark (bottom row). Blue text on red may even seem to vibrate on the screen, making that combination very difficult on the eyes.

Space

Space is not emptiness. It's an important design element. But blank space is a very precious commodity online.

Concern for space is a major reason to think mobile first! Working with the very limited space of the small screen can make designers and content writers conscious of how important it is to let go of the words. Trying to squeeze everything into the mobile screen just doesn't work, as you can see by comparing the screens in Figure 3-8.

More on tools to help you choose a color scheme:
http://designshack.net/articles/inspiration/25-awesome-tools-for-choosing-a-website-color-scheme

More on mobile: Wroblewski, *Mobile First*, 2011; Hinman, *The Mobile Frontier*, 2012

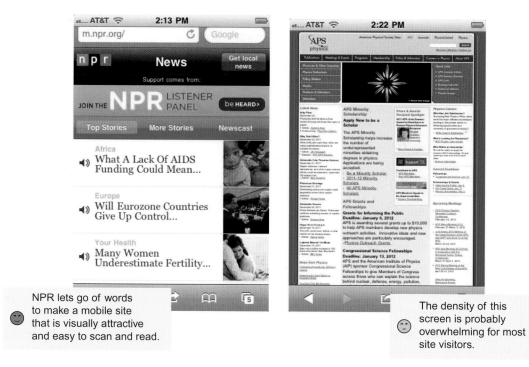

NPR lets go of words to make a mobile site that is visually attractive and easy to scan and read.

The density of this screen is probably overwhelming for most site visitors.

Figure 3-8 Space is a critical design element at all screen sizes.
www.npr.org (on an iPhone); www.aps.org (on an iPhone)

When you plan for space on your site, consider these six guidelines:

1. Create consistent patterns.
2. Align elements on a grid.
3. Keep active space in your content.
4. Beware of false bottoms.
5. Don't let headings float.
6. Don't center text.

1. Create consistent patterns

People love patterns. If the Search box is in the upper right on the home page, we expect to see it in that place on all the pages. If bulleted lists are slightly indented on the first few pages we look at, we expect all bulleted lists to be indented in the same way.

We are faster at understanding how the page is designed and at finding the specific part we need if the patterns are obvious and consistent across pages. Consistent patterns also help build site visitors' trust in the site, as well as confidence they'll have a successful experience.

We build our mental models of sites – our expectations for where different content elements are and what they look like – both from our experiences with other sites and with what we find on a particular site.

**More on patterns: Tidwell,
Designing Interfaces,
2nd edition, 2011**

2. Align elements on a grid

One of the most effective ways to create patterns that people quickly see and learn is to have only a few places across the page where content elements start. When people complain that a site is "cluttered" or "too busy" or "hard to use," they are often reacting to pages where elements are not lined up well.

Figure 3-9 shows how the New York Metropolitan Opera provides an easy-to-use site by setting up clear alignment and grids on each type of page.

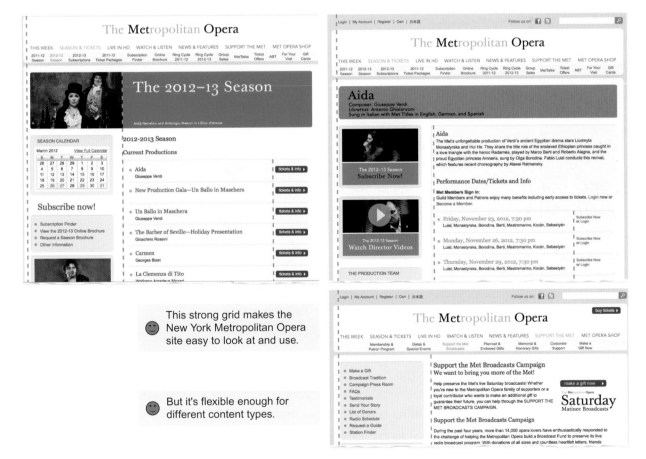

This strong grid makes the New York Metropolitan Opera site easy to look at and use.

But it's flexible enough for different content types.

Figure 3-9 The Metropolitan Opera's templates are very clear, with well-defined grids.
www.metoperafamily.org

3. Keep active space in your content

Too little space on a web page or app screen can make information very difficult to skim, scan, find, and read. Too much space in the wrong places can mislead people about whether the web page is finished and about how headings fit with the text.

Information designers distinguish between passive space and active space (Figure 3-10).

- **Passive space** is outside of the main content area; for example, the margins on a piece of paper.

- **Active space** is inside the main content area; for example, the space between paragraphs and between list items.

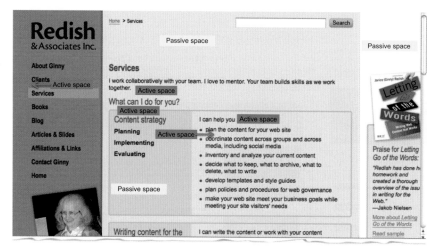

Figure 3-10 Active space helps people use web pages.
www.redish.net

Online, we can usually reduce passive space, but we must keep active space to help people make sense of the information. Create useful active space by:

- breaking the text into small chunks
- using lots of headings
- keeping paragraphs short and putting space between them
- turning sentences into more visual forms, like lists and tables
- putting space into lists
- including pictures and other graphics with a little space around them

Compare the active space that you saw in Figure 3-10 with the lack of active space in Figure 3-11.

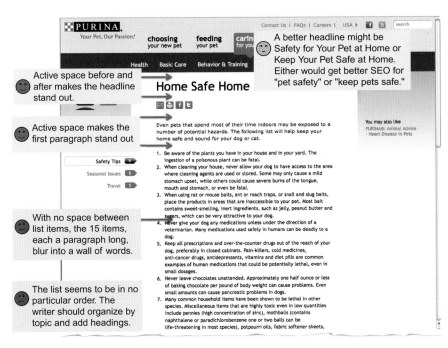

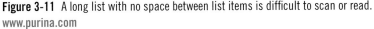

Figure 3-11 A long list with no space between list items is difficult to scan or read.
www.purina.com

On mobile screens, you have almost no room for passive space. But you must keep active space. For mobile web and app, let go of words. Keep only the content that you really need. Present that content in short pieces, lists, and visuals with a little space around each piece. Look back at Figure 3-8 and see how small amounts of active space make the NPR mobile screen work so well.

4. Beware of false bottoms

You don't control how much any particular site visitor sees without scrolling. What they see depends on whether they are looking at your site on a mobile, tablet, laptop, or large monitor. Even on a large monitor, it depends on the resolution they are using and how large a window they have open.

Over and over in usability testing, I've seen people stopped by a horizontal line or a block of space at the bottom of their screen. Even if the scroll bar shows that there's lots more, the message that the horizontal line or a large block of space seems to be sending overwhelms the message of the scroll bar.

Don't put a horizontal line or a large block of space across your web page. They stop people. Check your site on different devices, different size monitors, at different resolutions, and in different browsers to be sure that your spacing is not likely to mislead people.

5. Don't let headings float

When headings are the same distance from the text before them as they are from the text after them, our eyes don't know how to group the information on the web page. Compare Figures 3-12 and 3-13.

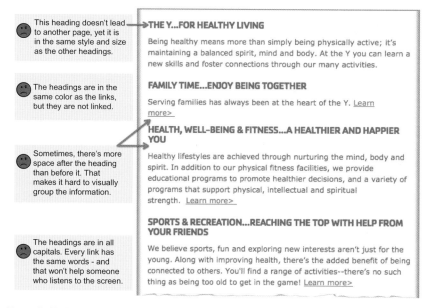

Figure 3-12 Floating headings make it hard to see how the content pieces connect to each other.
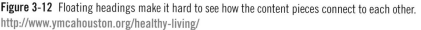
http://www.ymcahouston.org/healthy-living/

When headings come right on top of the text, your site visitors won't have to think about how the headings and text go together. To make headings work well, put more active space above the heading than between the heading and the text it goes with.

Floating headings come naturally with ordinary HTML. To put the headings directly on top of the text they cover, use a cascading style sheet (CSS). You get much more with a CSS than just solving the problem of floating headings, but it's worth learning about and using a

Headings – Chapter 9

The space between the introduction to a list and the first list item is a similar problem. Use a CSS to remove that space, too. Lists – Chapter 11

CSS even if this is the only problem that you have. Keeping the headings from floating is that important!

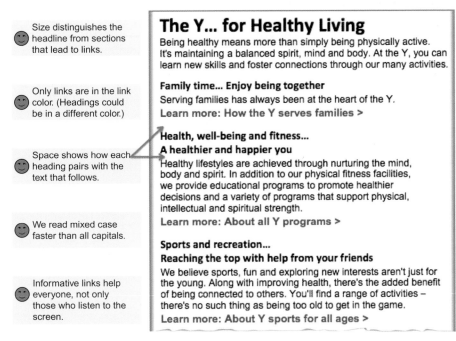

Size distinguishes the headline from sections that lead to links.

Only links are in the link color. (Headings could be in a different color.)

Space shows how each heading pairs with the text that follows.

We read mixed case faster than all capitals.

Informative links help everyone, not only those who listen to the screen.

Figure 3-13 My suggested revision (with help from designer Jeff Rum of Spark Enterprise)

By the way: If you want to use rules (lines) with your headlines or headings, consider putting them **over**, not under. That way, the rule helps your site visitors group the headline with the rest of the page and each heading with the text that follows.

6. Don't center text

 What is your reaction to the screen in Figure 3-14 (on page 60)?

Centered text violates our need for alignment. When the text is centered, our eyes have no "anchor" – no steady place to come back to at the start of each line. Centered text may be lovely on a wedding invitation, but it's tiring for reading.

Even menu items in a left or right navigation column are easier to skim and scan when they are lined up on the left. Column headings in a table work better when each heading starts at the left column edge rather than being centered over the column.

Left-aligned, ragged-right (not justified on the right) is best for all web writing.

Figure 3-14 Centered text is hard to read.
www.englewood-chamber.com

Unless you are writing poetry, don't center text *anywhere* on your web pages.

More on space in web design:
Lupton, *Thinking with Type*,
2nd edition, 2010

Typography

If you want people to read, you must give them legible text. Your choices of color and your use of space contribute to legibility (or lack of it). So, of course, do your choices of type – the defaults you set for type face (font) and type sizes, as well as line length, highlighting, and how you use capitalization.

As designers and content specialists working together, consider these six guidelines:

1. Set a legible sans serif font as the default.
2. Make the default text size legible for your visitors.
3. Set a medium line length as the default.
4. Don't write in all capitals.
5. Underline only links.
6. Use italics sparingly.

1. Set a legible sans serif font as the default

Most web sites use sans serif type, such as Arial, Tahoma, or Verdana.

A brief primer on fonts and type families

Note: This discussion applies to type in the Roman alphabet that English and many other languages use. We would need a different discussion for other writing systems.

If you open the font list in your word processing program, you'll see a long list to choose from. That list could be even longer. Thousands of fonts are available.

But all the fonts in that huge list fall into two major categories: serif and sans serif (plus the unusual, artistic fonts that you would only consider for very special situations).

To see the difference, look at a capital T in Times and in Tahoma.

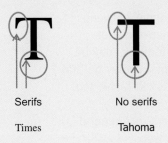

Serifs   No serifs

Times   Tahoma

Serifs are the "arms" and "feet" that extend down and out on the letters of serif fonts. *Sans* is French for "without." Sans serif fonts don't have the arms and feet.

Whether a font has serifs is not the whole story. Within each of those broad categories, fonts differ in other features such as how wide the rounded parts of letters like "b" and "d" are, how high lowercase letters like "x" are compared to the overall height of letters like "h," how clearly the font distinguishes between the letter "l" and the number "1," how close together the letters are to each other, and so on.

Even at the same point size, different fonts take up different amounts of space on the screen. Try it for yourself by typing the same sentence several times and then changing the font but not the point size for each rendition of the sentence.

Based on research in the mid-twentieth century, people often said that serif fonts were better for sustained reading. A common explanation was that the serifs at the bottom of the letters draw the eye horizontally along the line of type.

However, relying on that research for your web content may not serve your site visitors well for several reasons:

- The research is now more than 60 years old.
- Serif fonts were the norm then. People had little familiarity with sans serif.
- With just a point or two more space between lines of type ("leading" – a word from the days when printers put a slug of lead between rows of type), you can make even a paper document in sans serif very readable.
- On the web, we break information into small pieces with small paragraphs, short sentences, lists, and tables.

(An aside: Even on paper, you may want to use an appropriate sans serif. This book is in Trade Gothic, a sans serif font.)

Research on web content has not shown a consistent winner between serif and sans serif for either reading speed or comprehension. But preference almost always favors the familiar sans serif fonts. It may be familiarity; people see most sites in these sans serif fonts. It may be that a site in serif font looks like a paper document; it seems old-fashioned.

 Researchers who work with low-vision readers recommend familiar sans serif fonts for both paper and web.

Of course, you do not entirely control what your site visitors see. They may have their browser set to always show a particular font. However, as the default, select a highly legible sans serif font. Select one that most of your site visitors are likely to have available on their computers. If you choose an unusual font, most people won't see your content in that font because browsers only use what the specific computer has available. Do usability testing to make sure your default results in legible pages.

2. Make the default text size legible for your visitors

Online, you are balancing how much to say and the space for saying it. If you only have a certain amount of screen "real estate" for your content, you either have to write fewer words or make the type smaller. That's a good reason to let go of words and focus on your key messages. If the type is too small, people won't read what you wrote. Write less. Use type large enough for your site visitors to read easily.

 Consider all your personas. You may be much younger than many of your site visitors. You may have much better vision than they do. Most people develop vision problems as they age. Cater to them on your site.

3. Set a medium line length as the default

This is a paragraph of information written in Verdana with a line length of 100 characters per line. Although university students in one research study read lines that were this long faster than shorter lines, in another study, other students read the medium lines fastest. In both studies, the students preferred the medium line length. Do you find this comfortable to read?

This is a paragraph of information written in Verdana with a line length of 50 characters per line. This is the length that students preferred even when they read longer lines faster. Research on paper over many years found that people do best with lines of text about this long. Do you find this comfortable to read?

This is a paragraph of information written in Verdana with a line length of 25 characters per line. Whole paragraphs in very short lines are difficult for people because it's hard to get the meaning with so few words on a line. Do you find this comfortable to read?

The problem with very long lines of type is physical. Long lines are tiring to read. Our eyes have to move more to get to the end of the line. When moving back to the beginning for the next line, people sometimes skip a line or go back up a line.

The problem with very short lines is semantic – related to the meaning of the words. If the line is so short that people don't get a whole phrase, the copy can be hard to understand.

So set the default for classic web and tablet to be a medium line length (50 to 70 characters or about 8 to 10 words). Also, set your text to be fluid (liquid layout) so it adjusts and wraps well as people resize their windows or turn their mobiles from one orientation to another.

4. Don't write in all capitals

ALL CAPITALS TAKE UP 30 PERCENT MORE SPACE ON THE PAGE. THEY SLOW READING SPEED BY ABOUT 15 PERCENT. THEY ARE ALSO BORING. PEOPLE'S EYES GLAZE OVER, AND THEY TEND TO STOP READING. WHEN YOU WRITE WITH ALL CAPITALS IN EMAIL AND ON THE WEB, PEOPLE THINK YOU ARE SHOUTING AT THEM.

All capitals take up 30 percent more space on the page. They slow reading speed by about 15 percent. They are also boring. People's eyes glaze over, and they tend to stop reading. When you write with all capitals in email and on the web, people think you are shouting at them.

 Which paragraph did you read? Do you agree that all capitals are more difficult and less interesting to read?

Using capital letters for headlines, headings, and emphasis is a carryover from typewriter days when writers had very few options for varying the type in a document. We have better options today.

For web sites, follow these guidelines:

- Use ALL CAPITALS only for a single word or short phrase in specific circumstances where people expect it.

- Use **bold** or color for headlines and headings, not all capitals.

- Use uppercase and lowercase (like normal sentences) even for important information. If you put a whole paragraph in capital letters to make people pay attention to it, you will achieve exactly the opposite. Most people will ignore it.

FLASHLIGHT flashlight

 Which did your eyes gravitate to? Which did you figure out fastest?

The traditional explanation for why all capitals are more difficult to read is that the shape of a word in lowercase give us more information than the shape of the same word in all capitals. The letters that stick up (have "ascenders"; b, d, f, for example) and the letters that go down (have "descenders"; g, p, y, for example) give words different shapes. Those differences in shape are present in lowercase letters but not in capital letters.

For an argument against the "letter shape" explanation: Larson, 2004

5. Underline only links

On web pages, people assume that anything that is underlined is a link, no matter what color it is. Underlining for emphasis or to indicate a book title is an old-fashioned technique from typewriter days.

6. Use italics sparingly

Italics have always been the way to show a book title in a printed document. Use that in your web content. Otherwise, use italics sparingly. They work as a light form of emphasis, but an entire paragraph in italics is hard to read.

Don't use italics for headings. They don't stand out on the page. And people don't agree on how to put italics into a hierarchy of headings. When I show people sets of headings all at the same size where one is in **bold** type, one is in *italic* type, and one is in regular type, people always say the bold one is the highest level – the most important heading. But then I get mixed results for whether the heading in *italic* is more important or less important than the heading in regular type.

Use **bold** or color for all your headings. Change the size to show the levels.

Putting it all together: A case study

In the following case study, I take a web page through a series of changes so that you can see the effect of each design guideline.

Case Study 3-1	Revising a poorly designed web page

Consider this page about the White-naped Crane as it originally appeared on a web site about birds:

White-naped Cranes *Grus vipio*

White-naped Cranes breed in northeastern Mongolia, northeastern China, and adjacent areas of southeastern Russia.

Breeding habitat includes shallow wetlands and wet meadows in broad river valleys, along lake edges, and in lowland steppes or mixed forest-steppe areas. White-naped Cranes nest, roost, and feed in shallow wetlands and along wetland edges, foraging in adjacent grasslands or farmlands. During migration and on their wintering grounds, they use rice paddies, mudflats, other wetlands and agricultural fields. White-naped Cranes are excellent diggers. The White-naped Crane is often found in the company of other crane species , including Red-crowned, Hooded, Demoiselle, and Eurasian Cranes.

Mated pairs of cranes, including White-naped Cranes, engage in unison calling, which is a complex and extended series of coordinated calls. The birds stand in a specific posture, usually with their heads thrown back and beaks skyward during the display. In White-naped Cranes, the female initiates the display and utters two calls for each male call. The male always lifts up his wings over his back during the unison call while the female keeps her wings folded at her sides. All cranes engage in dancing, which includes various behaviors such as bowing, jumping, running, stick or grass tossing, and wing flapping. Dancing can occur at any age and is commonly associated with courtship, however, it is generally believed to be a normal part of motor development for cranes and can serve to thwart aggression, relieve tension, and strengthen the pair bond.Nests are mounds of dried sedges and grasses in open wetlands. Females usually lay two eggs and incubation (by both sexes) lasts 28-32 days. The male takes the primary role in defending the nest against possible danger. Chicks fledge (first flight) at 70-75 days.

 Do you agree that it is not as well designed as it could be?

You can probably identify several ways to make it easier for people to see it, read it, and get the information from it.

First, let's make it easier just to see by increasing the contrast between the background and the text.

White-naped Cranes *Grus vipio*

White-naped Cranes breed in northeastern Mongolia, northeastern China, and adjacent areas of southeastern Russia.

Breeding habitat includes shallow wetlands and wet meadows in broad river valleys, along lake edges, and in lowland steppes or mixed forest-steppe areas. White-naped Cranes nest, roost, and feed in shallow wetlands and along wetland edges, foraging in adjacent grasslands or farmlands. During migration and on their wintering grounds, they use rice paddies, mudflats, other wetlands and agricultural fields. White-naped Cranes are excellent diggers. The White-naped Crane is often found in the company of other crane species , including Red-crowned, Hooded, Demoiselle, and Eurasian Cranes.

Mated pairs of cranes, including White-naped Cranes, engage in unison calling, which is a complex and extended series of coordinated calls. The birds stand in a specific posture, usually with their heads thrown back and beaks skyward during the display. In White-naped Cranes, the female initiates the display and utters two calls for each male call. The male always lifts up his wings over his back during the unison call while the female keeps her wings folded at her sides. All cranes engage in dancing, which includes various behaviors such as bowing, jumping, running, stick or grass tossing, and wing flapping. Dancing can occur at any age and is commonly associated with courtship, however, it is generally believed to be a normal part of motor development for cranes and can serve to thwart aggression, relieve tension, and strengthen the pair bond.Nests are mounds of dried sedges and grasses in open wetlands. Females usually lay two eggs and incubation (by both sexes) lasts 28-32 days. The male takes the primary role in defending the nest against possible danger. Chicks fledge (first flight) at 70-75 days.

White background, but still in serif font, centered

Now, let's change from centered text to left-aligned. And let's break up the text more.

White-naped Cranes *Grus vipio*

White-naped Cranes breed in northeastern Mongolia, northeastern China, and adjacent areas of southeastern Russia.

Breeding habitat includes shallow wetlands and wet meadows in broad river valleys, along lake edges, and in lowland steppes or mixed forest steppe areas. White-naped Cranes nest, roost, and feed in shallow wetlands and along wetland edges, foraging in adjacent grasslands or farmlands. During migration and on their wintering grounds, they use rice paddies, mudflats, other wetlands and agricultural fields. White-naped Cranes are excellent diggers.

The White-naped Crane is often found in the company of other crane species, including Red-crowned, Hooded, Demoiselle, and Eurasian Cranes.

Mated pairs of cranes, including White-naped Cranes, engage in unison calling, which is a complex and extended series of coordinated calls. The birds stand in a specific posture, usually with their heads thrown back and beaks skyward during the display.

In White-naped Cranes, the female initiates the display and utters two calls for each male call. The male always lifts up his wings over his back during the unison call while the female keeps her wings folded at her sides.

All cranes engage in dancing, which includes various behaviors such as bowing, jumping, running, stick or grass tossing, and wing flapping. Dancing can occur at any age and is commonly associated with courtship; however, it is generally believed to be a normal part of motor development for cranes and can serve to thwart aggression, relieve tension, and strength the pair bond.

Nests are mounds of dried sedges and grasses in open wetlands. Females usually lay two eggs and incubation (by both sexes) lasts 28-32 days. The male takes the primary role in defending the nest against possible danger. Chicks fledge (first flight) at 70-75 days.

White background, left-aligned, seven paragraphs instead of three, but still in serif font

Next, let's change the font – at the same point size.

White-naped Cranes *Grus vipio*

White-naped Cranes breed in northeastern Mongolia, northeastern China, and adjacent areas of southeastern Russia.

Breeding habitat includes shallow wetlands and wet meadows in broad river valleys, along lake edges, and in lowland steppes or mixed forest steppe areas. White-naped Cranes nest, roost, and feed in shallow wetlands and along wetland edges, foraging in adjacent grasslands or farmlands. During migration and on their wintering grounds, they use rice paddies, mudflats, other wetlands and agricultural fields. White-naped Cranes are excellent diggers.

The White-naped Crane is often found in the company of other crane species, including Red-crowned, Hooded, Demoiselle, and Eurasian Cranes.

Mated pairs of cranes, including White-naped Cranes, engage in unison calling, which is a complex and extended series of coordinated calls. The birds stand in a specific posture, usually with their heads thrown back and beaks skyward during the display.

In White-naped Cranes, the female initiates the display and utters two calls for each male call. The male always lifts up his wings over his back during the unison call while the female keeps her wings folded at her sides.

All cranes engage in dancing, which includes various behaviors such as bowing, jumping, running, stick or grass tossing, and wing flapping. Dancing can occur at any age and is commonly associated with courtship; however, it is generally believed to be a normal part of motor development for cranes and can serve to thwart aggression, relieve tension, and strength the pair bond.

Nests are mounds of dried sedges and grasses in open wetlands. Females usually lay two eggs and incubation (by both sexes) lasts 28-32 days. The male takes the primary role in defending the nest against possible danger. Chicks fledge (first flight) at 70-75 days.

White background, left-aligned, seven paragraphs, sans serif font

Finally, let's revise it by reorganizing, letting go of words, putting in bold headings, and adding a picture. The page may grow a little longer, but isn't it more inviting and easier to get the information?

White-naped Cranes – *Grus vipio*

Breeding area
>   Northeastern Mongolia
>   Northeastern China
>   Adjacent areas of southeastern Russia

Habitat
>   Shallow wetlands and along wetland
>   edges, foraging in adjacent grasslands
>   or farmlands

White-naped Crane

>   During migration and on their wintering
>   grounds, white-naped cranes use rice
>   paddies, mudflats, other wetlands and
>   agricultural fields.

>   Breeding habitat includes shallow
>   wetlands and wet meadows in broad
>   river valleys, along lake edges, and in
>   lowland steppes or mixed forest steppe areas.

Nests
>   Mounds of dried sedges and grasses in open wetlands

Eggs
>   Usually two

Nesting behavior
>   Both sexes incubate the eggs, which hatch in 28-32 days. The male
>   takes the primary role in defending the nest against possible danger.
>   Chicks fledge (first flight) at 70-75 days.

White-naped Cranes are often found with other crane species
>   The White-naped Crane is often found in the company of other crane
>   species, including Red-crowned, Hooded, Demoiselle, and Eurasian
>   Cranes.

White-naped Cranes dance, as do other cranes
>   All cranes engage in dancing, which includes various behaviors such
>   as bowing, jumping, running, stick or grass tossing, and wing flapping.
>   Dancing is commonly associated with courtship, but it can occur at any
>   age. Dancing is generally believed to be a normal part of motor
>   development for cranes and can serve to thwart aggression, relieve
>   tension, and strength the pair bond.

Mated cranes call and display
>   Mated White-naped Cranes, like other crane pairs, engage in unison
>   calling, which is a complex and extended series of coordinated calls.
>   The birds stand in a specific posture, usually with their heads thrown
>   back and beaks skyward during the display.

>   In white-naped cranes, the female initiates the display and utters two
>   calls for each male call. The male always lifts up his wings over his
>   back during the unison call while the female keeps her wings folded
>   at her sides.

Summarizing Chapter 3

Key messages from Chapter 3:

- Integrate content and design from the beginning.
  - Answer content and design questions together.
  - Use real content throughout the process.

- Build in flexibility for universal usability.
  - Make adjusting text size obvious.
  - Make all the text adjust.
  - Allow other changes – contrast, keyboard, voice, and more.
  - Check the colors for color-blind site visitors.
  - Think about the cultural meaning of colors.

Color

- Work with your brand colors.

- Use light on dark sparingly.

- Keep the background clear.

- Keep the contrast high.

Space

- Create consistent patterns.

- Align elements on a grid.

- Keep active space in your content.

- Beware of false bottoms.

- Don't let headings float.

- Don't center text.

Typography

- Set a legible sans serif font as the default.

- Make the default text size legible for your visitors.

- Set a medium line length as the default.

- Don't write in all capitals.

- Underline only links.

- Use italics sparingly.

Starting Well:
Home Pages

People get to the information on web sites in many ways, as this illustration shows.

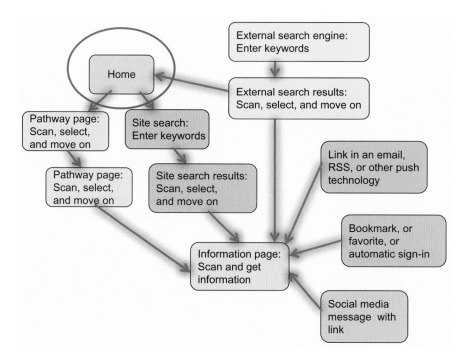

In this chapter, we're looking at home pages of information-rich and task-rich web sites whether people come to them on large screens, tablets, or mobile devices.

Blogs fit into this picture both as home page and as information page. The entire site may be a blog with the home page showing the latest post. A blog may be just one of many types of information on the site – reachable from the home page through a tab, link, or any of the other pathways in this picture.

Home pages – content-rich with few words

Home pages must satisfy six basic functions:

1. Be findable through search engines. (Which site should I go to?)

2. Identify the site. (Did I get where I thought I was going?)

3. Set the site's tone and personality. Inspire confidence and trust. (Who are you? Are you credible? Should I trust you?)

4. Help people get a sense of what the site is all about. (What can I do here?)

5. Continue the conversation quickly. (Can I start my task right here?)

6. Send each person on the right way. (Where's the link I need? Where's the Search box? Will Search help me?)

In this chapter, we'll see how to accomplish all six functions without asking people to read much.

1. Be findable through search engines

SEO | When people type keywords into a search engine like Bing, Google, or Yahoo, they almost always click on one of the first few items in the search results. If you want people to come to your site through these search engines, your site has to be near the top in the search results.

You can pay for placement with search engines, but I'm talking here about placement in the organic (not paid for) search results.

At the time I'm writing this, some key components of good SEO are

- keywords in the title that shows up at the top of the browser

- keywords in the URL

- keywords in the headline, headings, and copy

- content that others link to

SEO applies to *every* page in your site. We'll talk about SEO again in later chapters because headlines, headings, and content high on the page matter for SEO – and they have to be coded correctly to be counted.

Your keywords must match searchers' keywords

People type *their* keywords into the search engine. If you want people to find you, you must have *their* keywords in your site. If your words and theirs differ, your site won't come up for them.

Gaming the system doesn't work

Some people try to get high rankings by putting keywords all over the page – even as a background (called "black hat" techniques). But the

You want to be first in the search engine results because the top-ranked result captures about 42% of the traffic. (Halligan and Shah, 2009, p. 58)

search engine programmers know that. So the search engines throw out sites and pages that have the same words too many times on the page.

No one knows just what the threshold is for the search engines to say "too much," but you don't have to write a lot to get good SEO. Of course, in this book, I'm describing best practice ("white hat") SEO.

*Remark*able content matters

Search engines rank the quality of your site in part by how many other sites link to yours and the quality of those sites. As Brian Halligan and Dharmesh Shah say in their book, *Inbound Marketing*, "The best way to rank well in the Google search results is to **create content that is rank-worthy**." (emphasis added)

Halligan and Shah also say that you want *remark*able content, italicizing the front part of "remarkable" to remind us that the word means "worthy of other people's remarks." If you have a *remark*able content strategy and *remark*able content, you'll do well in SEO.

2. Identify the site

People want to know "Whose site is this?" "Did I get the site I was going to?" And you want them to recognize the site, relate to your brand, and develop brand loyalty so that they'll come back to the site.

Your site's logo, name, and tag line must identify it. Don't use a paragraph to explain the site. Don't put paragraph-long mission statements on the home page. Most people won't read them.

Instead, encapsulate your company or organization's key message in a memorable tag line – a short phrase that tells people how to think about the site.

Wilderness Travel does this well (Figure 4-1).

On tag lines and other aspects of home pages, pathway pages, and navigation: Steve Krug, *Don't Make Me Think!*, 2005

Wilderness Travel
Extraordinary cultural, wildlife and hiking adventures since 1978

Figure 4-1 Wilderness Travel gives you a good sense of what they do in just seven words and a date.
www.wildernesstravel.com

3. Set the site's tone and personality

Remember that your web site is part of a conversation. You set the tone for your side of the conversation by sharing the web site's personality.

Web sites definitely have personalities – expressed in the site's visual style (colors, graphics, typography) and content strategy (choice of content, writing style, words). Through those personalities, you establish trust with your site visitors (or not), credibility (or not), confidence that they will succeed (or not).

In 2001, the U.S. Internal Revenue Service (IRS, the tax collectors) had a home page that looked like a tabloid newspaper (Figure 4-2).

An interesting paper on web sites having personalities: Coney and Steehouder, 2000

Include notes about tone and personality in your style guide. Style Guide – Interlude 5 just before Chapter 15

Is a tabloid newspaper the right personality for the tax collectors' web site?

Does this home page make you feel the site is credible and trustworthy?

Figure 4-2 The web site of the U.S. Internal Revenue Service in 2001

What personality *should* the IRS site have?

Does the 2011 version in Figure 4-3 do a better job of matching the personality you expect from the IRS? It may not be as exciting as the Digital Daily, but it is much more appropriate and useful.

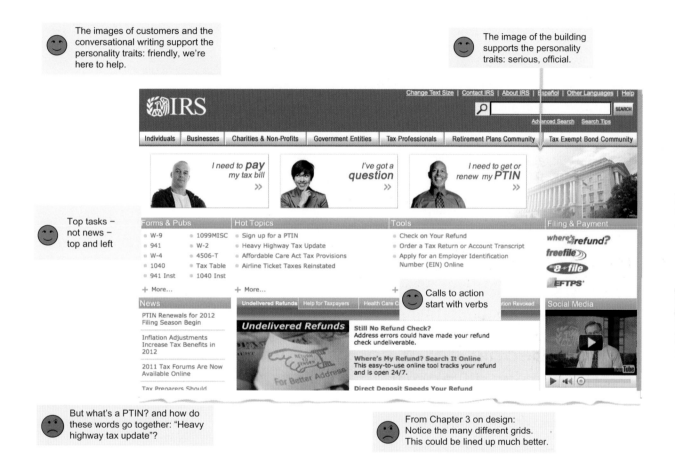

Figure 4-3 The web site of the U.S. Internal Revenue Service in 2011
www.irs.gov

As Margot Bloomstein, a content strategy consultant who helps organizations find the personality they want to express in all their interactions, says: What you want is "a brand that never breaks character—ever. This all comes down to how the content and visual design (along with interaction affordances and features) all work together to maintain a cohesive voice and consistently manifest the same communication goals, or message architecture."

Bloomstein, *Content Strategy at Work*, 2012

Who decides on the site's personality?

If you own the site (it's your blog; it's your company; you are an independent artist or writer; it's your Facebook wall), you decide on the tone and personality you want to project.

However, if you are part of a larger organization, it's not your decision alone. In fact, another group (Marketing, Corporate Communications, Web Services) may dictate aspects of the site's brand – colors, layout, writing style.

Don't arbitrarily reject those decisions. A lot of effort may have gone into choices within a content strategy, brand strategy, message architecture, social media strategy.

If you want to influence the site's personality, get involved. Communicate up the chain and across groups. Become part of whatever teams are working on these issues.

As you consider the right tone and personality for the site, think broadly about all the organization's site visitors, not just those who come for your part of the site. A web site is the whole organization's face to the world.

4. Help people get a sense of what the site is all about

The trick here is to satisfy Goldilocks: Both too little and too much can keep people from understanding what the site offers.

A useful home page

- makes it instantly clear what the site is all about
- is mostly links and short descriptions
- includes calls to action (verb phrases) for your primary site visitors that respond to the conversations they came to have

Smithville, a local broadband service provider in Southern Indiana, does this well while projecting its "we're local folks just like you" personality (Figure 4-4).

To help you understand how your site visitors would sort and group content:

- **Work with information architects. Morville and Rosenfeld, *Information Architecture*, 3rd edition, 2006**
- **Have users sort and group content cards.** http://usability.gov/methods/design_site/cardsort.html; **Spencer, *Card Sorting*, 2009**

Figure 4-4 You can get a lot across with few words.
www.smithville.net

5. Continue the conversation quickly

A successful web site picks up on the site visitor's conversation
right away.

Focus on your key visitors and their key tasks

If you try to give equal emphasis to all things for all people on your
home page, you'll end up satisfying no one. That's why the planning in
Chapter 2 is so important. Who are your primary personas? What are
their primary tasks (conversations)?

Look at what Tricare, the military's primary health care organization, did
when they considered these questions (Case Study 4-1).

Case Study 4-1 | **Focusing on personas and tasks**

The "old" Tricare home page looked like this:

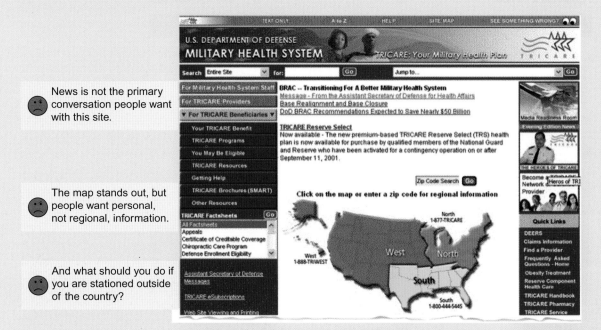

News is not the primary conversation people want with this site.

The map stands out, but people want personal, not regional, information.

And what should you do if you are stationed outside of the country?

When Dian Lawhon and her web team at Tricare considered this page, they thought about:

- Who comes to the site?
- What conversations do those site visitors want to have with the site?
- How well is the site conversing with those site visitors?

Among their primary site visitors are military families like Kyle and Susan.

What do we have to do to get the baby onto our health insurance?

The Tricare team realized that the old home page didn't make it easy for Kyle and Susan to quickly move ahead in the conversation they came to have with the site. So they redesigned the home page to look like this:

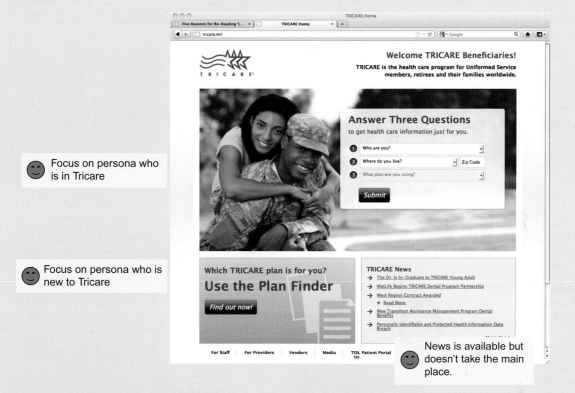

Focus on persona who is in Tricare

Focus on persona who is new to Tricare

News is available but doesn't take the main place.

The new Tricare web site is now a good conversational partner.

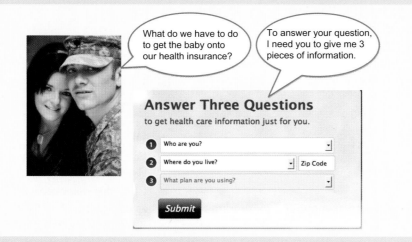

Tricare saw their satisfaction ratings go up 20 points after they launched the new site.

Let people start major tasks on the home page

The two primary conversations for Tricare are: I have a plan; answer my question about coverage. I'm new; help me choose a plan. The new site caters to both those conversations.

 What are the primary conversations for your site? How can you quickly move those conversations along?

To move the first of the primary Tricare conversations along requires that the site visitor fill out a brief form. In fact, many tasks people come to do involve forms.

It's been interesting to watch over the years as more and more forms come to the front of web sites. Years ago, travel sites required several clicks before you began to arrange your travel. Now they all let you start a reservation immediately (Figure 4-5).

More on all aspects of web forms, including realizing they are about relationship, conversation, and appearance: Jarrett and Gaffney, *Web Forms that Work*, 2009. Design details for forms: Wroblewski, *Web Form Design*, 2008

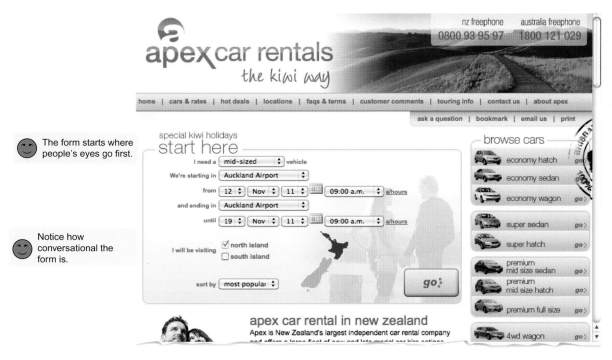

The form starts where people's eyes go first.

Notice how conversational the form is.

Figure 4-5 When the most common task on a site involves a form, it's a great idea to put the form high on the home page.

www.apexrentals.co.nz

Make sure the forms are high on the page

If you have forms on the home page, make sure they are easy to find – high enough to be seen immediately. The large pictures that many sites have on their web pages sometimes push critical tasks and critical information below what people see when the web page first comes up.

Don't put unnecessary forms up front

Starting people on forms they want or need on the home page is good. Forcing people to fill out forms that they don't want or need – or before they are ready to give you the information – is likely to be counterproductive.

Think carefully about the benefits and perils of asking for information when people are not ready to give it to you. If you ask too early, or you ask for too much, or you ask for information that people have to struggle to get for you, you risk losing more than you might gain. If you want people to spread the word in social media, don't annoy their friends by

As people move to higher screen resolutions, some of the worries I had about this in the first edition go away. However, check your site with various browsers and monitors. Also, remember that people are now working on tablets, mobiles, and some are still on old computers.

Yes, many people today scroll down web pages; but I still see many people in usability tests who don't scroll on home pages. If they expect something to be near the top of the page, they don't go looking for it further down.

asking new site visitors to fill out a form before getting what you offered through the social media link.

Consider the trade-offs. If you are asking people to register so you can market to them later, do you lose more than you gain by having people leave early? If people put in fake information just to get past your form, does that end up being a costly pain for you?

6. Send each person on the right way

The great irony of the home page is that it must both

- give people "the big picture" of all that is on the site
- help people move ahead in their conversation very quickly

For most sites, most site visitors' task on the home page is to figure out how to move beyond the home page! You want them to do that by moving forward – and not by leaving the site.

Web sites give people only two ways to move:

- Search.
- Choose a link.

Put Search near the top

If your site has search capability (and any large site should), put the Search box near the top of your web pages – and put it in the same place throughout the site. Don't expect people to scroll to the bottom to look for Search as the site in Figure 4-6 does.

Remember from Chapter 1: In the Nielsen and Loranger study, average time on the home page was 30 seconds.

People look for Search near the top.

The Search box is way down here.

Figure 4-6 Most site visitors will think this site has no search capability.
www.fi.edu

Having the Search box before other content also helps people who listen to the screen. Screen-reading software starts each page at the top. Imagine having to listen to the entire screen before finding where to type your search word.

Use your site visitors' words in your links

When people come to your web site to start a conversation, they have a topic or question in mind. And they are saying that topic or question to themselves in *their* words. When they see links with those words, they gain confidence that you will satisfy their conversation. If they don't see links with their words, they may conclude that you have nothing for them.

Don't use cute, made-up names for programs or projects or article headlines that aren't going to make good connections for your site visitors. Cute doesn't work if it doesn't help your site visitors know where to click.

Don't use your internal organization language for site visitors who don't know that jargon. And don't make people wonder which link to click on.

Headlines as links – Chapter 8
Other points about links –
Chapter 12

 Look at the web site in Figure 4-7. Then, think about Don and Mariella Garcia who need to finance their new car. (Their story was one of our scenarios in Chapter 2.) What would they click on at this credit union's site? Loans? Rates? Services?

If the tabs and links at your site confuse people, they may just leave without exploring further. You've lost their business before they've read any of your copy.

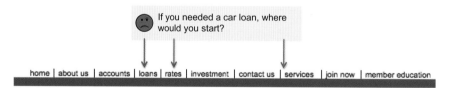

Figure 4-7 Home pages have to help people choose quickly and confidently. Confusing tabs may hinder your site visitors.

In mobile versions, strip down to the essentials

Mobile first! is a good mantra. It can help you focus on your primary personas and their primary conversations. It can help you let go of words.

Wroblewski, *Mobile First*, 2011; Hinman, *The Mobile Frontier*, 2012

On the small screens of mobile devices, your site visitors want to move ahead with the conversation even faster than they do when sitting at their desks. You don't have room for everything. So, the key is to figure out who wants to use your site on a mobile and what their top conversations are – and then make those options clear and easy to find and use.

Compare Lufthansa's web site and mobile app in Figure 4-8. The top task on the web site is booking a trip. The top task on the mobile is checking flight status. The link to book a flight is still there, just not first. And, of necessity, the form that's on the home page of the web site is one click away – but easy to get to – on the mobile.

The mobile app has key tasks in the order people are likely to want them.

The form has to be one click down, but it's easy to get to.

Figure 4-8 For your mobile site or app, focus on top tasks for site visitors who are using a mobile device. They may be different from top tasks for other situations.

www.lufthansa.com

Summarizing Chapter 4

Key messages from Chapter 4:

- Consider the entire site.
  - Your keywords must match searchers' keywords.
  - Gaming the system doesn't work.
  - *Remark*able content is what matters.

- Identify the site.

- Set the site's tone and personality.

- Help people get a sense of what the site is all about.

- Continue the conversation quickly.
  - Focus on your key visitors and their key tasks.
  - Let people start major tasks on the home page.
  - Make sure the forms are high on the page.
  - Don't put unnecessary forms up front.

- Send each person on the right way.
  - Put Search near the top.
  - Use your site visitors' words in your links.
  - In mobile versions, strip down to the essentials by thinking about who uses your site on a mobile and the information and tasks that they most want when using a mobile.

Getting There: Pathway Pages

On a web site with more than a few pages, you can't complete everyone's conversation in one click from the home page. But you must help people get to the information they need as effectively and efficiently as possible.

You do that by setting up useful, usable pathway pages.

On some sites, what I call pathway pages are known as landing pages. On other sites, they are gallery pages. What they all share is the primary function of helping site visitors scan, select, and move on.

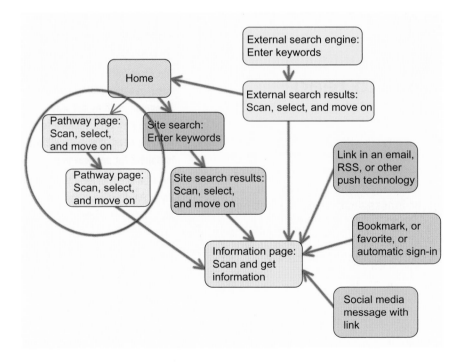

Your busy site visitors are trying to get to "the good stuff" – to whatever they are looking for – as quickly as possible. They don't want to stop and read along the way. They are navigating. They aren't "there" yet.

In this chapter, we explore these six points:

1. Site visitors hunt first.

2. People don't want to read while hunting.

3. A pathway page is like a table of contents.

4. Sometimes, short descriptions help.

5. Three clicks is a myth.

6. Many people choose the first option.

An information page can also be a pathway to related information or more details. More about that in the section on layering in Chapter 7.

1. Site visitors hunt first

When looking for information in a web site, we are bloodhounds. We try to find links with good "scent." We aren't interested in our surroundings. We don't want to be distracted until we've arrived at a good destination.

2. People don't want to read while hunting

On this hunt, our goal is to move ahead, not to stay on the pathway page. We're in "find" mode, not in "read" or "study" mode. Sure, we scan links. And we may read short descriptions. But we don't want to read long, dense paragraphs. That's why pathway pages aren't the right place for welcoming messages or long marketing messages.

Case Study 5-1 shows how little most people read on pathway pages.

The concept of "scent of information" comes from the work of Pirolli, Card, and their colleagues at Xerox's Palo Alto Research Center (now parc, a Xerox company).

The Xerox parc researchers talk about people as information foragers – sniffing our way through web sites, hunting for what we need. It's an excellent metaphor for pathway pages.

More on scent of information: Peter Pirolli at www.parc.com Jared Spool at www.uie.com

Case Study 5-1   Making links clear on a pathway page

The United States has no national registry for vital records, such as birth certificates. To get a copy of your birth certificate, you must find the right office in the state where you were born.

The U.S. government has a portal site that links people to the right place for many needs. In a usability test of that site, we gave people the scenario: "You need a copy of your birth certificate, and a friend said you could get to the right place from this site."

Everyone of the 16 people in our usability test found the link they needed easily. That brought up this web page:

At the time of the test, the portal site was called Firstgov.gov. It's now called USA.gov.

At the time of the test, the link to birth certificates was on the home page. Although it is now four levels down, the path to the right link is very smooth.

The page we are discussing in this case study is also the top search result if you search for "birth certificate" at USA.gov.

Site visitors may not connect "vital records" with "birth certficates."

Usability test participants clicked on B – over and over.

They did not read the paragraph.

What did people do on this page?

No one read the paragraph. Most clicked on B right way, often several times. They did this even though they were all sophisticated web users. They knew that gray meant the link was not available. But their need for their birth certificate overwhelmed the message that the gray B was sending.

What could we do to fix this web content?

Three actions:

- Cut the text drastically.
- Don't use the alphabet—it just confused people.
- Think about the essential message of the page. If this is a conversation, what must the page tell the person who comes to it?

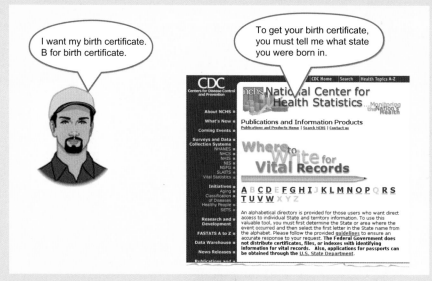

What happened?

The people who own this page could have solved the problem in several ways: a map or a dropdown box, for example. But the simplest way was a short instruction and a list of states – and that's what they did. Site visitors will scroll down a page like this where it is clear that other state names are further down the page.

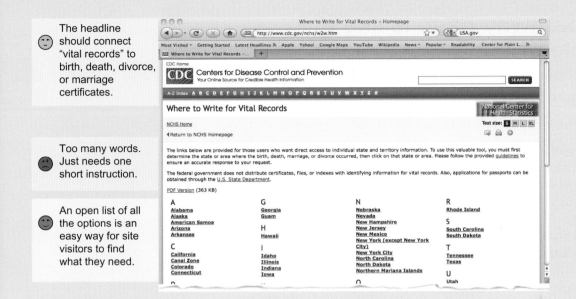

☹ The headline should connect "vital records" to birth, death, divorce, or marriage certificates.

☹ Too many words. Just needs one short instruction.

☺ An open list of all the options is an easy way for site visitors to find what they need.

Notice that the writers also took away the outdated visual metaphor of a pencil. But they've left the headline, Where to Write for Vital Records. They need to say "Vital Records" because that's what many state offices are called – and they can't change state office names. But they also should connect "Vital Records" to what site visitors are looking for – birth, death, divorce, or marriage certificates.

Over time, the writers have kept the wonderful solution of a clear list of states. But they've let the text creep back to being much more than necessary. All that this page really needs is the instruction: Click on the state or territory where the birth, death, divorce, or marriage occurred.

What do we learn from this case study?

Three key takeaways:

- Most people will not read a paragraph of text on a pathway page. They want the page to tell them what to do without having to read much.

- Using the letters of the alphabet may work well as an index – the way into a very long list of topics. But it does not work well for other uses.

- You are in a conversation with your site visitors. As you construct pathway pages, think of the message that the page must send to keep people on a good path.

3. A pathway page is like a table of contents

A table of contents must serve two functions. It must help people

- get a quick overview of what's offered
- pick the place they want to go to

Pathway pages in both information-rich sites and e-commerce sites serve these same two functions. You would not expect to see paragraphs of text or a large distracting picture mixed into a table of contents.

In the birth certificate example of Case Study 5-1, you saw how people skipped a paragraph of explanation. Case Study 5-2 from a more recent usability test with eye-tracking shows what people did on a page that had a large picture and a "congratulations" message.

Case Study 5-2	Getting people to the links quickly

Persona: Margot lives in Seattle, Washington, USA. She has just bought her first house and needs homeowner's insurance.

Scenario: A friend told her that the Office of the Insurance Commissioner (OIC) has good, impartial information: tips on what to consider and information about specific insurance companies.

Conversation:

So far on the web site:

1. Home page choices were:

   - Consumers, Agents/Brokers, Companies.
   - Margot chose Consumers.

2. Next page choices were:

   - Auto, Health, Medicare, Home, Life/Annuity, Long-term Care.
   - Margot chose Home.

And here's where Margot looked on the pathway page that came up:

Notice what Margot did and did not look at: She checked out the headline at the top of the page. She glanced to the right of the picture (probably to see if any text was there). She skirted the paragraph that starts "Congratulations." She jumped to the links. The first link says "How much coverage do you need?" Margot didn't look further. She clicked on that link.

Other usability test participants did what Margot did. So, the web team at OIC gave Margot and their other site visitors a pathway page that puts the links right at the top of the page.

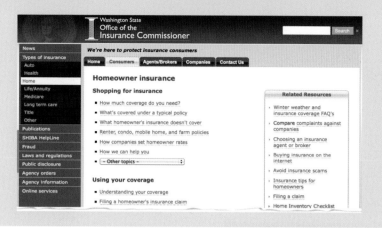

On pathway pages, help people move ahead quickly.

4. Sometimes, short descriptions help

If the links aren't instantly obvious, a few words of description may help your site visitors find what they need. Although people don't want to read paragraphs of text or uninformative marketing messages on pathway pages, they may want just a few words to help them decide which link to choose to move toward their goal. Shell does a pretty good job of this on their pathway page for Products and Services (Figure 5-1).

Figure 5-1 Short descriptions can help people choose on pathway pages.
www.shell.com

Watch the jargon

If the pathway page only uses your internal language, it won't work for site visitors who don't know that language. Use your personas to remember with whom you are conversing.

Don't assume a picture is enough

E-commerce sites often use product pictures as pathway pages. Jared Spool calls these "gallery pages" and points out how frustrating it can be to try to move ahead in your conversation with the site from a picture-only gallery page.

Spool, *Gallery Pages*,
http://www.uie.com/articles/
galleries_reprint

For some items – for example, clothing, crafts, handbags, shoes – we may get enough from the pictures to see meaningful differences. Even here, however, a few details help, as you see in Figures 5-2 and 5-3.

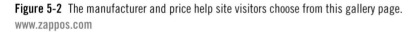

Figure 5-2 The manufacturer and price help site visitors choose from this gallery page.
www.zappos.com

Figure 5-3 Color choices, price, and rating may be what is most important to visitors to this site.
www.landsend.com

The key is to know what questions about the product are uppermost in your site visitors' minds. That's the conversation they want to have. You help them by answering those conversations on your gallery pages.

Technology products – for example, binoculars, cameras, computers, phones – are often not differentiated enough with just pictures. We need more information on the gallery page than you see in Figure 5-4.

Figure 5-4 These pictures won't help most site visitors even select what to compare. www.nokia.com

 And remember that some of your site visitors can't see any of those pictures. If you use picture-based gallery pages, you must have descriptive ALT-text for blind and low-vision site visitors. They have money. They come to buy. Don't abandon them part way through their conversations.

Write in fragments

The short descriptions on the Shell page in Figure 5-1 are each one or two complete sentences, and they work well. But so do the tidbits of information on the Zappos and Lands' End pages in Figures 5-2 and 5-3.

On gallery pages, you don't always need complete sentences. Short descriptions can be fragments or bulleted items. Your site visitors aren't in "read" mode; they're in "help me choose" mode.

5. Three clicks is a myth

Of course, everyone in the organization wants *their* content to be just one click from the home page. But you can only do that if the web site is tiny. Most web sites need pathway pages, so the question becomes: How short must the pathway be?

After watching hundreds of usability test sessions, my answer is that the smoothness of the path is more important than the number of clicks (within reason). If your site visitors are moving steadily on a successful path – following great scent of information – they won't even realize they've clicked four or five times instead of three.

Tom Brinck and his colleagues at Diamond Bullet Design revised a web site through a user-centered process, taking it from an internal-organization focus to a user-task focus. Much of the information on the new site ended up one level deeper – requiring one more click – but time to find the right information went way down and task success went up.

To organize – or reorganize – a site as Brinck and his colleagues did, follow the steps in Interlude 1 on content strategy. Also, do a card-sorting study and work with an information architect.

	Old version	New version
Task success	72%	95%
Average time to complete each task	132 seconds	50 seconds
Number of clicks to get to information: On average, one click **more** in the new version		

Source: From a study by Tom Brinck and colleagues.
http://www.asis.org/Bulletin/Dec-04/brinck.html

Don't make people think

Your site visitors want to get to the right place quickly *and efficiently*. If they have to stop and think about what to do at each step on the pathway, it's not efficient – nor is it quick.

The wording and guideline come from Steve Krug's *Don't Make Me Think!*, 2005.

Keep people from needing to go back

If people can't find the right link to move forward easily, they'll hop part way down one path, back up to try another path, down that second path, possibly back up again, and so on. Jared Spool calls this "pogo-sticking."

Don't make site visitors do this. They get frustrated and leave. If people use the Back button while trying to find what they need on your site, rethink your information architecture – your pathway pages.

6. Many people choose the first option

Humans don't act optimally. As Herbert Simon pointed out many years ago, we "satisfice." We trade time for benefit – often without realizing we are doing it. We make decisions based on what seems "good enough" without exploring all the options.

Busy site visitors click as soon as they see a link that looks as if it might work for them. And the younger your site visitors are, the more likely they are to jump to act.

- Think carefully about the order of information on pathway pages.
- Put the most important links high on the page.
- If you want people to select one option over another, put the one you want them to select first.

 Many site visitors who listen to the screen also choose the first option they hear that sounds reasonable. However, older site visitors – at least in the current generation – tend to be more cautious clickers, looking over all the options before choosing. But they, too, will usually decide that what comes first must be the best choice.

Summarizing Chapter 5

Key messages from Chapter 5:

- If your site is large enough, you may need pathway pages between the home page and the information people want.
- Pathway pages are just that – a way to navigate down a path to the information, product, service, or task the site visitor needs.
- Site visitors hunt like bloodhounds for what they need.
- They don't want to read while hunting.
  - They don't want to be distracted.
  - Welcoming messages and long marketing messages don't work well on pathway pages.
- A pathway page is like a table of contents. It should be mostly links.
- Sometimes, short descriptions help. However, remember these points:
  - Watch the jargon.
  - Don't assume a picture is enough with no description or specs (especially for technology products).
  - It's okay to write in fragments.
- Three clicks is a myth. The smoothness of the path is more important than the number of clicks (within reason).
  - Don't make people think on pathway pages.
  - Keep people from needing to go back.
- Many people choose the first option, so think carefully about what you put first.

Breaking up and Organizing Content

6

Huge documents, dense web pages, and most PDFs are like lectures where one person (the writer) takes up all the time and space. Successful web experiences are conversations.

Over the next four chapters, we'll look at various aspects of this key guideline: **Don't hog the conversation.**

We'll work on

- breaking up and organizing your content (this chapter)
- answering site visitors' questions, letting go of words, layering content, starting with key messages, and breaking up walls of words (Chapter 7)
- announcing your topic with an informative headline (Chapter 8)
- writing useful headings within the topic (Chapter 9)

In this chapter, we tackle four important guidelines:

1. Think "information," not "document."
2. Divide your content thoughtfully.
3. Consider how much to put on one web page.
4. Use PDFs sparingly and only for good reasons.

1. Think "information," not "document"

Most people come to the web for information, not for a complete document. They don't want the manual; they want instructions for the task they are doing. They don't want the handbook; they want the answer to a question. They want usable, manageable pieces.

Right information in the right amount at the right time to the right person in the right medium should be your mantra. Deciding how to do that is part of your content strategy.

Need: Right information in the right amount

 Do you get benefits – health, retirement, vacation – from your employer? How do you get information about those benefits?

In the old, paper-based days, you probably had a three-ring binder of all the information about all your benefits. But did you ever read it all the way through? Probably not.

And even if you read it through once, you almost certainly *used* it differently. You went to it only when you had a question. And you wanted to find just the answer to that question as quickly as possible.

You were having a conversation with the benefits information – a conversation that you started. You wanted the book divided into many topics with easy access to just the one you needed at that moment.

Problem: Little pieces of paper get lost too easily

 What if, instead of the binder, your employer gave you a set of paper index cards with one topic per card all shrink wrapped? Would you have been happy?

I'm sure you said no. Even though you only want one topic, that stack of paper index cards would be hard to store and use.

Solution: Online, "index cards" work well

As we move away from paper, the problem of losing those separate cards goes away. You can think about information in much smaller pieces – satisfying each conversation on a separate index card.

Binders, books, large reports make sense in the paper world.
They are a way to physically keep different topics together. If each
topic were on a separate card, the cards might get mixed up or lost.

Online, we don't need to hold the cards together physically.
Thinking about just how much makes one good conversation
often means breaking up information into different "cards" =
web pages.

Of course, you'll have web pages = index cards of different lengths –
some covering just one question, some covering several questions that
are all part of the same conversation. And you need to make each web
page = index card easy to find through good pathway pages and writing
that matches site visitors' search terms.

Thinking of content as index cards brings us to questions about how
best to break up and organize content. At a high level of organizing

information across a web site, that's information architecture. Let's start there. Then, we'll move down to look at issues in breaking up and organizing specific sections of a web site.

2. Divide your content thoughtfully

Information architecture is a critical part of carrying out your content strategy: How do you divide up and organize the wonderful, valuable content throughout your site? In this section, I'll explore these seven ways with you:

- Questions people ask
- Topic or task
- Product type
- Information type (for example, policies or procedures)
- People
- Life event
- Time or sequence

Card sorting is a great usability technique for finding out how the people whom you want to use your site would sort and group the content. http://usability.gov/ methods/design_site/cardsort .html; Spencer, *Card Sorting*, 2009

Divide web content by questions people ask

Many site visitors come with a specific question. Using those questions is a great way to break up and organize your content at all levels of a site.

On writing good questions:
Chapter 8 – headlines
Chapter 9 – headings

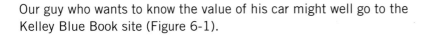

Our guy who wants to know the value of his car might well go to the Kelley Blue Book site (Figure 6-1).

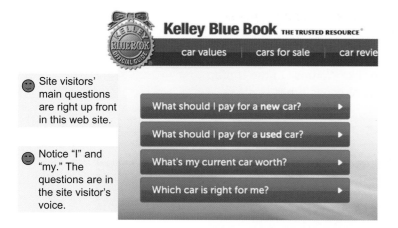

Site visitors' main questions are right up front in this web site.

Notice "I" and "my." The questions are in the site visitor's voice.

Figure 6-1 The folks at Kelley Blue Book know that most people come with one of these four questions.
www.kbb.com

Divide web content by topic or task

Topics are categories of information that are natural groupings for people's questions. Tasks are actions people want to or should take. Tasks answer "How do I...?" questions.

For both topic and task, use your site search analytics to know what people are looking for and the words they use.

The distinction between topic and task may be fuzzy. For example, on the day I grabbed the screen in Figure 6-2, the most popular topic at the Fitbie web site was Simple Ways to Cut 500 Calories. The topic answers the site visitor's conversation: "I need to lose some weight. I know I have to cut calories. How do I do that?" It's a topic that leads to calls to action and tasks.

For topic and task, the question to consider is "granularity" – "grain size" – how much of one task or topic to put together on one web page. Consider some of the other ideas in this section. Also see the next part of this chapter.

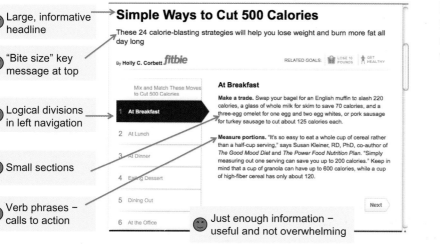

Large, informative headline

"Bite size" key message at top

Logical divisions in left navigation

Small sections

Verb phrases – calls to action

Just enough information – useful and not overwhelming

Figure 6-2 A topic that is broken into small pieces and well organized
www.fitbie.msn.com

Divide web content by product type

Most e-commerce sites use product type as a major divider for their information architecture. That works when site visitors know what type of product they are looking for. A grocery chain, like Waitrose in the United Kingdom, typically divides its site by the type of goods it has to offer (Figure 6-3).

Figure 6-3 E-commerce sites often divide their offerings by product type.
www.waitrose.com

Divide web content by information type

Most sites organize by type of information for at least some of their content: News goes in its own section. Perhaps Events is a section by itself. E-commerce sites often have a separate section on how to use or take care of their products.

Separating and linking related information

Setting up your information architecture by type of information is often a good content strategy. But so is making sure that site visitors can easily move laterally to related information that sits in a different category. For example, link both ways between

- a policy and the procedures for carrying out that policy
- tips or advice about a topic and products related to that topic
- the news release about a research study and the research report

"How do I...?" questions are different from "Can I...?" questions.
"How do I...?" is about tasks or procedures.
"Can I...?" is about policies.

The University of Otago in Dunedin, New Zealand, keeps policies and procedures on separate, but linked, pages, as you see in Figures 6-4 and 6-5.

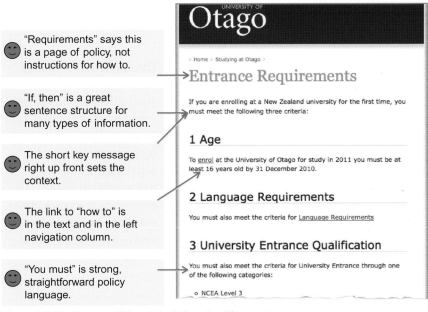

Figure 6-4 Enrollment policies at the University of Otago
http://www.otago.ac.nz/study/entrance

The link to policies is in the text and the left navigation column.

This short list of steps gives students a "big picture" of the process.

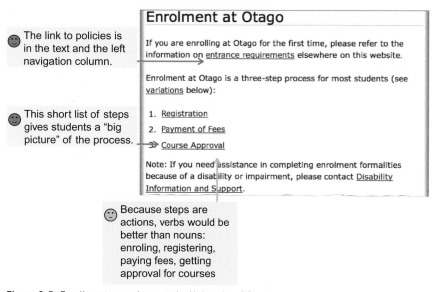

Enrolment at Otago

If you are enrolling at Otago for the first time, please refer to the information on <u>entrance requirements</u> elsewhere on this website.

Enrolment at Otago is a three-step process for most students (see <u>variations</u> below):

1. <u>Registration</u>
2. <u>Payment of Fees</u>
3. <u>Course Approval</u>

Note: If you need assistance in completing enrolment formalities because of a disability or impairment, please contact <u>Disability Information and Support</u>.

Because steps are actions, verbs would be better than nouns: enroling, registering, paying fees, getting approval for courses

Figure 6-5 Enrollment procedures at the University of Otago
http://www.otago.ac.nz/study/enrolment

Moving the conversation ahead through related links

On each web page, ask yourself: Where would site visitors want to go now? It might be to a related piece that is in a different "information type" bucket. When you include those related links, you help people get to the next part of the conversation they want to have.

Although many sites are much better at this type of cross-linking than they used to be, I still see missed opportunities. Sometimes, the lack of linking is a sign that one part of the organization doesn't know that another has relevant information. Break down those silos!

Meshing marketing calendars and editorial calendars

I also see marketing sites where the tips or advice ("features," "articles") don't directly relate to any product. The content writers seem to be in a different world than the product marketers.

If that's true for your site, get the marketing team and the editorial team together. Include them both on the team developing the content strategy.

Make sure they understand the content strategy and their roles in carrying it out. They must work together to see that every piece of content on the site supports the business goals.

Expand your content strategy beyond a single silo, department, group, or medium. Do a content inventory and content audit to find all the information on a given topic, wherever it is in the organization. Use content strategy and information architecture to organize your web site to meet site visitors' needs – not to reflect internal structures.

Divide web content by people

Another useful way to divide and organize your web content is to think about who is going to use the information. Separating information for different site visitors may work well at many levels within a site.

Dividing by people on the home page

On some web sites, it makes sense to keep information for different people totally separate and have your site visitors self-identify right on the home page. The Tricare site in Chapter 4 (Case Study 4-1) now clearly divides information for new people from information for people already on one of the Tricare plans.

Here's another example: Husqvarna, a Swedish company that sells mowers, trimmers, chainsaws, and more, divides site visitors into five groups, as you see in Figure 6-6.

Figure 6-6 Choosing your role narrows your product choices.
www.husqvarna.com/us

Consider, however, these three concerns:

- People have to instantly identify the right group for what they want.
- They have to want to be associated with the name you give their group.
- The same person may be in different groups on different visits.

People have to instantly identify the right group. If your site visitors have to think about which link to choose – or if they might start down a wrong path – this way of dividing information may be more frustrating than helpful.

They have to want to be associated with the name you give their group. Having a section for "Geeks" probably wouldn't be well received at many sites, but it works well for the Exploratorium – a hands-on museum of science for kids of all ages (Figure 6-7).

The Exploratorium is more than a museum. It's a hands-on adventure for "kids" of all ages.

who are you? Tell us who you are and we'll help get you started.

Educators   Parents   Artists   Scientists

Geeks   Teens   Museum Professionals   Curious?

Inviting people in with these roles might not work for other sites, but it seems fine here – even though you could be a geek and a teen, a parent and curious.

Figure 6-7 If you organize content for different groups, be sure those groups like the names you choose.
www.exploratorium.edu

The same person may be in different groups on different visits. Each visit to your site is a separate conversation. And people can wear many different hats. So they may come one day in one hat for a conversation with one part of your site and then come again in a different hat for a conversation with a different part of the site. You need to help them see clearly which group they belong to for each conversation.

For example, I own a business in which I am both an employer and an employee. If I were in the United Kingdom and had to deal with the tax office, how would I choose the right group at the HMRC web site (Figure 6-8)?

Consider whether some people will feel excluded or confused if you divide information by "who you are."

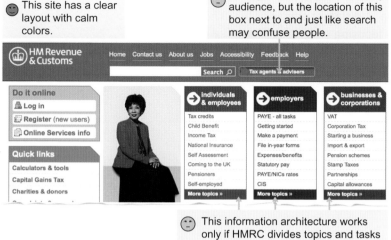

☺ This site has a clear layout with calm colors.

☹ Tax agents must be a secondary audience, but the location of this box next to and just like search may confuse people.

☹ This information architecture works only if HMRC divides topics and tasks into these categories the same way that site visitors divide what falls under each "hat" that they wear.

Figure 6-8 The same person may be an employee, an employer, and owner of a business. www.hmrc.gov.uk

Dividing by people below the home page

Having different content for different site visitors doesn't have to start at the home page. It may be relevant only for some of your content. In Chapter 2 (Figure 2-3), you saw how the U.S. National Cancer Institute offers two sets of information for each type of cancer, suggesting one set for patients and their families and the other for health professionals.

Here's an example from an e-commerce site: Figure 6-9 shows how Bed, Bath, and Beyond helps both gift getters and gift givers on the page for Wedding and Gift Registry.

☺ If you want to get gifts, you start here.

☺ If you want to give gifts, you start here.

Figure 6-9 You might divide information by role for content below the home page. www.bedbathbeyond.com

Divide web content by life event

On some sites, the content is for people at different stages of life. These sites are often about babies or elders – focusing on getting started or on retiring. Figure 6-10 shows how Baby Center takes families from before pregnancy through their child's life stages.

Figure 6-10 The chronology of life is the major organizer for this web site.
www.babycenter.com

Divide web content by time or sequence

Our seventh and last way of dividing content is by time or sequence. Something happens first, then something else, and so on. For example, Bank of America takes site visitors through a series of interactive videos to help them make good decisions about buying a home (Figure 6-11).

Figure 6-11 Although you can work through these interactive videos in any order, the sequence helps site visitors see the steps in buying a home.
http://myhome.bankofamerica.com

Don't organize by your org chart!

I've shown you several ways that work well for organizing web sites. The one way that does not usually work well is having the web site mirror your internal organization.

Your content and information architecture should not rely on your site visitors knowing the internal workings of the agency, company, or nonprofit.

Most site visitors do not know what topics or tasks belong to which part of the organization. Nor do they care! They just want to satisfy their goals, their needs, their conversations. Your web site and social media succeed only by satisfying your site visitors.

3. Consider how much to put on one web page

So far in this chapter, we've talked about web content as index cards rather than big documents. We've talked about ways to think about content for your content strategy and information architecture. Now we need to talk about "grain size." How much information should you put together on one web page?

One page or separate pages? To decide wisely, ask yourself these questions:

- What does the site visitor want?
- How long is the page?
- What's the download time?
- How much do people want to print?
- What will I do for small screens – and for social media?

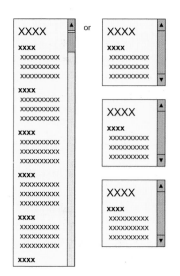

What does the site visitor want?

What conversation does the site visitor want to have with the site? How much information does the site visitor need to satisfy that conversation?

If the content that you now have on one page is actually for different conversations, perhaps it should be divided into several small pages (the index cards we talked about at the beginning of the chapter). Here's an example:

In the first edition, I showed a page from the Australian bookstore, Dymocks. At that time, Dymocks had every bit of their customer service information on one extremely long web page (Figure 6-12). Whether you were looking for the company's privacy policy, how to use its shopping basket, or whether you can return an item, you got to the same web page. You then had to find your question among the 23 topics on that one extremely long web page.

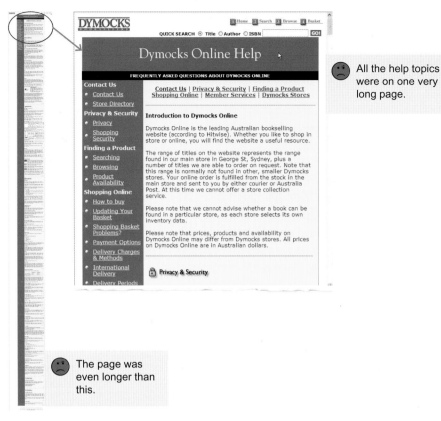

Figure 6-12 Dymocks' Help page in 2006

The only conversation that page supported well was the very unlikely one, "I want to read all of your customer service policies and procedures." Much more likely conversations for customer service are ones like these:

None of these site visitors wants to see the entire customer service page. They each want only the answer to their question – by itself.

For almost all site visitors, a more useful interaction design would be a pathway page with each topic leading to an "index card" – a web page that covers just that topic. That's what Powell's of Portland, Oregon, has been doing for many years (Figure 6-13).

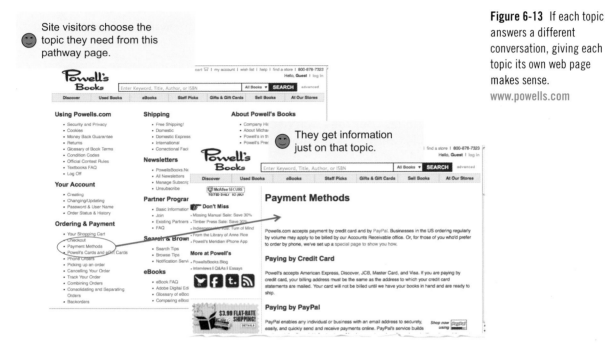

Site visitors choose the topic they need from this pathway page.

They get information just on that topic.

Figure 6-13 If each topic answers a different conversation, giving each topic its own web page makes sense.
www.powells.com

I'm happy to report that Dymocks got at least part of the message. Their web site now breaks that long page into 12 pages (Figure 6-14).

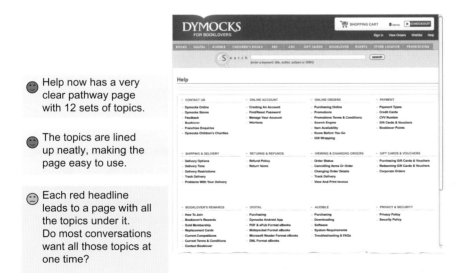

Help now has a very clear pathway page with 12 sets of topics.

The topics are lined up neatly, making the page easy to use.

Each red headline leads to a page with all the topics under it. Do most conversations want all those topics at one time?

Figure 6-14 Dymocks' Help page in 2012
www.dymocks.com.au

For large documents, large reports, large sets of disparate information, use the index card model: Create a mini web site with a table of contents (pathway page) where each link leads to a separate page for that part of the document or report or for each topic in the set.

How long is the page?

Even in the Powell's model, you have to consider how much information you have on each topic: How long would each "index card" have to be to cover everything about a single topic?

Most people today will scroll vertically (not horizontally) if the page layout indicates that the page continues. But they won't scroll forever. Think of three or four scrolls' worth as a maximum length for a web page.

What's the download time?

You may be working on a very fast connection. Your site visitors may not. And consider the mobile experience. On mobiles, downloads can happen very slowly, even if the provider claims high speed connections.

Conversations should proceed smoothly. If people have to wait a long time for your response, they may be annoyed – especially if your response includes much more than they wanted.

On the other hand, if you break the information onto many small pages and your site visitors need all of it to get what they need, waiting for each one to load may be annoying. You're conversing in fits and starts, not smoothly. And the time between pages may make it hard for site visitors to put the information together in their heads.

So you have to think about the issue of download time together with the issues of how much of the information people want and how connected it is in their minds.

How much do people want to print?

If people want just one part of the information and have to print pages and pages to get it, they waste ink, paper, and time. That's frustrating. If you break the information into very short pieces and people have to print several web pages in succession to get what they need, that's also frustrating. So you have to consider who will want to print and what they will want to print.

Write informative titles or headlines for each topic. Write informative headings for each section that you break out from a large document or report. Headlines – Chapter 8 Headings – Chapter 9

Make sure that your pages print well. Always include a way for people to print the content without losing the end of each line of text.

To cover many possibilities, you can offer options as the U.S. National Cancer Institute does for some of its content (Figure 6-15).

Page Options

- 🖨 Print This Page
- 🗐 Print This Document
- 🔍 View Entire Document
- ✉ Email This Document
- 🗎 View/Print PDF
- ▮ Order Free Copy
- ✚ Bookmark & Share

Figure 6-15 You can offer different ways to print a topic.
www.cancer.gov

You can also show the information as small index cards but print it as one page. The Mayo Clinic does this as you can see in Figures 6-16 and 6-17.

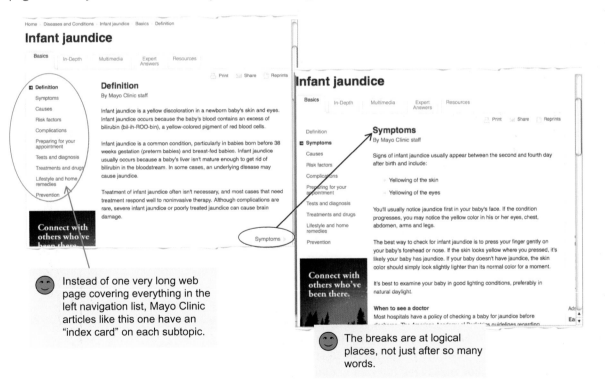

Instead of one very long web page covering everything in the left navigation list, Mayo Clinic articles like this one have an "index card" on each subtopic.

The breaks are at logical places, not just after so many words.

Figure 6-16

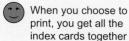

When you choose to print, you get all the index cards together as one article.

Infant jaundice
By Mayo Clinic staff

Original Article: http://www.mayoclinic.com/health/infant-jaundice/DS00107

Definition

Infant jaundice is a yellow discoloration in a newborn baby's skin and eyes. Infant jaundice occurs because the baby's blood contains an excess of bilirubin (bil-ih-ROO-bin), a yellow-colored pigment of red blood cells.

Infant jaundice is a common condition, particularly in babies born before 38 weeks gestation (preterm babies) and breast-fed babies. Infant jaundice usually occurs because a baby's liver isn't mature enough to get rid of bilirubin in the bloodstream. In some cases, an underlying disease may cause jaundice.

Treatment of infant jaundice often isn't necessary, and most cases that need treatment respond well to noninvasive therapy. Although complications are rare, severe infant jaundice or poorly treated jaundice can cause brain damage.

Symptoms

Signs of infant jaundice usually appear between the second and fourth day after birth and include:

- Yellowing of the skin
- Yellowing of the eyes

You'll usually notice jaundice first in your baby's face. If the condition progresses, you may notice the yellow color in his or her eyes, chest, abdomen, arms and legs.

The best way to check for infant jaundice is to press your finger gently on your baby's forehead or nose. If the skin looks yellow where you pressed, it's likely your baby has jaundice. If your baby doesn't have jaundice, the skin color should simply look slightly lighter than its normal color for a moment.

It's best to examine your baby in good lighting conditions, preferably in natural daylight.

When to see a doctor
Most hospitals have a policy of checking a baby for jaundice before discharge. The American Academy of Pediatrics guidelines regarding jaundice recommend that your newborn infant be examined for jaundice whenever a routine medical check is done and at least every eight to 12 hours while in the hospital.

Your baby should be checked for jaundice when he or she is between three and seven days old, when bilirubin

Figure 6-17 You can separate parts of an article online and put them together for printing. www.mayoclinic.com

SEO |

The Mayo Clinic gets great SEO for this article for both *infant jaundice* and *baby jaundice* at Google, Yahoo, and Bing. The headline is right on target. Each section has the keywords in the first line. I'm not sure how search engines count this, but it's interesting to note: Although the article is broken into "index card" pieces, each piece is actually a section of the same URL.

What will I do for small screens – and for social media?

The index card model is really important for mobile. In fact, planning for mobile may help you break up and organize your content into very small chunks, as the writers at the U. K. government site, Directgov, have done (Figure 6-18). And, as you write those small chunks, you can think of extracting key messages for your social media conversations.

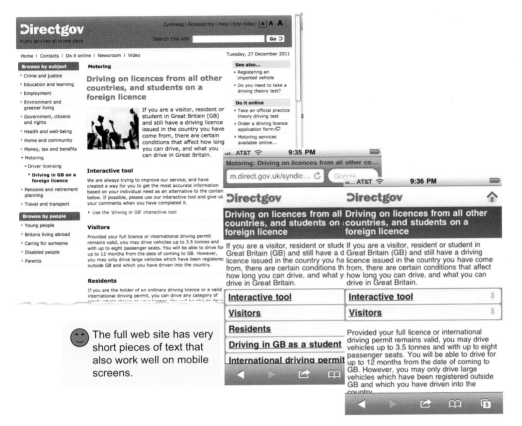

Figure 6-18 If you break up and organize into small pieces, you can make both your full web site and your mobile version converse well with site visitors.
www.direct.gov.uk

4. Use PDFs sparingly and only for good reasons

PDF is a way to publish documents online that anyone can open, read, and print as long as they have Adobe Acrobat Reader. A PDF file keeps the layout, page breaks, and fonts of the original document or slide deck.

PDF = portable document format

PDF from Adobe Systems, Inc.

www.adobe.com

Never say "never"

I'm sure you see how different a PDF is than the conversational, index card model that I'm advocating. However, I'm not going to say, "Never put up a PDF file." As always, it comes down to your goals, your site visitors, and their conversations. And often it also comes down to budget. But remember that in most cases, PDF is a way to *deliver print information*.

When might a PDF file be appropriate?

If you are using your web site to distribute white papers, annual reports, journal articles, or other material that you expect people to print and use on paper, and if your site visitors are comfortable with PDF files, PDF may be the right way to go.

Distribution is the great advantage that the Internet has over paper, even for paper documents.

- You save printing and shipping costs; you shift printing to readers.
- Many people would rather go online than trudge down to the physical library.
- People can get what they want any time – no need to know when the library is open; no need to work only in daytime.
- Searching online may be quicker than hunting in the library – no need to understand the way the library organizes journals; no need to hunt through the library shelves; no worries that someone has already taken out that issue or cut out the article.
- Even people who don't live near a library or who are in countries where mail delivery is slow or unreliable can get instant access.

But you don't need PDF to get information to anyone, anywhere, at any time. The Internet serves all these distribution needs through regular web pages, too.

Another appropriate use of PDF is fillable forms, where you need people to fill out what is essentially still a paper form. With PDF, you can set up the form so people fill it out online and send it to you online.

Sometimes, having both PDF and HTML is best

The web sites of most professional journals give subscribers the option of both PDF and HTML versions of articles. In my usability studies for two different journals, I found the same results: Subscribers like having both versions. They use them differently. When they need to study the article carefully offline, they save or print the PDF. When they want to skim the article, check a fact, grab a quote, or use a graphic (with permission and credit), they choose the HTML.

For white papers, annual reports, and other compilations of information, you might also want to offer both PDF and HTML of the entire document.

But you also should consider setting up the content in small, reusable pieces that you put together in different ways.

For example, the white paper might be a PDF that you want people to download. But you might also have a series of blog articles from different points in the white paper. You might extract key message tidbits for social media messages. You might pull pieces of the information into HTML pages. And in all of these formats, you link to the other options. This increases your inbound links, helps your SEO, and contributes to marketing your content.

When is a PDF file not appropriate?

For many situations, however, PDF is not the way to build a useful, usable web site – especially when the PDF is the only way you offer the information. PDF is a poor choice when your site visitors

- don't want the whole document
- are mostly on mobile devices
- don't want to print
- are not comfortable with PDF files
- need accessible information (And you should always consider accessibility!)

When people don't want the whole document

If your site visitors come for information and the PDF has more than they need, a PDF defeats the very purpose and nature of the web.

Yes, PDF files are searchable, but people don't want to first navigate or search to get the document and then have to navigate or search in a different way within the document.

Yes, you can have a linked table of contents that lets people jump to a specific place in a PDF document; but most PDF files are just put up on the web with no attention to internal links.

When people are mostly on mobile devices

Reading a PDF on the small screen of a smart phone has to be a pretty excruciating experience.

When people don't want to print

Why make the document look just like paper if it is not meant to be used on paper?

For example, a two-column layout works well on paper. It doesn't work well on the screen if you can't see the entire page without scrolling.

When people are not comfortable with PDF files

If your site visitors include many people from the general public, don't assume that they all know what PDF is, have the software downloaded, or are willing to download anything new. If some of your site visitors are on slow connections, think about their frustration in waiting for a large PDF to open when all they need is a small part of the information.

When people need accessible information

AAA Adobe Acrobat now supports setting up a PDF for assistive
ACCESS technology to read well. But . . .

- For a PDF to work well with a screen-reader, the author has to set up the file with correctly marked headings, appropriate tags for images, and other elements that the screen-reader needs. Many PDFs aren't well set up.

- If you just scan a document, it becomes a graphic file and is not accessible. You can make scanned documents accessible through optical character recognition (OCR), but many people don't.

Many people who use screen-readers still bypass PDF files. They have seen few examples to change their expectation that the document will not be accessible.

For help in making new or existing PDFs accessible: http://www.adobe.com/accessibility/products/acrobat/

For help in making a scanned file into an accessible PDF: http://wac.osu.edu/pdf/scan/pdffromscan-textonly.html

Why else is a PDF not appropriate?

Two more reasons for not using PDFs:

PDF files are optimized for the printed page

A typical PDF is in portrait orientation. Most site visitors are looking at landscape-oriented screens.

PDF files usually come from paper documents

If the author was still in "paper mode," or "document mode," or "book mode" when writing what becomes the PDF file, it's very likely that the writing isn't going to work well on the web. The paragraphs will be too long. The headings will be too sparse. The author likely assumed that people would read the document from first page to last.

Most old PDFs just aren't good at conversing with your site visitors. For all these reasons, make part of your content strategy a plan to remove old paper-based PDF files – turning those that still have important information into usable, useful web content.

Summarizing Chapter 6

Key messages from Chapter 6:

- Think "information," not "document."
- Divide your content thoughtfully by
  - questions people ask
  - topic or task
  - product type
  - information type
  - people
  - life event
  - time or sequence
- Consider how much to put on one web page.
  - What does the site visitor want?
  - How long is the page?
  - What's the download time?
  - How much do people want to print?
  - What will I do for small screens – and for social media?
- Use PDFs sparingly and only for good reasons.

Focusing on Conversations and Key Messages

7

In Chapters 4 and 5, we looked at home pages and pathway pages – at responding well to the conversations your site visitors start by getting them quickly to where they need to go. In Chapter 6, we began to focus on not hogging the conversation – breaking up and organizing information to match your site visitors' needs. In this chapter, we continue to focus on not hogging the conversation within a single web topic.

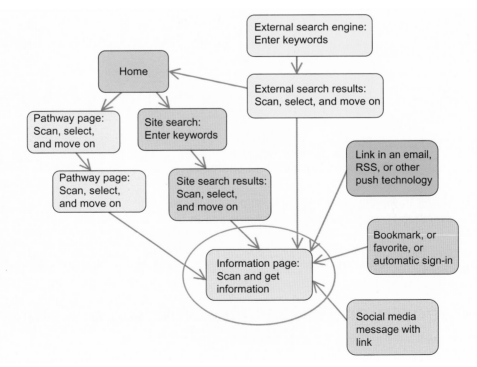

What do you do when you get to an information page – to the page that you think holds what you came to the site to find? Do you immediately start to read it all or do you first skim and scan?

Most people don't jump right in and read. They first scan to decide:

- Did I get where I thought I was going?
- Is what I'm looking for here?

They look at the headline (the level 1 heading). They look for keywords and key messages. From the information design – the visual layout, how short the sections are, how clear the other headings are – they very quickly decide what to do. Most of all, they are focused on *their* goal and *their* conversation. You need to focus on that, too.

Seven guidelines for focusing on conversations and key messages

These seven guidelines will help you converse successfully with your site visitors while getting across your most essential messages:

1. Give people only what *they* need.
2. Cut! Cut! Cut! And cut again!
3. Think "bite, snack, meal."
4. Start with your key message.
5. Layer information.
6. Break down walls of words.
7. Plan to share and engage through social media.

Guidelines like these should be part of your content strategy.

SEO | Following these guidelines will also help optimize your site for search engines. Keywords in headlines and in the first few lines of content on the page will help your SEO – *as long as those keywords match what site visitors put into their searches.*

1. Give people only what *they* need

A good mantra for web sites and social media is **less is more**.

What do your site visitors want to know? Need to know?

- Do they really care about the entire history of your project? Probably not.

- Do they want to hear how much you welcome them before you show them what you have to offer at what price? Probably not.

That content may be important to *you*, but if it isn't important to your site visitors, drop it entirely, put it at the bottom of the page, or layer it through a link to a deeper page.

Revising content you already have

Try this process to improve the way your site converses on a specific topic:

Checklist 7-1
Process for Selecting Web Content

1. **Put the content you now have on the topic aside.**

   I know this is difficult, but you should rethink your topic without being constrained by what the site now says.

2. **Check strategy and architecture.**

   Find out how this topic fits (or not) into your organization's content strategy, marketing strategy, social media strategy, and information architecture. Should you drop it entirely? Should you include it? If it doesn't fit, stop here.

3. **Adopt your persona's perspective.**

   Think about the topic from your site visitors' point of view. Which persona(s) is this for? Put yourself in those personas' place.

4. **List questions.**

   What would those personas ask about the topic? (Use all the sources in Chapter 2 to find out what your site visitors want to know about this specific topic.)

5. **Put the questions in logical order.**

   Which question would the personas ask first? Which next? Go through your list until you have all the questions in an order that is logical to your site visitors.

6. **Cut, paste, rewrite, edit.**

   Now, go back to the content you set aside in Step 1. Use it as source material to answer the questions you have written down. (It's okay to cut and paste as long as you edit what you paste so that it's a good, clear answer to the question.)

7. **See what's left.**

   Look over what is left in your original. Do your site visitors care about any of what is left? Is any of it critical for your site visitors to know? If they care or if it is critical, write a question that your site visitors might ask so that you can give them the answer.

8. **Get more answers.**

   If you have questions in your list for which you do not have an answer, find the right person and get the information. If it's a question people will ask, taking this step will save phone calls later.

9. **Read your new draft.**

   Does it flow logically? Are the questions in your site visitors' words? Are the answers short, straightforward, and clear?

10. **Discard what you have not used.**

    If your site visitors neither need nor care about the information, why include it? This may be the most difficult step of all, but remember that the web is about what people want and need to know, not about saying all there is to say on a topic.

Writing new content

The process for new content is very much the same. You can just leave out the heart-wrenching first step. Start with Step 2.

For Step 6, you won't have old copy as source material. You may have other source material. You may have subject matter experts to work with (or you may be the subject matter expert).

For Step 7, instead of looking over your original, look over all your source material or talk again with your subject matter expert.

Case study 7-1 shows how we might apply this persona-based, conversation-and-key-message-based process to write the content inviting people to participate in a contest.

Case Study 7-1	Using personas and their conversations to plan your content

What if you had to create the content for this web topic?

International Aviation Art Contest
"Create an Air Show Poster" is the theme of this year's contest for children ages 6 to 17.

Following our process, you would ask yourself:

- What do I want to achieve?
  - Have lots of young people enter the contest.
  - Get great entries that we'll want to show.
  - Only get acceptable entries (right people, right theme, right materials, follow the rules) – I don't want people to be unhappy because they couldn't find or understand the information they needed.
- Who are my primary personas for this content? (With whom am I conversing?)
  - Parents
  - Teachers
  - Children old enough to participate (I don't expect the 6-year-olds to read this. They'll hear about it from a parent or teacher, so this persona is most likely a teenager.)
- What will they want to know?

Thinking of people's questions is a great way to analyze web content even if you do not end up using question-and-answer format in your writing.

Continuing to think about these personas and their conversations, you might end up with these questions in this order:

- Who can enter?
- Deadline: When is the entry due?
- Prizes: What can I win?
- Theme: What must the poster show?
- Media: What types of art are acceptable?
- Judging: What will the judges look for?
- Where do I send my entry?

In addition to these questions from your personas, you may have information that people need but that they may not have thought about and so wouldn't ask about. For example, in this case, you know that an adult must certify that the child did the work. So you add another question to the list:

- Who must certify that the child made the poster?

Because people have to do that before they send it in, you might put that question next to last in your ordered list.

You now have an outline for your content, and that might lead you to create a page like this:

International Aviation Art Contest

This year's theme: A poster for an air show

Who can enter?
All children from age 6 to age 17 may participate. The child's age on December 31, 2012 is what counts.

Deadline: When is the entry due?
Entries must be postmarked by **January 11, 2013**.

Prizes: What can I win?
Entries will be divided into three age groups:
6 to 9 years; 10 to 13 years; 14 to 17 years.

The contest starts on the state level.

State prizes
Winners and runners-up in each state get a certificate and recognition from their state. The top three entries in each age group from each state go on to the national competition.

National prizes
Judges will pick a national winner and two runners-up in each age group. They all get certificates, ribbons, and a framed photograph of their artwork -- and their work will be sent on to the international competition. The first place national winners also get a professional work of art from the American Society of Aviation Artists.

International prizes
Winners in the international competition get certificates and gold, silver, or bronze medals.

Media: What types of art are acceptable?
- Size should be 11 inches by 17 inches.
- **8½ by 11 is not acceptable because of international rules.**
- All artwork must be handmade by the child.

Acceptable media	NOT acceptable media
watercolor	pencil
acrylic or oil paints	charcoal
indelible markers	other nonpermanent media
colored pencils	computer generated work
felt-tip pens	collage work involving the use of photocopies
soft ball-point pens	
indelible ink	
crayon or similar indelible media	

What will the judges look for?
The judges will look for creative use of the theme in relation to aviation.

Who must certify that the child made the poster?
A parent, guardian, or art teacher must certify that the entire artwork is the original work of the child.

Make sure the certificate is fastened to the poster with tape or glue. Also, **please print the name of the artist on the back of the poster and please print legibly.**

Where do we send the poster?
Get the <u>Entry Form for the 2012 International Aviation Art Contest</u>.

When it is ready, send the poster with the appropriate paperwork to your <u>state's sponsor office</u>.

My version, adapted from facts about the actual contest

2. Cut! Cut! Cut! And cut again!

People read on the web and in social media when they need the information or it engages them. But they don't want to read long, meandering paragraphs. They want to grab information quickly.

Checklist 7-2
Process for Cutting Down to Essential Messages

1. **Start with your new draft.**

   Go through the steps in Checklist 7-1.

2. **Focus on the facts. Cut the flab.**

3. **Focus on your site visitors and what they want to know.**

   Cut out words that talk about you or the organization – unless your site visitors want or need that information.

4. **Put your new draft away for a day or two.**

   Then, take it out and see if you can cut some more without losing your essential messages.

5. **Read it out loud.**

   Ask a colleague to read it out loud. Ask a few representative site visitors to read it out loud.

6. **Listen carefully and revise.**

Don't ask people for their opinion of the content. Ask them to tell you what the content said. What's important is whether they "got" their answers and your key messages.

As an example for the first two guidelines in this chapter, look at Figure 7-1. It's from the web site of a university's medical center.

 What would you say are the writer's goals, the personas, and the personas' goals and conversations for this content?

My analysis:

- Writer's goals:
  - People will make appointments efficiently.
  - They will call the right number for their situation.
  - They will be happy with the process of making an appointment.

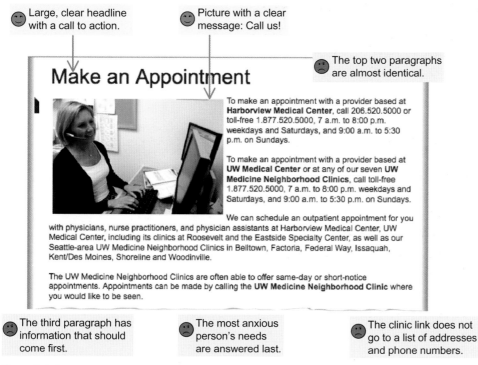

Large, clear headline with a call to action.

Picture with a clear message: Call us!

The top two paragraphs are almost identical.

The third paragraph has information that should come first.

The most anxious person's needs are answered last.

The clinic link does not go to a list of addresses and phone numbers.

Figure 7-1 Paragraphs are not the best way to convey this information quickly.
http://uwmedicine.washington.edu

- Personas for this web content:
  - Someone who is ill or hurt (anxious, in pain)
  - A family member of someone who is ill or hurt (also anxious)
  - A person needing a routine check-up (may be anxious about having to deal with medical situations)

- Personas' goals:
  - Get an appointment at the right place at a good time
  - Spend as little time as possible on the phone

- Personas' conversations (questions):
  - How do I make an appointment?
  - What if I need an appointment right away?
  - What's the phone number?
  - When will you answer the phone?

Given that analysis, we might revise the content into Figure 7-2.

My revision has 40% fewer words (157 to 93). We could cut it even more by not having the first sentence under the first question (157 to 81; 48%

fewer words). I included that sentence as reassurance to the personas and to explain why they had to go to a neighborhood clinic and not the main medical center. Writing always requires judgments like this.

A more informative headline ☺ has info that was buried in the third paragraph.

The most anxious persona's ☺ content comes first.

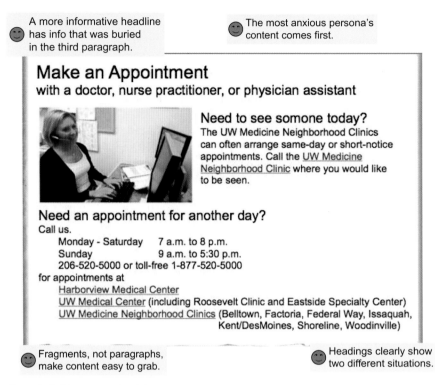

Make an Appointment
with a doctor, nurse practitioner, or physician assistant

Need to see somone today?
The UW Medicine Neighborhood Clinics can often arrange same-day or short-notice appointments. Call the UW Medicine Neighborhood Clinic where you would like to be seen.

Need an appointment for another day?
Call us.

Monday - Saturday   7 a.m. to 8 p.m.
Sunday   9 a.m. to 5:30 p.m.
206-520-5000 or toll-free 1-877-520-5000
for appointments at
Harborview Medical Center
UW Medical Center (including Roosevelt Clinic and Eastside Specialty Center)
UW Medicine Neighborhood Clinics (Belltown, Factoria, Federal Way, Issaquah,
                                                        Kent/DesMoines, Shoreline, Woodinville)

☺ Fragments, not paragraphs, make content easy to grab.

☺ Headings clearly show two different situations.

Figure 7-2 My suggested revision

3. Think "bite, snack, meal"

What if you have a lot of information on a topic, but some people just want the "soundbite," others want a little more, and a few want all the details? You can satisfy all those conversations by thinking "bite, snack, meal."

I learned this wonderful concept from Leslie O'Flahavan and use it with her permission.

www.ewriteonline.com

Bite: the kernel

Snack: the main fruit

Meal: the whole thing - meat and potatoes

Bite = headline, link, or both plus a very brief description.

Snack = key message or brief summary. The snack can be a bit on the home page, a separate bold or italic line at the top of an article, the first bit of information in a blog post, or the summary to a very large report.

Meal = the details. The meal can be the rest of an article or blog post, a deeper web page linked from the snack, or the full report.

Figure 7-3 from REI, a major seller of outdoor clothes and gear, shows how you can apply "bite, snack, meal" to an article.

How to Choose Bike Shoes

😊 The picture and headline on a pathway page = bite

😊 The headline with the article matching the link = bite repeated

How to Choose Bike Shoes

You can ride a bike in just about any shoes, but anyone who rides regularly can benefit from shoes designed specifically for bicycling. Shoes compatible with "clipless" pedal systems are a logical step up if you seek greater cycling efficiency. This article discusses your bike shoe options.

😊 The first paragraph elaborating the point = snack

Why Bike Shoes?

If you ride using flat (platform) pedals, you've no doubt seen riders zipping by you with their feet firmly anchored to their pedals and wondered if that might be a wise choice for you. Fear not, bike shoes and clipless pedals are part of a natural progression to make your riding more efficient and less tiring.

😊 The whole article = meal Notice how easy the meal is to digest with a question heading and personal pronouns.

Compared to typical athletic shoes, cycling shoes are designed with **stiffer soles to provide more efficient energy transfer** as you pedal away. These stiff soles provide other benefits, too. They protect your feet while riding and support the full length of your feet to reduce cramping and fatigue. The uppers are also relatively rigid for extra support.

Cycling shoes are usually paired with a compatible pedal to hold your feet securely on the bicycle. The so-called **clipless shoe-pedal combination** offers unmatched control with a minimum amount of your pedaling energy lost before it reaches the rear wheel.

Quick Overview

In a hurry? Here's an overview of the most popular shoe-pedal attributes:

	Road Biking	Mountain Biking, Casual or Touring
Outsole type	Smooth	Lugged
Outsole rigidity	Very stiff	Stiff
Cleat style	Protrudes from sole	Recessed into sole
Clipless pedal style	3-hole (Look style)	2-hole (SPD style)

For a closer look at your options, read on.

😊 Each short description and picture of a type of bike shoe ends with a link to the specific shoes of that type that REI offers. Great example of finding marketing moments

Types of Bike Shoes

If you're considering clipless pedaling but are unsure where to start, don't worry. Your choices can be quickly paired down by the type of riding you intend to do. We cover shoe shopping in this article, but you may want to shop for pedals first (see our Q&A discussion below for more information).

😊 If you decide that you need to consider pedals first, this link = bite for the article on pedals.

For pedal information, see the REI Expert Advice article on How to Choose Bike Pedals.

Casual (Sport) Riding Shoes

If you ride casually (say, 5 miles or less)

Figure 7-3 The bite (on a pathway page) leads to the snack (top of the article) and then to the meal (rest of the article).

www.rei.com

Bite, snack, meal brings together two very important guidelines for
successful web writing:

- Start with your key message.
- Layer information.

Let's explore those concepts in the next two sections.

4. Start with your key message

Whatever your key message is, put it first. Put it in the headline
(the bite) and elaborate it quickly in the beginning of the text
(the snack).

For some people, that will be enough. They get the point. They don't
need more. For others, a good bite and snack will entice them further
into the content. If you don't capture readers' attention with a good bite
and snack, they are likely to leave.

Many site visitors read only a few words of a page – or a paragraph –
before deciding if it is going to be relevant and easy for them to get
through.

Key message first = inverted pyramid style

Journalists and technical writers know that many readers skim headlines
and the first paragraphs of articles. That's why they write in inverted
pyramid style – with the main point first.

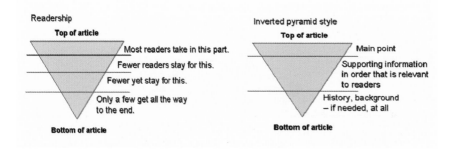

For many web content writers, however, inverted pyramid style requires a
major shift in thinking and writing. For school essays and reports, you
were probably taught to write in narrative style, telling a whole story in

chronological order and building to the main point at the end – the conclusion. That's not a good style for the workplace or the web.

Busy site visitors want the conclusion first.

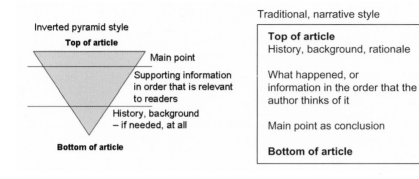

Although it may be difficult at first to start with the conclusion, it's a very useful skill. As Chip Scanlan says:

> [Inverted pyramid style] is also an extremely useful tool for thinking and organizing because it forces the reporter to sum up the point of the story in a single paragraph. Journalism students who master it and then go on to other fields say it comes in handy for writing everything from legal briefs to grant applications.

And, I'll add, for writing successful web content.

Scanlan's blog on inverted pyramid is at http://www.poynter .org/how-tos/newsgathering-storytelling/chip-on-your-shoulder/ 12754/writing-from-the-top-down-pros-and-cons-of-the-inverted-pyramid/, **updated March 2, 2011.**

Figures 7-4 and 7-5 show the difference between narrative style and inverted pyramid style, respectively, through two articles on the same topic.

Greenland Ice Is Melting – Faster and Faster!

A new paper by scientists of Utrecht University, Institute for Marine and Atmospheric Research, in collaboration with colleagues from the Netherlands Royal Meteorological Institute, Delft University of Technology, Bristol University (UK), and the Jet Propulsion Laboratory (USA) was published in *Science* recently. The work used the Regional Atmospheric Climate Model to calculate surface processes over Greenland, statellite radar measurements to determine iceberg production, and ice sheet mass loss from the Gravity Recovery and Climate Mission (GRACE) satellites.

Figure 7-4 The headline and first 75 words – narrative style – no key message
www.enn.com

> **Greenland Ice Melting Faster Than Expected**
>
> The Greenland ice sheet is melting faster than expected, according to a new study led by a University of Alaska Fairbanks researcher and published in the journal *Hydrological Processes*.
>
> Study results indicate that the ice sheet may be responsible for nearly 25 percent of global sea rise in the past 13 years. The study also shows that seas now are rising by more than 3 millimeters a year – more than 50 percent faster than the average for the 20th century.

Figure 7-5 The headline and first 80 words – inverted pyramid – key message and data
www.sciencedaily.com

 Did the second version do a better job of engaging you? With the first version, did you stop reading part way through the first paragraph?

Eye-tracking shows the need for key message first

Like many other usability specialists, I've seen a lot of this behavior: Site visitors read a bit at the top and then skim until something catches their attention. That could be a bold heading, a bulleted list, or a word that they are searching for. Eye-tracking data often confirms this observation.

Figure 7-6 shows accumulated eye-tracking data (a heat map) for a web information page. Notice how people looked in an F pattern – across the lines at the top of the information and then at the beginning of the bulleted list. Notice how, after the first few lines, they looked more at the beginning of lines than all the way across. Notice how reading trails off down the page.

 Blind web users act similarly. They scan with their ears. They listen to only a few words before deciding whether to keep going. With their screen-readers, blind web users can jump to the next link or the next heading or to the next paragraph – and they do so at an amazingly rapid pace.

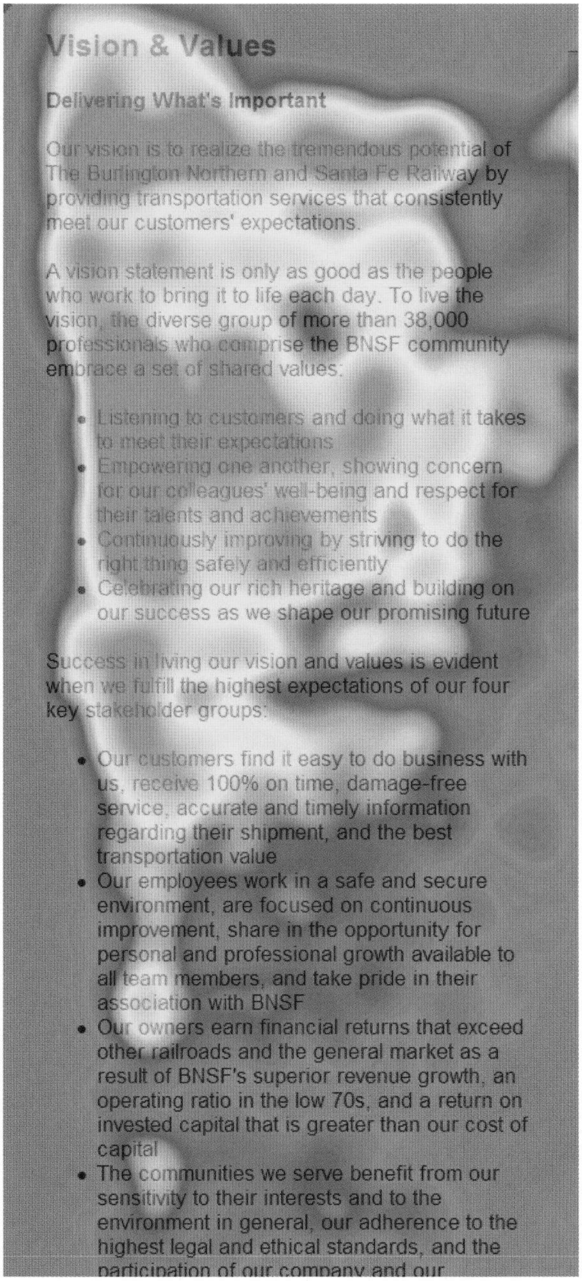

Figure 7-6 This heat map from eye-tracking shows the typical F pattern of web reading on information pages. Readers looked most at the first paragraph and then at the beginning of bulleted lists. The colors show the concentration of eye fixations, with red indicating the heaviest concentrations and blue the least.

Eye-tracking by Jakob Nielsen and Kara Pernice, Nielsen Norman Group. Used with permission. For more about the study this picture came from, see www.useit.com/eyetracking and *Eyetracking Web Usability*, 2010.

5. Layer information

Layering is a way of dividing web information. When done well, layering

- keeps site visitors from being overwhelmed
- helps site visitors who want different levels of information

Bite, snack, meal is one way to layer. In the next two sections, I show you examples of layering by:

- opening extra information on top of what site visitors or app users are doing
- progressively disclosing information within the content, letting people open and close pieces as needed

Layering with an overlay

You can take advantage of layering to provide definitions, technical details, or other "extra" information. When you provide rollovers or open a small secondary window on top of the main page, your site visitors don't lose the context.

Figure 7-7 shows how Traffic.com gives details of traffic problems.

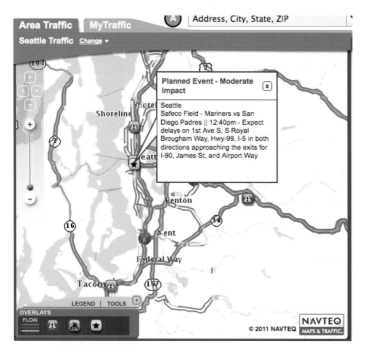

Figure 7-7 Clicking on any warning symbol on this traffic map brings up a small overlay with details of the problem — a good use of layering without losing context.
www.traffic.com

Even on tablets and mobiles, I see some interesting uses of overlays. For example, Figure 7-8 shows the details for an airline flight over the map showing the flight's route. Other overlays allow you to add flights to track and choose which of the flights you are tracking to look at. The app tracks flights in real time.

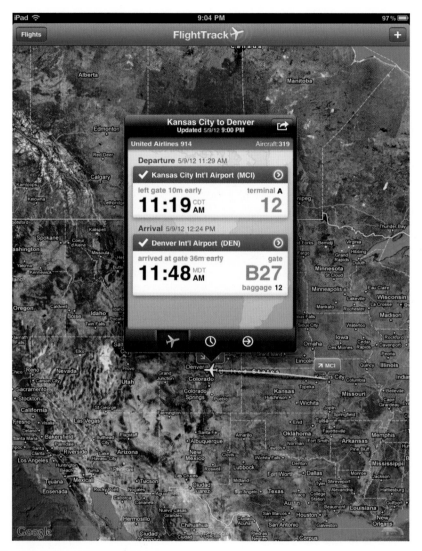

Figure 7-8 An overlay on a tablet app.

Layering with progressive disclosure

You can layer within the context in even more innovative ways. Case Study 7-2 shows how a team in Washington state helps injured workers file and follow their claims.

Case Study 7-2	Opening layers on the same web page

You can use progressive disclosure – opening and closing overlays – to give site visitors what they need without leaving the main content. Let me show you how the web team at the Washington State Department of Labor & Industries (L&I) approached and solved the problem of helping injured workers understand the process for claiming benefits.

Purposes, personas, conversations

They started with our three planning questions.

What does the agency want to achieve?

- Fewer phone calls
- Complete, correct claims
- Satisfied clients

Who is the agency conversing with?

The site is for people like Joe.

Joe

- 26 years old
- construction worker
- high school graduate; no college
- married, no children yet
- likes to be outdoors
- has an old home computer his brother gave him
- doesn't use the computer much
- is in pain from his injuries
- is skeptical about whether the government agency is going to be helpful if he tries to get information about what to do

Joe fell off a scaffold on a construction job last week. He knows he's lucky that he's going to be okay. But he sprained an ankle, injured his back, and broke his arm. He won't be able to work for a while.

Joe is worried about money. His wife, Lily, works in retail, but they won't be able to get through the month with just her salary. They're going to be relying on the checks he should get from the government agency that handles benefits for injured workers.

His employer and the doctor both told him .he has to file a claim to get paid while he is out of work because he is injured. He wants to be sure that he files the claim correctly so he starts getting paid quickly.

What does Joe want from the site?

- File the claim correctly so he starts getting paid quickly.
- Understand what happens next.

Constraints

The writers have to explain a complicated process that they cannot change.

Solution

Thinking about their goals; Joe, the injured worker, and his questions; and the content they needed to provide, the L&I team created a mini web site with

- each phase in the process as a tab
- one page for each phase
- layering within the page where links open to more information without changing the underlying page

The three screens that follow show you how this works.

Injured? What you need to know

en Español

Contact Us

| Phase 1
Injured at work | Phase 2
File a claim | Phase 3
Approved claim
OR
Phase 4
Rejected claim | Phase 5
Getting back to work | Phase 6
Closed claim |

Injured at work.

If you are injured at work or develop an occupational disease and your claim is accepted, workers' compensation (L&I or your self-insured employer) pays for medical care directly related to your accident or illness. If you are unable to work following your injury, you may be eligible for a portion of your lost wages. Most important, L&I or your self-insured employer may help coordinate a safe and timely return to work.

If your employer is self-insured, your rights and benefit entitlement don't change, but who manages your claim and the process is different. Your employer, not L&I, handles your paperwork and pays for the claim.

About a third of all Washington employees work for self-insured employers. **Read** A Guide to Industrial Insurance Benefits for Employees of Self-insured Businesses (F207-085-000) **to better understand employee benefits.**

Make sure you:

⊙ Get first aid.

See a doctor if needed.

Tell your employer.

Find out:

What your employer needs to do.

What your doctor needs to do.

What to do if injured while working out of state.

⊂ More about workers' comp claims

⊂ Claim information online in Claim & Account Center 🔒

Get first aid.

Many falls, cuts, and sprains can become serious injuries if they aren't treated right away. If it's a minor injury, get first aid at your workplace.

Did you know?

In Washington, all employers are required to have a first-aid kit at the workplace.

The screen for phase 1 of the process

www.lni.wa.gov

Injured? What you need to know

en Español

Contact Us

Phase 1 **Injured at work**	Phase 2 **File a claim**	Phase 3 **Approved claim** OR Phase 4 **Rejected claim**	Phase 5 **Getting back to work**	Phase 6 **Closed claim**

Injured at work.

If you are injured at work or develop an occupational disease and your claim is accepted, workers' compensation (L&I or your self-insured employer) pays for medical care directly related to your accident or illness. If you are unable to work following your injury, you may be eligible for a portion of your lost wages. Most important, L&I or your self-insured employer may help coordinate a safe and timely return to work.

If your employer is self-insured, your rights and benefit entitlement don't change, but who manages your claim and the process is different. Your employer, not L&I, handles your paperwork and pays for the claim.

About a third of all Washington employees work for self-insured employers. **Read** A Guide to Industrial Insurance Benefits for Employees of Self-insured Businesses (F207-085-000) **to better understand employee benefits.**

Make sure you:

Get first aid.

See a doctor if needed.

▶ Tell your employer.

Find out:

What your employer needs to do.

What your doctor needs to do.

What to do if injured while working out of state.

Tell your employer

If you are injured on the job or diagnosed with an occupational disease, let your employer know right away. Employers need to know about injuries and be familiar with the situation when the L&I paperwork arrives so that they can help you plan your return to work.

Questions workers have

What if I can't do my job?

How will my injury affect my employer's costs?

What if my employer wants me to see a company doctor?

What if my employer wants a company nurse or representative to accompany me to the doctor?

What if my employer says my company is self-insured?

I'm afraid to report my injury because I don't want to get fired. What do I do?

The same screen after you have clicked "Tell your employer."

Injured? What you need to know

en Español

Contact Us

Phase 1	Phase 2	Phase 3	Phase 5	Phase 6
Injured at work	**File a claim**	**Approved claim**	**Getting back to work**	**Closed claim**
		Phase 4		
		Rejected claim		

Injured at work.

If you are injured at work or develop an occupational disease and your claim is accepted, workers' compensation (L&I or your self-insured employer) pays for medical care directly related to your accident or illness. If you are unable to work following your injury, you may be eligible for a portion of your lost wages. Most important, L&I or your self-insured employer may help coordinate a safe and timely return to work.

If your employer is self-insured, your rights and benefit entitlement don't change, but who manages your claim and the process is different. Your employer, not L&I, handles your paperwork and pays for the claim.

About a third of all Washington employees work for self-insured employers. Read A Guide to Industrial Insurance Benefits for Employees of Self-insured Businesses (F207-085-000) to better understand employee benefits.

Make sure you:

Get first aid.

See a doctor if needed.

Tell your employer.

Find out:

What your employer needs to do.

What your doctor needs to do.

What to do if injured while working out of state.

Tell your employer

If you are injured on the job or diagnosed with an occupational disease, let your employer know right away. Employers need to know about injuries and be familiar with the situation when the L&I paperwork arrives so that they can help you plan your return to work.

Questions workers have

What if I can't do my job?

If you have work restrictions, your doctor will explain them on the Activity Prescription Form (F242-385-000).

How will my injury affect my employer's costs?

What if my employer wants me to see a company doctor?

You may see a company doctor if you wish, but you have the right to choose your own doctor.

What if my employer wants a company nurse or representative to accompany me to the

The same screen after you have clicked on two of the questions

When I show this example, people ask me how it's done and whether it's accessible for people who listen with screen-readers. The answer is yes. It's done with Show/Hide in Javascript.

Show/Hide does not reload the page. Reloading a page is a problem for people with screen-readers because the screen-reader assumes it is a new page and starts reading again from the top of the page. With progressive disclosure (Show/Hide), when a screen-reader user clicks on a link that opens text just below or next to the link, the screen-reader continues reading whatever is open – thus, reading the newly shown information as intended.

6. Break down walls of words

As you put together all the guidelines in this chapter about giving people only what they need; cutting your content down to essentials; thinking in terms of "bite, snack, meal"; putting the key message first; and layering information, also remember the message of Chapter 3: design matters. Information design matters. If your content looks too dense, people won't even discover that it has what they need.

Walls are barriers. Large blocks of text that look like wall-to-wall words are barriers. Whether your site visitors are on large screens, tablets, or mobiles, very short paragraphs or bullet points work best.

Lots later on how to break down walls of words:

Headings – Chapter 9

Short sentences – Chapter 10

Lists and tables – Chapter 11

On the web, each small section needs its own heading. Each question and answer needs the question as a heading and the answer in short sentences or as a bulleted list.

Case Study 7-3 shows how changing from a paragraph to a bulleted list increased business for an e-commerce company.

Case Study 7-3	Breaking down walls of words made the difference!

When CompareInterestRates.com tried a variety of changes to their online form, the only one that made a significant difference was revising the introduction at the top of the form from paragraphs of text to a bulleted list. Here's how the original started:

Request a Personalized Rate Quote

Tired of calling a list of mortgage providers only to be asked the same questions over and over again? Let our lenders and brokers come to you! By providing the following information, one or more companies in your area will provide a "personalized quote" on your borrowing request. Most will respond in less than 24 hours. Please complete this form as thoroughly as possible.

We respect your privacy. This is a confidential request and your personal information will only be sent to lenders and brokers in your area who are customers of CompareInterestRates.com For more information, see our privacy statement.

Property State | Please Choose One ▼

The top of the old form

What they tried

Working with Caroline Jarrett, a usability consultant, the client tried several variations of the form, with combinations of these changes:

- including a photo or not (and variations of the photo by size and content)
- placement in the window (centered or left-justified)
- color in the fields or no color
- colored background behind the form (blue or yellow) or no color
- reworking the text at the top

What they measured

This was a typical A/B test measuring conversion rates. People got to the form by clicking on a web page ad or through a sponsored link on a search engine page. Each person saw only one version – but it might be any one of the several versions: A, B, C, D, and so on. What mattered was what percentage of the people who saw each version actually completed and submitted the form, requesting a personalized quote for mortgage rates.

What they found

The new forms increased conversion rates from 5% to 7.3% in one stream of traffic and from 10% to 12.5% in another stream of traffic. In the world of conversion rates, that is excellent improvement.

At first, however, it was not clear which change was contributing most to the success. With detailed statistical analysis, it became clear that **only reworking the text at the top had a significant impact.** Here's one of the variations showing the bulleted list at the top instead of a wall of words.

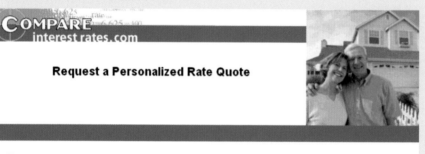

Usability testing with eye-tracking supported the conclusion from the conversion rate study. All the participants in the usability test preferred the bullet points.

A great site where you can see many tests like this, pitting versions against each other:
www.whichtestwon.com

You get to see if you can pick the winner and then you find out if you were right. Lots of fun – and lots of great examples.

See Jarrett and Minott, 2004, for the complete story of this study.

7. Plan to share and engage through social media

The need to be succinct in social media reinforces all the guidelines in this chapter. Whether you are working within the 140 characters of Twitter, putting a message on your Facebook wall, posting to Google+, describing a video or slide deck you are sharing through YouTube or SlideShare, or using another social media program, you only have room for your key message.

Think "bite, snack, meal." Put the bite into your social media message. Make it engage people so they click on the link to a specific snack in your web site. If you have more for them, let the snack lead to a fuller meal. But remember to make even the meal easy to digest – no walls of words, please.

Summarizing Chapter 7

Key messages from Chapter 7:

- Give people only what they need.
- Cut! Cut! Cut! And cut again!
- Think "bite, snack, meal."
- Start with your key message. Write in inverted pyramid style.
- Layer information.
- Break down walls of words.
- Plan to share and engage through social media.

If you are a copy writer – whether you work freelance, for an agency, or inside an e-commerce company – everything in this book is relevant to you. This interlude just adds a few points about marketing online.

Marketing on the web is different: Pull not push

In traditional, paper-based, direct marketing, you start the conversation. You send information to people. When they get it, they don't have their own need, their own agenda, in mind. You are putting a need in front of them and hoping that it resonates with them.

That's a "push" technology – you push information out to potential customers.

Of course, push also exists in the web world. You probably have many people who have registered to receive e-marketing from you (e-specials, e-newsletters). You encourage people to follow you on Twitter and friend you on Facebook so you can push ideas and enticements out to them.

But most visits to your web site probably don't come directly from that e-marketing. Most web contacts are part of a "pull" technology.

People come to your web site of their own choice because they think you might have something they want to buy. And that changes everything. They start the conversation.

As a marketing specialist, you may have been trained to think about how to draw people *in* to your products. On the web, however, your first worry should be how to *not drive away* the people who have chosen to come to your site.

Because site visitors are usually very focused on whatever brought them to the site, they are very likely to bypass any messages that don't help them satisfy the conversation they came for – until they've met their need. Then, you can entice them to consider more.

Join the site visitor's conversation

Our gal looking for a service provider got to this provider's site and immediately saw a tab called Solutions. Opening that tab, she saw the options were For Home, For Business, and so on. She clicked on For Home expecting to get plans, prices, perhaps bulleted lists of what she would get for each plan. She didn't expect what she got (Figure Interlude 2-1).

Look back:

Case Study 5-2: The site visitor didn't read the paragraph that starts with "Congratulations."

Case Study 7-3: The "after" version that got much better conversion gets right to the point. The "before" version starts with a marketing pitch that doesn't help the conversation.

Figure Interlude 2-1 On this page, the company just talks about itself. It doesn't join the conversation the site visitor started. It's pushing too much marketing too soon. www.hughes.com

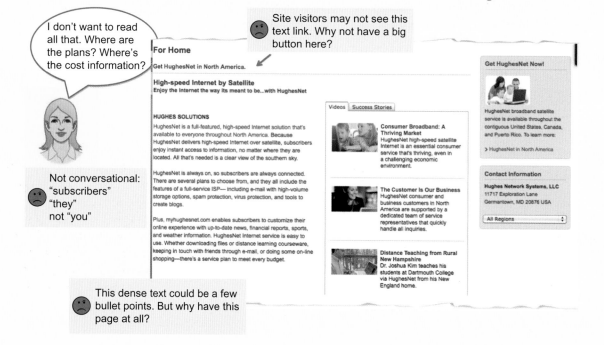

The site does have what our gal is looking for (Figure Interlude 2-2). But from the screen she's on, she'll find it only if she notices the links (in text; no buttons) – and if she's not turned off by the dense paragraphs of "read about us" marketing.

Figure Interlude 2-2 Successful marketing makes itself part of the conversation that the site visitor started.
www.hughesnet.com

Find the right marketing moments

The way to market on a web site is to join the conversation that site visitors bring to you. Then, you can cross-sell and upsell – but only *after* your site visitors have satisfied at least part of the conversation they started with the site.

I call these times when site visitors are ready to hear what you have to offer, "marketing moments."

A "marketing moment" is a time and place on the web site when site visitors are ready for a marketing message. A marketing moment is not meant to distract your site visitor. A marketing moment is a natural follow-on or complement to what your site visitor is doing.

Figure Interlude 2-3 shows you how Amazon.com is a master at marketing moments.

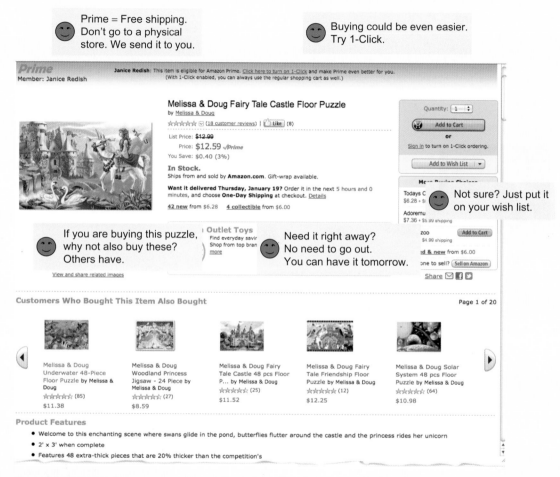

Figure Interlude 2-3 Amazon.com and many other online sellers find many marketing moments — within the site visitor's conversation.

www.amazon.com

Don't miss good marketing moments

I'm amazed at how many sites put lots of marketing upfront (too early in the conversation) and then don't market later when that would be the way to keep the conversation going.

This web page is very clean. Just the facts.

But what do you do if you want a loan?

The page has no links to help you move ahead.

You have to know to go back to the navigation and now select Products.

Figure Interlude 2-4 This credit union makes the rates easy to see with no marketing fluff before the numbers. But it also strands its site visitors.
www.foundersfcu.com

For example, the Founders credit union does a great job of getting people directly to the facts they are looking for. But then it misses the opportunity to market to them from the facts (Figure Interlude 2-4).

Never stop the conversation

The missed marketing moment on the Founders site also brings the conversation the site visitor started to a screeching halt. That's not a good idea.

Always let your site visitors decide when they have what they need. Don't let the site stop the conversation.

You can include many ways to continue the conversation:

- Give site visitors related links.
- Market related opportunities.
- Offer live chat.
- Engage site visitors in your social media.
- Allow them to provide recommendations, comments, or other feedback.
- Give them "contact us" information in the main content area as well as in the global navigation.

If you walk your personas through their conversations, you'll see when you might be cutting off a conversation too early.

You can keep the conversation going – in fact, you can encourage the conversation to continue – as Signal Financial does in Figure Interlude 2-5.

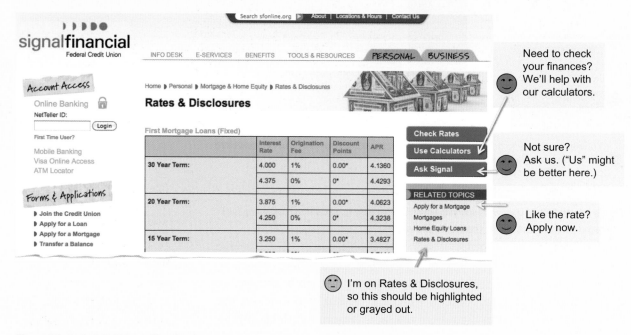

Figure Interlude 2-5 This credit union does not waste people's time with "we're wonderful" marketing messages. Instead, it markets well by encouraging site visitors to continue the conversation. It captures the marketing moment.
www.sfonline.com

Announcing Your Topic with a Clear Headline

Headlines online have to do even more than headlines in print. On paper, you usually see the headline and the article together on the same piece of paper. Online (and especially on a mobile), the headline often appears first by itself as a link. It has to do a lot of work, conveying enough context to

- entice and engage the people for whom it leads to useful content
- *not* entice people who will be frustrated because it is a wrong choice for what they need
- signal to search engines what the content that follows is all about

How much do Americans pay for fruits and vegetables?

That's where the information I need will be.

🙂 This link from the Economic Research Service leads to just what you expect – data on the price of apples, peas, and other produce.

Roadmap for performance-based navigation

I'm a private pilot. I'll click on this and order road maps.

🙁 In a usability test with people who fly their own planes, some thought this was a link to road maps. It's not. It's the title of the government agency's strategic plan.

This chapter is about the first level heading of your content (<H1>).

Journalism and copy writing = headline

Technical and business communication = title

But in the web world, "title" has a special meaning: <Title> is different from <H1>. That's why I'm using "headline" here.

SEO | A headline (<H1>) with keywords that match what site visitors search for can help your ranking with search engines. Note that proper coding is critical. Use the <H1> tag. Just using bigger, bolder letters doesn't tell search engines or screen-readers that this is a first-level heading.

Seven guidelines for headlines that work well

1. Use your site visitors' words.
2. Be clear instead of cute.
3. Think about your global audience.
4. Try for a medium length (about eight words).
5. Use a statement, question, or call to action.
6. Combine labels (nouns) with more information.
7. Add a short description if people need it.

1. Use your site visitors' words

Headlines that work well in your web conversations have words that make good connections in site visitors' minds.

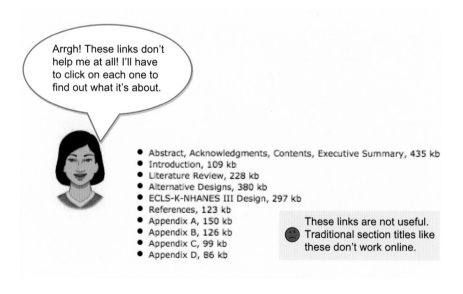

2. Be clear instead of cute

Of course, humor has its place. But a cute heading that doesn't match what site visitors are looking for is likely to fail in two ways:

- Site visitors scanning links on the page may not connect what they want with the cute phrasing you've used.
- A search engine may not place the article high in its results because the headline doesn't have the keywords it is matching.

Caroline Jarrett, co-author of the wonderful book *Forms That Work – Designing Web Forms for Usability*, tells a story about herself:

For one of her monthly online columns about designing forms and surveys, Caroline tackled the question of whether to use an even or odd number of response categories in a survey. She called the article, "Piggy in the Middle." It didn't get a lot of clicks. In hindsight, that's no surprise. How would anyone know what it was about?

In contrast, the column that Caroline published in the same series with the headline "Sentence or Title Case for Labels?" got 100 times as many visitors. Why? At least in part, it must be that the headline clearly foreshadowed the content – and it showed up well in search engine results.

3. Think about your global audience

If you want what you write to have a global reach, be aware of abbreviations, acronyms, and idioms that only locals understand.

This headline appeared not only in the local edition of the *New York Times*, but also in the global edition (*International Herald Tribune*).

☺ Headline = bite. Statements with key messages make good bites.

L.I. Harvests May Signal a Comeback for Scallops

☹ New Yorkers may instantly understand that L.I. = Long Island. (Parts of New York City are on Long Island.) But will other readers around the world?

4. Try for a medium length (about eight words)

Outbrain looked at the click-through rates from headlines or page titles of 150,000 web articles.

This feature	Improved click-through
Thumbnail image with headline	27% higher than no image
Eight words in headline	21% higher than other lengths
Odd number "5 keys to…"	20% higher than even number
Colon or dash and subtitle	9% higher
Headline as question	higher (% not specified)

Source: Kelly Reeves, 5 Tips to Improve Your Headline Click-through Rate, June 3, 2011.
http://www.contentmarketinginstitute.com/2011/06/headline-click-through-rate/

This finding is very similar to Jared Spool's earlier finding that links of 7 to 12 words work best (Figure 8-1).

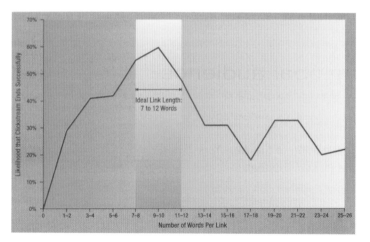

Figure 8-1 Jared Spool and his colleagues found that links of 7 to 12 words worked best in getting people to the information they were seeking. *Designing for the Scent of Information.* www.uie.com

Why do medium-length links work well? They probably

- have better "scent" (see Chapter 5)
- use more keywords that site visitors are looking for and that search engines can match
- are questions, statements, or calls to action that resonate with your site visitors

5. Use a statement, question, or call to action

Lots more about these different types in the next chapter on headings.

Statement headlines put the key message first (see Chapter 7). They are likely to bring questions to site visitors' minds. (See the next chapter for how to follow the key message with a good set of questions and answers.)

Question headlines let the site visitor start the conversation – if the headline is a question that your site visitors would ask.

Calls to action encourage people to act.

Figure 8-2 gives you an example of each type of headline.

A statement – key message – bite – can work well as a headline

Robots may dominate rugby by 2050

www.voxy.co.nz

A question can be a great headline – if the question resonates with site visitors.

IS POWER PROTECTION COSTING YOU MORE THAN IT SHOULD?

A simple change in your power system can pay for itself many times over — and return thousands of dollars to your IT budget.

www.powerquality.eaton.com

A verb phrase makes a call to action. It's a great headline when you want people to act.

Cuba Travel News: Fly Off to Havana (Now Legally)

June 30, 2011 | Doug Stallings
Posted in Trip Ideas & Itineraries | Tagged: Cuba

Americans can once again travel to Cuba legally on a cultural tour—and without applying to the U.S. Department of the Treasury for a special license to travel.

(More)

www.fodors.com

Figure 8-2 Statements, questions, and calls to action work well as headlines.

Look again at Figure 8-2. Notice the way the three headlines use capital letters. Which is easiest to read?

Did you say the one about robots? When planning your style for headlines and headings, consider using sentence capitalization [Robots may dominate…] rather than all capitals [IS POWER PROTECTION…] or even initial capitalization (also called "title case") [Cuba Travel News…]. You don't need capitals. Bold, color, and text size are better ways to show that this is your headline.

Look back at Chapter 3 for more on why not to use all caps.

6. Combine labels (nouns) with more information

Nouns by themselves announce topics. They often work as links for entire sections: News, Shoes, Site Map. They don't work well as headlines for articles or information pages because they don't draw readers in. They often don't give enough specifics for people to know that's what they want.

The Outbrain study found that combining the topic label with a call to action or other phrase worked better than a label by itself.

Colon or dash and subtitle	9% higher

Which of these articles do you think our gal will read? Which headline would pull you into the article?

I'm so stressed.
I'm going crazy.
I have too much to do.

Stress relief:
When and how to say no
from www.mayoclinic.com

Stress Management

7. Add a short description
if people need it

A headline should serve by itself as the "bite" that entices people to want the snack and then the meal. But you won't always be able to write a headline where that bite is enough for everyone.

Offer a brief description. Figure 8-3 shows how Fidelity Investments helps site visitors choose the link they need after they choose the tab for Guidance and Retirement.

Also see the example from shell.com **in Chapter 5.**

Figure 8-3 A brief description can help people select the right link.
www.fidelity.com

Summarizing Chapter 8

Key messages from Chapter 8:

- Use your site visitors' words.
- Be clear instead of cute.
- Think about your global audience.
- Try for a medium length (about eight words).
- Use a statement, question, or call to action.
- Combine labels (nouns) with more information.
- Add a short description if people need it.

Including Useful Headings

Let's move from the headline at the top of your content to the headings inside the content. Headings – short and in bold or **color** – divide your web content on a single topic into manageable pieces.

In a typical conversation, the people who are talking to each other take turns. Headings – especially question headings – are your site visitors' turns in the conversation.

Good headings help readers in many ways

Well-written headings in well-organized content help readers

- scan to get the gist
- find just the section they need
- follow the flow of your story
- get a quick "bite" of context for each section
- manage the amount they deal with at one time

Thinking about headings also helps authors

Headings form an outline of what you are going to write. Planning the headings is a way of analyzing the information you have, grouping it well, and putting it in an order that is logical for your site visitors.

Headings with keywords your site visitors are using in their searches help your SEO.

People who listen want to scan just as sighted people do. They can have their assistive software jump from heading to heading – but only if the headings are properly tagged.

Compare Figures 9-1 and 9-2. Which version of the information on physical exercise would you be more likely to read and use?

For both SEO and accessibility, you must tag headings properly: <H1>headline text</H1>, <H2>heading text</H2>, and so on. Bigger, bolder text that is not tagged won't be seen as a heading by either search engines or accessibility software.

Physical Exercise

The hardest part of an exercise routine is getting started. Once you've established a regular pattern of exercise, you'll find yourself following it. So, how do you get started? Well, first of all, consult your doctor. Your doctor can recommend the specific kinds of exercise for your own individual needs. Generally, however, these guidelines should get you going.

First of all, exercise will only become a habit if it's fun! Pick something you will enjoy doing. If you like being with a group of people, try a team sport like basketball or soccer. You don't have to be a super athlete. Anyone can exercise. Social activities like dancing and mall-walking are also good. If you're more of a loner, try bicycling or swimming.

Don't kid yourself. Be honest about what you realistically think you can do. If you have always hated to climb stairs, step aerobics probably isn't for you. Maybe a walk around the neighborhood would be more pleasant. Many people today are walking toward fitness.

Consider your current state of physical fitness. If you haven't exercised in years, you'll definitely want to start with some modest activities. As you get adjusted, you can increase your activity.

Consider your schedule. Are you a morning person? Then plan to exercise in the morning. If you're addicted to your snooze button, plan to exercise in the evening. Start with just a small block of time, maybe fifteen minutes. As you get into your routine, you probably won't mind increasing to twenty, and then thirty, minutes. In order to be effective, you'll need to repeat your exercise routine 3 or 4 times per week.

Will you exercise at home or at a fitness center? Selecting a fitness center can be a challenge, but you may find the community support motivational. Will you need any special equipment? The variety of exercise equipment available for purchase today can be overwhelming. Be sure to buy the proper equipment.

Figure 9-1 The original web text with no headings

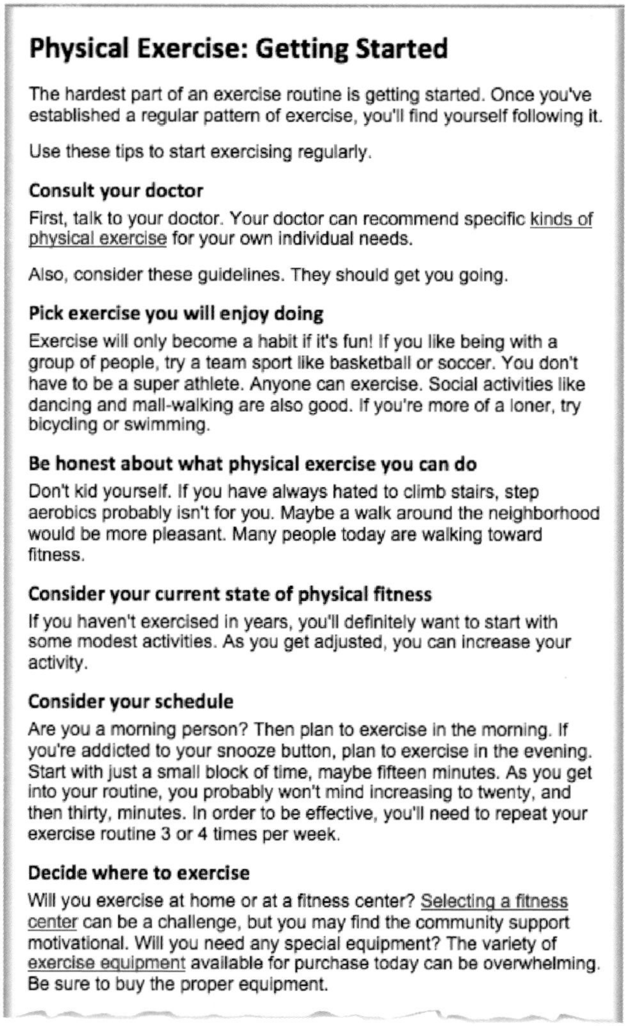

Physical Exercise: Getting Started

The hardest part of an exercise routine is getting started. Once you've established a regular pattern of exercise, you'll find yourself following it.

Use these tips to start exercising regularly.

Consult your doctor

First, talk to your doctor. Your doctor can recommend specific <u>kinds of physical exercise</u> for your own individual needs.

Also, consider these guidelines. They should get you going.

Pick exercise you will enjoy doing

Exercise will only become a habit if it's fun! If you like being with a group of people, try a team sport like basketball or soccer. You don't have to be a super athlete. Anyone can exercise. Social activities like dancing and mall-walking are also good. If you're more of a loner, try bicycling or swimming.

Be honest about what physical exercise you can do

Don't kid yourself. If you have always hated to climb stairs, step aerobics probably isn't for you. Maybe a walk around the neighborhood would be more pleasant. Many people today are walking toward fitness.

Consider your current state of physical fitness

If you haven't exercised in years, you'll definitely want to start with some modest activities. As you get adjusted, you can increase your activity.

Consider your schedule

Are you a morning person? Then plan to exercise in the morning. If you're addicted to your snooze button, plan to exercise in the evening. Start with just a small block of time, maybe fifteen minutes. As you get into your routine, you probably won't mind increasing to twenty, and then thirty, minutes. In order to be effective, you'll need to repeat your exercise routine 3 or 4 times per week.

Decide where to exercise

Will you exercise at home or at a fitness center? <u>Selecting a fitness center</u> can be a challenge, but you may find the community support motivational. Will you need any special equipment? The variety of <u>exercise equipment</u> available for purchase today can be overwhelming. Be sure to buy the proper equipment.

Figure 9-2 My suggested revision with headings

Both versions are conversational. They have the same words and the same organization. The difference is only in whether you *show* the organization, break up the text, and make the key messages stand out.

Eleven guidelines for writing useful headings

These 11 guidelines will help you help your site visitors:

1. Don't slap headings into old content.
2. Start by outlining.

3. Choose a good heading style: questions, statements, verb phrases.

4. Use nouns and noun phrases sparingly.

5. Put your site visitors' words in the headings.

6. Exploit the power of parallelism.

7. Use only a few levels of headings.

8. Distinguish headings from text.

9. Make each level of heading clear.

10. Help people jump to content within a web page.

11. Evaluate! Read the headings.

1. Don't slap headings into old content

Going through existing content and putting in a heading every so often does not produce good information. Poorly written, arbitrary headings may confuse your site visitors instead of helping them.

Put headings into old content as a *first* step

To become familiar with the content you have, go through it, trying to write a heading for each paragraph. That can be a useful *first* step in revising.

- If you find it difficult to write a heading for a section of text, it probably means the section is not clear or covers too many points all jumbled together. Clarify the content. Break it into smaller sections.

- If you find yourself writing the same heading over different sections of content, it probably means the material is not well organized. Reorganize it to be logical for your site visitors.

Next, list the headings as if they were a table of contents. Do they make a good outline? Do they make sense as a whole? Do they flow? Is this what site visitors want to know? Are these the key messages you should be giving? If not, step back and revise, or even start with a new outline.

Thanks to Caroline Jarrett for teaching me this technique of putting headings into old content as a *first* step in revision. But as Caroline says, "Don't stop there."

2. Start by outlining

An outline is just your headings in order. Don't stress about using Roman numerals, letters, or an elaborate numbering scheme. If you just put down the headings you are going to use in the order you are going to use them, without any text under them, you have an outline.

If you use more than one level, indent a bit for the second level of your outline. You'll see the pattern you are creating.

Figure 9-3 shows the outline for the web content in Case Study 7-1 about the International Aviation Art Contest.

International Aviation Art Contest
Who can enter?

Deadline: When is the entry due?

Prizes: What can I win?

> **State prizes**
>
> **National prizes**
>
> **International prizes**

Media: What types of art are acceptable?

What will the judges look for?

Who must certify that the child made the poster?

Where do we send the poster?

Figure 9-3 The outline for a web topic

I'm now adding to the advice that I gave in Chapter 7, Checklist 7-1. There, I suggested starting by writing the questions that people ask and then putting those questions into an order that will make sense to your site visitors. What do you then do with the questions you've listed?

- Sometimes, you'll keep those questions as your outline, and, therefore, your headings.
- Sometimes, you'll decide that questions aren't the best headings for your material. You may turn the questions into statements (key messages).
- If you find you have all "How do I...?" questions, turn them into action phrases with verbs ("Do x" or "Doing x").
- And sometimes, if you are just labeling parts, it's okay to use nouns as headings.

Let's explore when, why, and how to use each of these types of headings: questions, statements, verbs, nouns.

3. Choose a good heading style: Questions, statements, verb phrases

Your three main choices for headings are questions, statements, or verb phrases (calls to action).

Questions as headings

When you write questions as headings, you play out both sides of the conversation. You put the site visitor on the page with you – the site visitor asks the question; you answer it.

As I said in Chapter 1, I'm not suggesting that you make your entire site one big section of frequently asked questions (FAQs). Site visitors might never find their specific question. I am suggesting questions and answers (Q&A) as an appropriate writing style for the main content *on each specific topic*.

Questions make very useful headings in all these different types of web content:

- articles
- blogs
- explanations
- handbooks
- introductions to manuals
- policies
- press releases
- regulations
- troubleshooting information

Using Q&A can draw people into a web page. For example, seeing the question, "Why immunize?" on the web site of the U.S. Centers for

If your site has both a main page of content on a topic and a separate page of FAQs on the same topic, think about whether you really need both.

Did the team have to write the FAQ page because the content on the main page wasn't satisfying site visitors' conversations? If so, you probably don't need both.

But don't get rid of the FAQs! Take away the other page. Use or rewrite the FAQ page as the *main page of content* on that topic and don't call it FAQs.

Disease Control and Prevention may draw parents into that article.
(Figure 9-4).

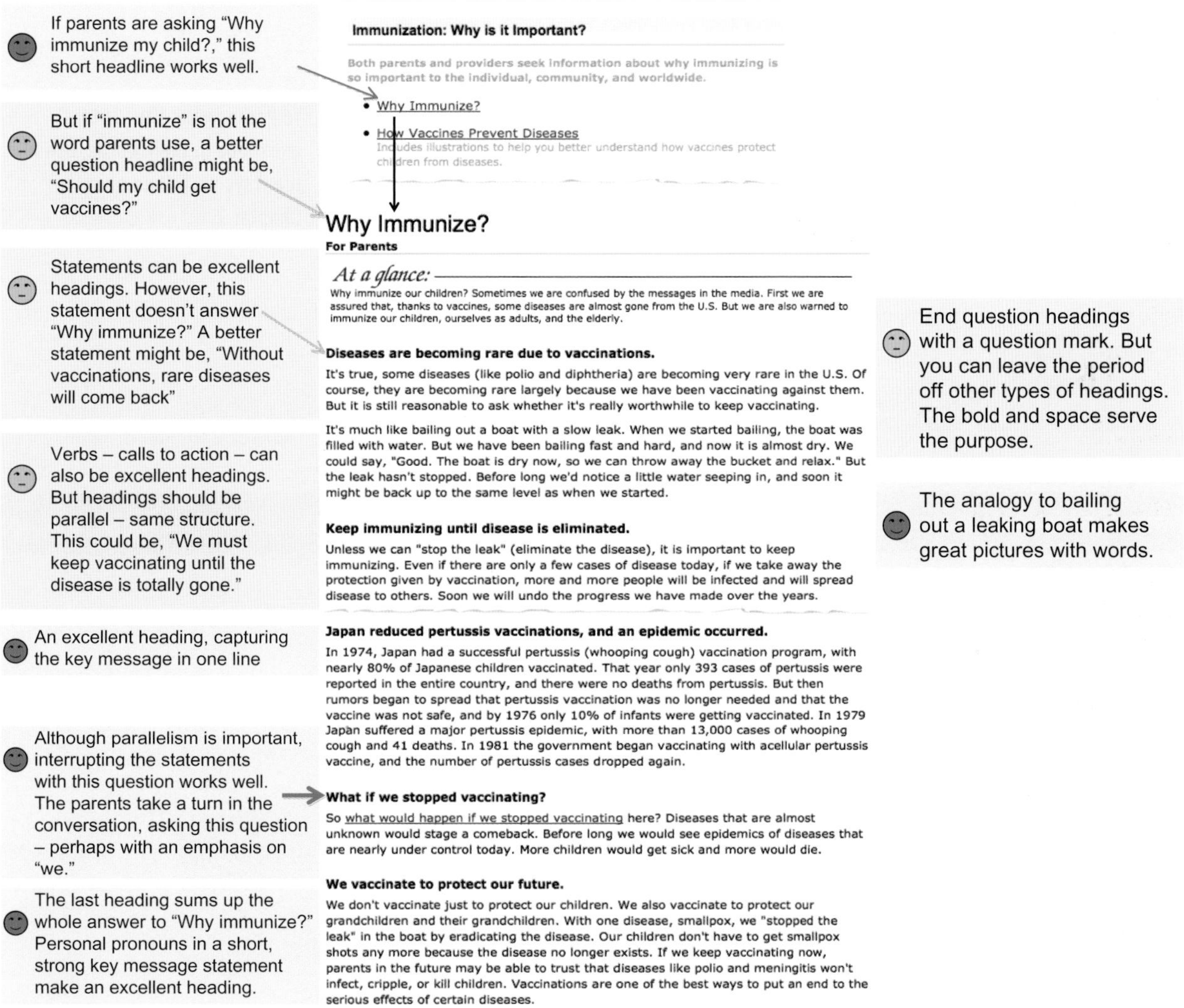

If parents are asking "Why immunize my child?," this short headline works well.

But if "immunize" is not the word parents use, a better question headline might be, "Should my child get vaccines?"

Statements can be excellent headings. However, this statement doesn't answer "Why immunize?" A better statement might be, "Without vaccinations, rare diseases will come back"

Verbs – calls to action – can also be excellent headings. But headings should be parallel – same structure. This could be, "We must keep vaccinating until the disease is totally gone."

An excellent heading, capturing the key message in one line

Although parallelism is important, interrupting the statements with this question works well. The parents take a turn in the conversation, asking this question – perhaps with an emphasis on "we."

The last heading sums up the whole answer to "Why immunize?" Personal pronouns in a short, strong key message statement make an excellent heading.

Immunization: Why is it Important?

Both parents and providers seek information about why immunizing is so important to the individual, community, and worldwide.

- Why Immunize?
- How Vaccines Prevent Diseases
  Includes illustrations to help you better understand how vaccines protect children from diseases.

Why Immunize?
For Parents

At a glance:

Why immunize our children? Sometimes we are confused by the messages in the media. First we are assured that, thanks to vaccines, some diseases are almost gone from the U.S. But we are also warned to immunize our children, ourselves as adults, and the elderly.

Diseases are becoming rare due to vaccinations.

It's true, some diseases (like polio and diphtheria) are becoming very rare in the U.S. Of course, they are becoming rare largely because we have been vaccinating against them. But it is still reasonable to ask whether it's really worthwhile to keep vaccinating.

It's much like bailing out a boat with a slow leak. When we started bailing, the boat was filled with water. But we have been bailing fast and hard, and now it is almost dry. We could say, "Good. The boat is dry now, so we can throw away the bucket and relax." But the leak hasn't stopped. Before long we'd notice a little water seeping in, and soon it might be back up to the same level as when we started.

Keep immunizing until disease is eliminated.

Unless we can "stop the leak" (eliminate the disease), it is important to keep immunizing. Even if there are only a few cases of disease today, if we take away the protection given by vaccination, more and more people will be infected and will spread disease to others. Soon we will undo the progress we have made over the years.

Japan reduced pertussis vaccinations, and an epidemic occurred.

In 1974, Japan had a successful pertussis (whooping cough) vaccination program, with nearly 80% of Japanese children vaccinated. That year only 393 cases of pertussis were reported in the entire country, and there were no deaths from pertussis. But then rumors began to spread that pertussis vaccination was no longer needed and that the vaccine was not safe, and by 1976 only 10% of infants were getting vaccinated. In 1979 Japan suffered a major pertussis epidemic, with more than 13,000 cases of whooping cough and 41 deaths. In 1981 the government began vaccinating with acellular pertussis vaccine, and the number of pertussis cases dropped again.

What if we stopped vaccinating?

So what would happen if we stopped vaccinating here? Diseases that are almost unknown would stage a comeback. Before long we would see epidemics of diseases that are nearly under control today. More children would get sick and more would die.

We vaccinate to protect our future.

We don't vaccinate just to protect our children. We also vaccinate to protect our grandchildren and their grandchildren. With one disease, smallpox, we "stopped the leak" in the boat by eradicating the disease. Our children don't have to get smallpox shots any more because the disease no longer exists. If we keep vaccinating now, parents in the future may be able to trust that diseases like polio and meningitis won't infect, cripple, or kill children. Vaccinations are one of the best ways to put an end to the serious effects of certain diseases.

End question headings with a question mark. But you can leave the period off other types of headings. The bold and space serve the purpose.

The analogy to bailing out a leaking boat makes great pictures with words.

Figure 9-4 This web topic about vaccinations has some good headings and some that we might improve.
www.cdc.gov

When writing questions as headings, consider these four points:

- Answer your site visitors' questions.
- Write from your site visitors' point of view.
- Keep the questions short.
- Consider starting with a keyword.

Answer your site visitors' questions

Web writers sometimes just put their internally focused information into Q&A style. That doesn't satisfy site visitors' conversations. To write successful Q&A, you must understand your site visitors and what *they* want to know.

Case Study 9-1 shows you how one group changed from internally focused questions to answering what site visitors really want to know.

To gather your site visitors' questions in their words, use all the ways we talked about in Chapter 2.

Case Study 9-1	Answering your site visitors' questions

If you want to complain about a bank in the United States, you might get to the web site of the federal Office of the Comptroller of the Currency (OCC). They regulate *nationally chartered* U.S. banks and federal savings associations.

However, they are not the right place to go if your complaint is about another type of financial institution, such as a credit union or state-regulated bank. Few people know if their bank is nationally chartered or state regulated.

In the first edition of *Letting Go of the Words*, I showed the OCC page as it was then:

In the first edition, I asked questions like these about this page:

 How well does this meet the needs of the site visitors it is for? Think about the mental state of people who are upset enough to complain to the government about a bank. Is their first question

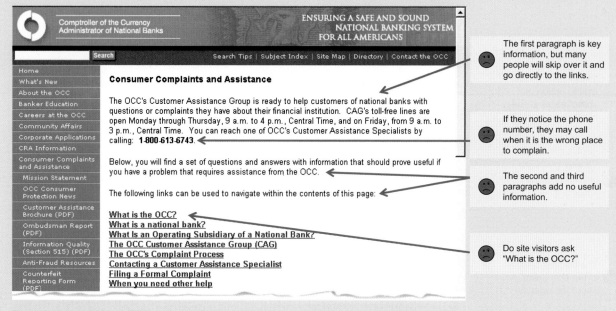

The web page in 2006 with my comments from the first edition of *Letting Go of the Words*

"What is the OCC?" Would they click on "What is a national bank?" when they don't yet know it is a question that is important for their problem?

> I'm really angry at what my bank did! It's intolerable. I'm going to file an official complaint with the government. How do I do that?

To their credit, the web team at the OCC came up with a great new solution to the problem that I raised. They created a site just for consumers, called helpwithmybank.gov. Here's their new page:

Headline is a clear call to action that matches what site visitors came to do.

✓ and 1 encourage site visitors to act.

The content talks to the site visitor, not about the agency.

The reference to another "appropriate regulator" in Step 1 should be a link to Who Regulates My Bank. Site visitors may not notice the link on the right.

The new page (new web site) for consumers who have a complaint

www.helpwithmybank.gov/complaints

SEO | The URL, the headline, and the content all help with the site's great SEO. It's the top search result at Bing, Google, and Yahoo for the search string: complain about my bank.

Write from your site visitors' point of view

Write as if you were recording both sides of the conversation. One good way to do that is to use

- "I" for the site visitor in the question
- "you" for the site visitor in the answer
- "we" for the organization

Figure 9-5 shows you how doctors from the American College of Radiology and the Radiology Society of North America talk to patients on their web site, RadiologyInfo.org.

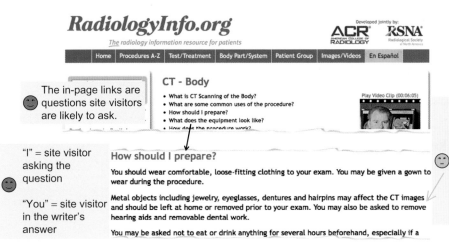

The in-page links are questions site visitors are likely to ask.

"I" = site visitor asking the question

"You" = site visitor in the writer's answer

How should I prepare?

You should wear comfortable, loose-fitting clothing to your exam. You may be given a gown to wear during the procedure.

Metal objects including jewelry, eyeglasses, dentures and hairpins may affect the CT images and should be left at home or removed prior to your exam. You may also be asked to remove hearing aids and removable dental work.

You may be asked not to eat or drink anything for several hours beforehand, especially if a

Most of the answer is fine – short, direct, active. But this could be better: "…and should be left at home or removed prior to your exam." Better: End the sentence after "images." Rewrite the rest as a new active sentence: "Leave them at home or remove them before your exam."

Figure 9-5 In Q&A style, "I" works well in the question with "you" in the answer.
www.radiologyinfo.org

Keep the questions short

People often skim a heading just enough to decide, "yes, that's what I want to know." They're anxious to get to the answer.

Why short? At least three reasons:

- Long questions take up precious space.
- Headings are in **bold** or color, and large blocks of **bold** or color are difficult to read.
- Despite the power of headings, some site visitors use the headings only as landing spots to see where new sections start. They don't actually read the headings.

Cut your questions to essentials, just as you cut your content to essentials. If you find yourself writing a long question, ask yourself:

- Is the section too long?
- Am I trying to cover several questions at once?
- Should I divide this content into more than one question and answer?
- Am I putting information in the question that should be in the answer?
- Am I using more words than necessary while still connecting with my site visitors and improving SEO?

As with many aspects of content strategy and content writing, you must balance competing demands. Keep headings short, but try to get keywords in at least a few of your <H2> headings as well as your <H1> headline. For example, in Figure 9-5, I might suggest adding "for my CT scan" to "How do I prepare?"

Consider starting with a keyword

Although questions work wonderfully well as headings, they have one downside. They don't start with a keyword for the specific topic.

 Site visitors who listen to the screen often move rapidly from heading to heading, listening only to the first bit of each one. Sighted web users similarly scan down the page often taking in only the first part of a heading.

A solution that can sometimes help is to combine a keyword with the question, as in Figure 9-6.

Signature: Who must sign the application?

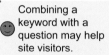 Combining a keyword with a question may help site visitors.

Deadline: When is the application due?

Figure 9-6 Dual headings like these help people who are scanning rapidly with their ears or their eyes.

However, don't start every <H2> or <H3> heading with the same keywords. That would make the content very difficult to scan. If the keywords would be the same for each heading, put them in only some of the headings and don't put them first. You'll still get some SEO benefit and people will be able to use your content.

Statements as headings

When you write statements as headings, you assume the site visitor has asked the question. You keep your site visitors in mind and talk directly to them, without putting them on the page with you.

Statement headings work well in the same types of web pages as questions. With statement headings you make your key messages stand out on the page in large bold or colored type. That's what you see in Figure 9-7.

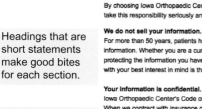

How We Protect You

Our Privacy Promise to You

By choosing Iowa Orthopaedic Center, you have expressed confidence in our ability to serve you. We take this responsibility seriously and diligently safeguard your personal information.

We do not sell your information.
For more than 50 years, patients have trusted Iowa Orthopaedic Center with their personal and medical information. Whether you are a current or former patient, Iowa Orthopaedic Center is committed to protecting the information you have shared with us. This commitment to conduct business honestly and with your best interest in mind is the foundation of our Privacy Promise to you.

Your information is confidential.
Iowa Orthopaedic Center's Code of Ethics requires that patient information be held in strict confidence. When we contract with insurance companies to process information, the contract strictly limits how they use information supplied by Iowa Orthopaedic Center and requires they have strong security protections.

We protect your information.
Iowa Orthopaedic Center maintains practices to ensure the security and confidentiality of your personal information. We have physical security at our buildings, passwords to protect our databases, compliance audits, and world-class virus/intrusion detection software in place. Within Iowa Orthopaedic Center, access to member information is limited to those who need it to perform their jobs.

We Collect Information to Serve You
Collecting information about patients makes it possible for Iowa Orthopaedic Center to deliver the kind of personalized service you expect.

At Iowa Orthopaedic Center, we collect and share information within Iowa Orthopaedic Center.

Headings that are short statements make good bites for each section.

You don't need periods at the end of headings.

Sentence capitalization, like the first three headings, is best for statement headings.

Figure 9-7 Short statements with key messages work well as headings.
www.iowaorthopaediccenter.com

Verb phrases as headings

Many web conversations are site visitors asking "How do I...?" If you have one "How do I...?" question with many other types of questions, it's fine to leave that as a question.

However, if you have a series of questions, all of which would start "How do I...?," people may have a hard time finding the one they want.

Which set of headings is most difficult to scan and use?

How do I set up an account?	Setting up an account	Set up an account
How do I view my profile?	Viewing my profile	View my profile
How do I change my profile?	Changing my profile	Change my profile
How do I pay online?	Paying online	Pay online
How do I get help?	Getting help	Get help

When you find yourself writing "How do I...?" over and over, take away the repeated words and start each heading with the action word.

Two good ways to write action headings (and action links) are with

- gerunds (the form that ends in "-ing")
- imperatives (the "Do this ..." form of the verb)

Example with –ing: Look ahead at Case Study 9-2.

Example with imperatives: Look back at Figure 9-2.

4. Use nouns and noun phrases sparingly

I see a lot of nouns as headings. They work sometimes. But more often than not, they don't work because site visitors don't know the nouns or don't give the nouns the same meaning the writer did. Nouns as headings often don't help either writer or site visitor understand the flow of the writing – why one section logically comes before or after another section.

Nouns label things. They aren't conversational. Unlike questions, statements, and action phrases, which provide context and explanation, a noun has to carry all the meaning of the heading in a single word.

Sometimes a label (a noun) is enough

Yes, sometimes, a label is all you need. Figure 9-8 shows a gaze plot – an eye-tracking picture of one person looking for tax forms and instructions about charitable contributions. In this case, the nouns in alphabetical order as topic headings worked well.

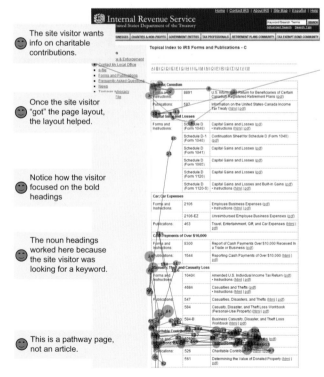

The site visitor wants info on charitable contributions.

Once the site visitor "got" the page layout, the layout helped.

Notice how the visitor focused on the bold headings

The noun headings worked here because the site visitor was looking for a keyword.

This is a pathway page, not an article.

Figure 9-8 An eye-tracking gaze plot showing the path the site visitor took on this page from the U.S. Internal Revenue Service's web site. The page has noun headings as topic labels. They worked in this case because the site visitor was seeking the same word the site was using.
www.useit.com/eyetracking

But nouns often don't explain enough

With nouns as headings, getting the information into logical order may be difficult. Case Study 9-2 shows how I might revise a set of noun-based headings in the information section of an e-commerce site.

Case Study 9-2	Turning nouns into better headings

Let's look at L.L.Bean's online Help Desk page on Tracking Your Order.

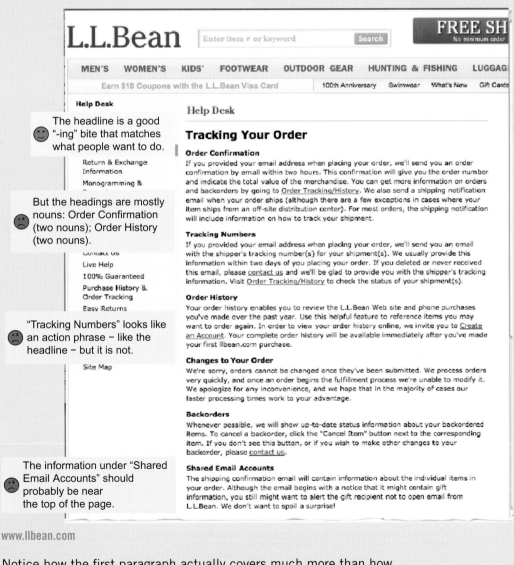

www.llbean.com

Notice how the first paragraph actually covers much more than how they'll confirm your order. Notice that the last paragraph has a good suggestion that you might miss because the heading doesn't tell you *why* you should care about shared email accounts.

If we rethink the actions this content describes, we might break it up more, use verb phrases, and put a set of same-page links at the top. Here's what I might do to revise this content:

Bringing all the headings together at the top gives people an overview and an easy way to get to one section. (See Guideline 10 later in the chapter.)

The long first paragraph of the original covered three topics. I split it into three separate sections.

I broke the pattern of "-ing" headings for the one about keeping gifts secret. I did that to get readers' attention.

I rewrote most headings as action phrases. Notice that the site visitor is the "actor" for the actions.

Hear the conversation with "we" and "you." Conversational questions or statements would work as headings here, too.

Tracking Your Order

Getting confirmation of your order
Getting an email when we ship your order
Gift order for someone on the same email? Don't let us spoil the surprise!
Following your order with its tracking number
Checking your order in Order Tracking/History
Changing an order
Checking all your orders for the past year

Getting email confirmation of your order

If you gave us your email address when you placed your order, we'll send you confirmation of the order by email within two hours. This confirmation will give you
*   the order number
*   the total value of the merchandise

Getting an email when we ship your order

If you gave us your email address when you placed your order, we'll also send an email to tell you when we've shipped your order. (Exception: If your item ships from an off-site distribution center, you won't get this email.) We usually provide this information within two days after you placed your order.

For most orders, this email will tell you how to track your shipment.

Gift order for someone on the same email? Don't let us spoil the surprise!

The email that we have shipped your order will include information about the individual items in your order. Although the email begins with a notice that it might contain gift information, you still might want to alert the gift recipient not to open email from L.L.Bean. We don't want to spoil a surprise!

Following your order with its tracking number

You can track your shipment by using the shipper's tracking number(s) in the email we send when we ship your order.

If you deleted or did not get this email, please contact us and we'll be glad to give you the shipper's tracking information.

Checking your order in Order Tracking/History

You can always check the status of your order by going to Order Tracking/History.

Changing an order or backorder

Order. We're sorry, orders cannot be changed once they've been submitted. We process orders very quickly. Once we have started to put your order together, we can't stop the process. We apologize for any inconvenience. We hope that for most cases our faster processing time works to your advantage.

Backorder. Whenever possible, we show up-to-date information about backordered items. You may change or cancel a backordered item. To cancel a backorder, click the Cancel Item button next to the item you want to cancel. If you want to make other changes to your backorder, please contact us.

Checking all your orders for the past year

If you set up an account at llbean.com, you can look at all the orders you've placed on the L.L.Bean web site and by phone during the past year. You can use this feature to check your current order(s), review past orders, and find items you may want to order again.

To view your order history online, create an account. Your complete order history will be available immediately after you've made your first llbean.com purchase.

My suggested revision.

5. Put your site visitors' words in the headings

The headings in your web content must resonate with your site visitors. If you write headings with words your site visitors don't know, they may not recognize that the heading is what they need. That content also might not show up when your site visitors search – either at your site or at an external search engine.

6. Exploit the power of parallelism

People are very pattern-oriented. It's faster and easier to scan a set of headings when all are in the same sentence structure.

Do It Yourself: Wallpaper	**Do It Yourself: Wallpaper**
Everyone loves wallpaper	Getting ready to put up wallpaper
Preparation	Preparing the walls
Removal of wallpaper	Removing old wallpaper
Straight line marking	Marking a straight line
Cutting the wallpaper	Cutting the wallpaper
Wallpaper soaking	Soaking the wallpaper
Hang the first sheet	Hanging the first sheet

 Did you find the headings on the right quicker and easier to scan and remember?

Be consistent (parallel) in the style you use within the same level of heading. Change styles as you change the heading level. Look back at the outline of the International Aviation Art contest (Figure 9-3): I used questions for level 1 and noun phrases for level 2. Making each heading level its own style helps people see the pattern and hierarchy of your writing.

If you break the pattern, do it for a good reason. Notice how I broke my pattern for one heading in the revised L.L.Bean content. I did it to make that point stand out. The point about keeping your gift a secret is not part of the flow of the process that the other headings describe. It's an "aside," so changing the heading pattern there was purposeful.

7. Use only a few levels of headings

If you think of content as conversation and index cards, you'll realize that the best content is in small pieces with lots of headings – but that the hierarchy of those headings shouldn't go very deep.

A typical web article or blog should have

- one <H1>; that's your headline (see Chapter 8)
- at least two or more <H2> headings
- rarely, <H3> headings

If you find yourself needing a lot of level 3 headings or any level 4 or 5 headings, consider reorganizing the information into a better set of index cards.

And, of course, as you think about mobile, you'll realize how much you need to break up content and how few levels of headings you can use. Figure 9-9 shows a good example from WebMD's mobile content on health conditions.

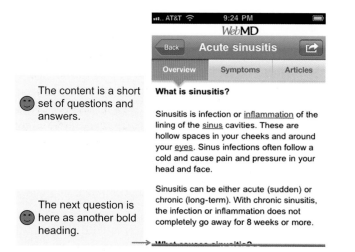

Figure 9-9   Mobile content needs headings, too. In general, keep to one level of heading within the text.
www.webmd.com

8. Distinguish headings from text

Here, I'm using "headings" to include all levels (your <H1> headline and all the levels of headings in your content under the headline).

Make headings easy to see at glance. Use **bold** or a **color** that stands out and consider these points:

- Don't use blue for headings. Save blue for links. Most site visitors assume that anything in blue is a link, even if it is not underlined.
- Don't use your web site's link color as a heading color. You don't want site visitors to be frustrated trying to click on a heading when it is not a link.

- Don't make **bold** versus color the only difference between heading levels. People have a hard time figuring out whether **bold** is more important than color or vice versa.

- Avoid *italics*. They are not as effective as **bold** to indicate a heading. *Italics* don't stand out enough on the screen.

- Underline a heading only if it is a link. Most site visitors assume that anything that is underlined is a link.

- Avoid ALL CAPITALS for all the reasons we talked about in Chapter 3.

- If you use color for headings, make sure the color is legible against the background of your web page. Before you choose a color, reread the section on color-blindness in Chapter 3.

9. Make each level of heading clear

To help site visitors, you must distinguish headings from text and also make the hierarchy of the headings (the different levels) obvious. Good ways to differentiate levels include size, spacing, and placement.

This guideline focuses on information design. It connects back to Chapter 3. Designers, content strategists, and web writers must collaborate to get designs that make headlines and headings truly usable to site visitors.

- **Size.** We all associate size with hierarchy – bigger is more important. Type size for the headline <H1> should be bigger than for the headings <H2>. If you use <H3> headings and don't change the placement, make them smaller than your <H2> headings.
  - Make sure the size difference is obvious – but not too huge. About three points difference is often good – making the headline about 150% of the text size and the headings about 125% of the text size. Less difference may be too subtle; much more may waste too much precious screen space.

- **Spacing.** The headline might also have more space after it than other headings. (Look back at the discussion around Figures 3-12 and 3-13 for why it's critical to put headings close to the text they introduce.)

- **Placement.** You can indent a level of headings. Or you can use bold or colored run-in text (not tagged as a heading) – as in this bulleted list.

While we are discussing design for headings, let me add three more really important guidelines:

- **Don't center headlines or headings.** If people are scanning down the left margin of the content, they'll miss the centered headings. If they go to the centered headings, their eyes will want to keep going to the right instead of back to the left margin of the text.

- **Put lines (rules) over, not under.** You don't need lines with headings, but if you use them, consider putting them over (not under) the headings. Lines under push the eyes up into the previous block of text. Lines over help to put each heading together with the text it covers.

Make sure everything enlarges together. When your site visitors change the text size, everything should get bigger or smaller proportionately. It doesn't help your vision-impaired site visitors if the headline or headings stay small when the text gets big enough to read.

10. Help people jump to content within a web page

If your web page has several sections with a heading over each section, consider giving people a table of contents at the top. By listing the headings at the top as links, you help your site visitors

I'll call these "same-page links" here. I've also heard them called "anchor links" and "in-page links."

- get a quick overview of what's on the page
- jump to a specific part of the page

Figure 9-10 is a good example of same-page links from a U.K. group that is very concerned about making its web site easy to use. (Thanks to Tom Brinck for suggesting this example.)

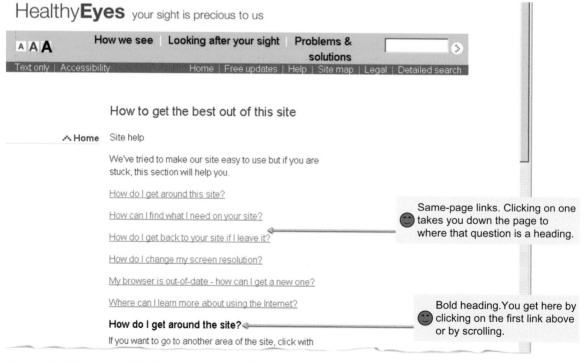

Figure 9-10 Gathering up all the headings into a set of links at the top of the content helps people. They can see what the content covers and get quickly to one part.
www.healtheyes.org.uk

Put same-page links first under the headline

Watching people in usability testing, it's striking to see how quickly they focus on the links as soon as a new screen appears. When the screen has links at the top of the content area, most site visitors skip whatever comes before that set of links.

Don't put off-page links at the top of the content area

Your site visitors bring expectations to your content. If they see links at the top in the main content area, they assume they are links to content further down that page. Don't confuse them. Meet their expectation.

Don't put same-page links in the left navigation column

Links in a colored bar to the left of the main content on most web pages take site visitors to *other* topics. Don't put your same-page links there.

I recall a "before we revise it, let's see how people use it" usability test where this is what happened:

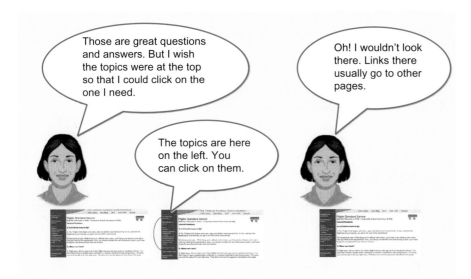

The client heard the message. Their new site always has same-page links at the top of the content area. Links on the left go to other web topics.

11. Evaluate! Read the headings

How do you know that you have good headings? Of course, the best way is to do usability testing. Before you do that, however, you can do this review yourself:

Reviewing as a persona –
Chapter 14

Usability testing – Chapter 15

1. Review your plan for the content.
   * What do you want to happen because you wrote this content?
   * Who are you in a conversation with? Which persona(s) is this content for?
   * What conversation did the persona start with the web site that brought that person to this content?

2. As that persona, read the headline and the headings without any of the text under the headings.

3. Answer these questions:
   * Do you ("channeling" the persona) understand what each heading means by itself?
   * Do the headings tell a coherent story? Do they flow logically from one to the next?
   * Do the headings successfully give you a "big picture"? Can you get the gist of the information on the topic?
   * If you wanted only some of the information, is it clear where you would go for the specific information you wanted?

If you answer "no" as your persona to any of these questions, the headings are not working well. You may need better headings. You may need to rethink, reorganize, and rewrite the content.

Summarizing Chapter 9

Key messages from Chapter 9:

* Good headings help readers in many ways.

* Thinking about headings also helps authors.

* Don't slap headings into old content.

* Start by outlining.

* Choose a good heading style: questions, statement, verb phrases.
  - Answer your site visitors' questions.
  - Write from your site visitors' point of view.
  - Keep the questions short.
  - Consider starting with a keyword.
  - Use key message bites as headings for sections.

     – Give calls to action with imperatives.

     – Use gerunds ("-ing" forms) for activities that aren't direct calls to action.

- Use nouns and noun phrases sparingly.

- Put your site visitors' words in the headings.

- Exploit the power of parallelism.

- Use only a few levels of headings.

- Distinguish headings from text.

- Make each level of heading clear.

- Help people jump to the content they need on the page.
  - Put same-page links first under the page title.
  - Don't put off-page links at the top of the content area.
  - Don't put same-page links in the left navigation column.

- Evaluate! Read the headings.
  - Review your content by "channeling" relevant personas.
  - Read only the headings and see if the content is useful to the personas.

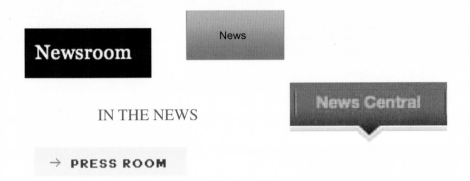

The Internet has radically changed the audiences, life span, distribution, and uses of press releases; but press releases haven't changed to meet the needs of web users. They should.

If your web site includes news briefs in any of their various forms – press releases, news items, announcements – this interlude is for you.

The old life of press releases

A typical press release is one or two pages about a key event, key person, new results, or new information. Press releases were originally designed to get information to newspaper and broadcast reporters with the hope that they would feature the news that day – or in their next edition or next broadcast.

Newspapers, magazines, radio, and TV are still there – now online as well as in print or voice or visually. And reporters still need press releases. But...

The new life of press releases

Reporters are often now writing for the web – not for paper. And the press release doesn't just go to reporters. It's posted on the organization's web site. It lives on, having many uses other than serving reporters. Consider the many differences between the life of a typical press release ten years ago and now.

	Old world: Print and broadcast	**New world: Web**
Audience	Media people: journalists and reporters	Everyone!
Life span	One day? Less? May be filed for future use	Forever!
Distribution	Sent only to specific people	Available through home pages and search engines – including external search engines
Use	Often expanded by talking to a media relations specialist and other people	As a summary, fact sheet, or basic information, either standing alone or linked to more details elsewhere on the web site

You – or others – may link to your press release from blogs, tweets, Facebook walls, Google+ posts, and other social media. You would probably be happy if online curators call attention to your press release. Your entire press release as you wrote it may show up on other web sites – and could stay there even if you archive it or take it down on your site.

In fact, the SEO of your site is likely to increase the more others link to your press releases. All of that good attention brings you many more site visitors who are not reporters. It brings you ordinary people who don't think of what they get to as "press release" or even "news story." They think of it as "information" and expect it to look like other web-based information.

Let me tell you several real-life stories about that.

How do people use press releases on the web?

Story 1: Press release as summary

The new life of press releases hit home to me when I was usability testing a web site meant for researchers and research librarians. The first scenario went something like this: "You have heard that researchers at … just released a new report on … and you want to see what they have to say on that topic."

Include your plans for press releases and other news in your content strategy. Will you leave them up forever? Move them off the site after two years? Put them in a section called Archive after one year?

The client and I thought that participants would look for the new report. Some did. But half first clicked on the tab for Press. One said, "I always look for a press release first. A good press release summarizes the key findings. Then I'll decide if I really want the report."

Great idea. At the time, however, the press releases on this web site were just copies of paper documents. They didn't even link to the full report. They do now!

Story 2: Press release as fact sheet

In another usability test – this time of a health information site for the general public – some people searched, and old news items (press releases) showed up in the search results. Several participants chose a link to a press release, without realizing that's what it was.

Because they weren't reporters, they didn't recognize that what they got was a press release. They assumed it was a fact sheet. For them, it was simply information on the topic they were interested in.

They wondered why the pages didn't look like other pages on the web site. They complained about the lack of headings and the wall-to-wall text that are still common in press releases.

Participants also assumed that the contact name on the web page was the researcher. Again, because they weren't familiar with press releases and were using the pages as information, they didn't realize the name was a media contact. And the press release page just gave a name and phone number – not a title or department.

Story 3: Press release as basic information

In a third project, I was helping a web team do a content inventory of what they had available on each of the main topics the site covers. To everyone's surprise, most of the information was in old press releases. But with long paragraphs and no headings, they weren't serving well as web content.

 What are your press releases like? How well do they serve as summaries for the public? As fact sheets? As basic information? How well do they fit into the look and feel of your site? How well do they work as web writing?

> Link press releases and other news to relevant information on the web site – full reports, pages about people, other information you have on the topic, and so on.

> Include a date on all press releases, including the year. The press release may still be on the web site next year or even two years from now.
>
> In deciding whose name(s) should be on the press release, think about both the short-term and long-term life it will have. Give titles and departments as well as names.

Story 4: The press call up

I once had several reporters as participants in a usability test. They all said they had no time or patience for trying to use the organization's web site. They knew whom to call. *They* were not reading news on the web site.

So perhaps the news section of your web site isn't primarily for reporters. Maybe it is for all your *other* site visitors who will expect what they find to be like other articles on the web site – with lots of headings, key message first, short paragraphs, bulleted lists, and so on.

What should we do?

Write for the web. Think about visuals as well as words. Plan for mobile and social media.

Write for the web

Write press releases with all your site visitors and the "forever" web life span in mind. Move from the typical press release style in the left column of this table to the web-based information style in the right column.

Many press releases have great headlines – key message bites. It's what happens after the headline that concerns me most.

Typical press release	Web-based information
No date, or date with no year	Full date including year, with month spelled out so date is not ambiguous
No headings after the headline	Broken into sections with well-written, bold headings
Long paragraphs	Very short paragraphs, bulleted lists, tables, graphics, videos, audio
No links	Links to full report, additional information, other relevant pages on the site, relevant people
Full page, looks like a paper document	Fits into the template of other information topics on the site
Name and phone number of media relations specialists, often without saying who they are	Names, titles, departments for each person; links to email or information about that person

Think about visuals as well as words

Everything is online. Every newspaper and magazine has an online presence. Every radio station has a web site. Today's news isn't only in words or voice – and television isn't the only visual outlet for news.

Make your news visual, too. Figure Interlude 3-1 shows how the U.S. National Science Foundation makes its news stories visual. Almost every story has at least one picture. Many have several. Some have video, too.

 Key message statement = good bite as headline

 One added sentence = a good snack

The full date with the year acknowledges the long life of online news.

But then 20 paragraphs with no headings. Headings would help Perhaps:

People have the same cycle all week

Data came from 2.4 million users, 84 countries

Text analysis shows people's moods

and so on

Press Release 11-209

Twitter Helps Determine "Morning People" and "Night Owls"

Sociologists use online social networking site to track people's moods in 84 countries

Using data from Twitter, researchers analyzed 509 million messages to explore people's mood cycles. Credit and Larger Version

September 29, 2011

It's true. The daily grind dealing with bosses, colleagues and repetitive work sours people's moods. But researchers say the cause may be something more than the work itself; people's biological clocks may be sending a message.

"Though it might seem intuitive to suggest that the decrease in mood level during the midday hours is a result of workday-related stress," said Scott Golder, lead researcher for a study appearing today in the journal Science, "it turns out we see the same rhythmic shape on the weekends, when people typically are not working. This suggests to us that something more enduring is going on, such as the effect of biological processes and sleep."

Golder, a graduate student in sociology at Cornell University, and sociology professor Michael Macy, recently analyzed text messages from 2.4 million users of the online social networking service Twitter to explore the daily, weekly and seasonal variations in the mood of people from 84 countries around the world.

Using Twitter.com's data access protocol, Golder and Macy collected up to 400 public messages from each user in the sample for a total of more than 509 million messages authored between February 2008 and January 2010. The researchers excluded users with fewer than 25 messages.

Twitter's 140 character limit on message length allowed them to chart the "positive" and "negative affect," or mood, of user communications using a prominent lexicon for text analysis, the Linguistic Inquiry and Word Count (LIWC). LIWC permitted measurements of an individual's spontaneous expressions, i.e. his or her positive affect--enthusiasm, delight, activeness and alertness--and negative affect--distress, fear, anger, guilt and disgust.

Golder and Macy found that individuals awaken in a good mood that deteriorates as the day progresses, which may be more

 Science

The researchers' work is described in the September 30, 2011 issue of the journal Science. Credit and Larger Version

Relevant color images at the top relieve the text. (Videos and audio files work well here, too.)

After the article, you find
• links to relevant people
• clear info on who they are
• links to relevant information

Figure Interlude 3-1 Think more about how your news looks and works on the web.
www.nsf.gov

Plan for mobile and social media

Your news is likely to show up on mobile and in social media –
either because you posted it there or because someone else did.
Plan for that from the beginning. Think "bite, snack, meal." Figure
Interlude 3-2 shows a good use of social media leading to a news story.

Figure Interlude 3-2 Think about how your headline, opening sentence, and visuals will work
in Twitter, Facebook, and other social media.
www.sciencealert.com.au

Does it make a difference?

Yes. A client and I tested different styles. We took a press release that
had all the features in the table under "typical" and redrafted it to have
the features under "web-based information." We included it as just one
of several situations we were looking at in a usability test.

In one scenario during the usability test, participants got to a press release that we had not changed. In another scenario, they got to the one we had changed. (The two were on different topics but were similar in length and level of detail. Both were information based on studies that researchers in the organization had done. Both came up as primary choices when people searched for their respective topics. So both were acting as fact sheets.)

Many participants noticed and commented spontaneously on the difference. Their comments were in favor of the one we had changed.

At the end of the session, we pointed out the two examples again and asked for a preference. All but one of the 16 participants preferred the one with headings and links – the one that was much more like good web writing. The only participant who differed said, "I always print the web pages I want."

Tuning up Your Sentences

10

Now, let's work on writing the paragraphs, sentences, and words of your web content.

As part of your content strategy, you must decide on the tone, voice, and style for your web messages, always remembering the key message of this book: content = conversation.

Writing conversationally is not "dumbing down"

Language changes over time. It always has. Our expectations of appropriate style also change over time. They always have.

Over the past century, the style for communicating useful information has become much less formal. And that trend has accelerated greatly with the Internet and social media.

Writing conversationally in plain language with short sentences and short words is not dumbing down. It's communicating clearly. **It's respecting your busy site visitors' time.**

Write so that busy people understand what you are saying the first time they read it.

As you write:

• Picture the people you are talking with. Which persona(s) are you conversing with?

Lists and tables – other good ways to tune up your sentences – next chapter

Keep photos and short descriptions of your personas with you as you write. Let them join your family on your desk, your corkboard, or a corner of your screen.

- Get into a conversation with those personas. If you were on the phone (speaking or texting), what would they ask you about this topic?
- Reply to them as if you were speaking or texting with them.

Ten guidelines for tuning up your sentences

1. Talk *to* your site visitors – use "you."
2. Use "I" and "we."
3. Write in the active voice (most of the time).
4. Write short, simple sentences.
5. Cut unnecessary words.
6. Give extra information its own place.
7. Keep paragraphs short.
8. Start with the context.
9. Put the action in the verb.
10. Use your site visitors' words.

1. Talk *to* your site visitors – Use "you"

Converse. Make the information inviting and personal by addressing your site visitors directly, as Etsy.com does in Figure 10-1.

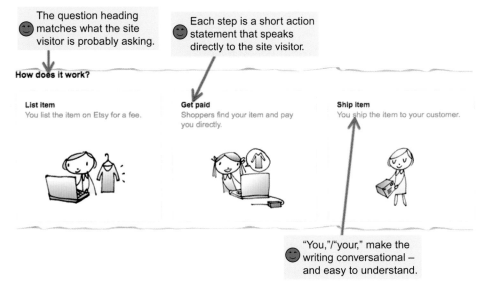

Figure 10-1 Etsy.com wants to attract artisans to sell their craft pieces through the site. The friendly writing and pictures make the site inviting.
www.etsy.com

Use the imperative in instructions

If you are giving hints or tips or instructions, use the imperative (List, Get, Ship from the example in Figure 10-1). That's a "you" form without stating "you." When you write with imperatives you are talking directly to your site visitor. You are conversing. Figure 10-2 shows a list of imperatives in tips about finding the right house to buy.

Some good house-hunting tips

Imperative = personal, friendly, conversational = call to action.

- Take pictures inside and outside the home.
- Bring a spouse, family member, or friend.
- Make sure the house fits into your budget.
- Ask about utility and maintenance costs.
- Think of commuting time and costs.

The line (rule) would be better over the heading, rather than under it.

Figure 10-2 These tips are easy to scan, read, and remember because they each start with a short, plain, imperative verb.
www.freddiemac.com

Use "you" throughout

If you can address your site visitors directly, do so – and do so throughout the content that is meant for them.

In Case Study 10-1, the writer talks directly to the site visitor with the imperative verb "ask" but never uses the pronoun "you." Why not? If the writer talked to "you," the doctor, the content would be both more understandable and more engaging.

Case Study 10-1	Addressing the reader directly

Consider this excerpt. It's for doctors who are considering moving to a different state where they will have to get a new state license to practice medicine. It's the first few sentences of a web paragraph that goes on for more than 200 words.

> When contacting a licensing board for the first time, ask for a copy of its current licensing requirements and the average time it takes to process applications. This will provide the physician with a solid idea of when to consider closing an existing practice and/or plan a move as well as with information about the potential problem areas to be addressed in completing an application. While initial

www.ama-assn.org

 Could we improve this?

I think so.

Consider the situation

Let's start with our three planning questions:

- What does the writer want to achieve?
  - Help doctors relocate.

- Who is the primary persona? With whom is the writer conversing?
  - Medical doctor – very smart, knows a lot, but also is very busy, dealing with many things related to the move, doesn't want to spend a lot of time reading about this topic.

- What's the conversation? What does the doctor want to know?

The family has decided to move. I know it will be a hassle – closing this office, opening a new one, getting a new license. And I'm still so busy here. Can you help me plan to move my medical practice?

Critique the original

The advice starts with an implied task. It doesn't tell the reader to do the task.

"Ask" is an imperative verb. It addresses the reader directly.

When contacting a licensing board for the first time, ask for a copy of its current licensing requirements and the average time it takes to process applications. This will provide the physician with a solid idea of when to consider closing an existing practice and/or plan a move as well as with information about the potential problem areas to be addressed in completing an application. While initial

The second sentence is 39 words long and includes several points.

The "physician" is the person the writer is talking to. The writer has already spoken directly to the physician with the imperative "ask." Why not continue to speak directly to the physician with "you"?

The first sentence mentions two points:
• requirements
• time

The second sentence explains why the two points are important, but it gives the rationale for time before the rationale for requirements.

Revise

Start with an imperative, rather than just implying the action "contact."

Talk directly to the doctor. Use "you."

Separate contacting from asking. Give each action its own sentence.

Use a bulleted list, even for two items like this.

Divide the information into two shorter paragraphs.

Contact the licensing board where you want to practice. Ask for
• a copy of its current licensing requirements, and
• the average time it takes to process applications.

Reading the requirements will help you understand any potential problems you may have in applying. Finding out about the processing time will help you plan when to close your current practice or when to move.

Break the original second sentence into two short sentences. Put them in the same order as the two bulleted items.

Give each reason its own sentence. The average sentence length drops from 33 to 16 words.

I've applied several other guidelines in addition to using "you." They all help make the information much easier for busy doctors to grasp quickly. When you write well, you apply lots of guidelines at the same time.

Use "you" to be gender-neutral

In English, the third-person singular pronouns (he, she, him, her, his, hers) are gender-specific. When you use these pronouns, some site visitors will think that you mean only people of that gender. To avoid even the perception of being exclusionary, avoid gender-specific writing when you are writing about or to both men and women.

Figure 10-3 is a paragraph from the current version of an example that I used in the first edition. The topic is mailing a package of food from Australia to the United States. In some cases, the sender has to tell the U.S. Food and Drug Administration about the package before mailing it.

The writers for the Australian Post Office have made some of the changes I recommended in the first edition of *Letting Go of the Words*, but not others. And now a key sentence has a gender-specific pronoun where it should not. We could easily avoid the gender-specific pronoun by talking directly to people, as I do in Figure 10-4.

Articles of food which are non-commercially prepared by an individual in (his) own residence and sent to another individual as a (non-commercial) gift are exempt from submission of this prior notice.

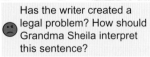 Has the writer created a legal problem? How should Grandma Sheila interpret this sentence?

Figure 10-3 The pronoun "his" is not appropriate in this sentence.

www.auspost.com.au

If (you) prepare the food in (your) own house (as personal items, not for sale) and send that food to another person as a not-for-sale gift, (you) do not have to fill out the "prior notice" form.

 "You" makes the sentence apply to everyone.

Figure 10-4 My suggested revision

If you use a noun like "employee" or "customer," you may have a problem referring to that person later in the sentence or paragraph. Workarounds like combining the two genders into "s/he" or "he or she" are awkward. The blue box, "More on gender-neutral writing," gives you several ways to avoid the problem.

More on gender-neutral writing

Four techniques for removing gender from your pronouns:

- Use "you."

  ☹ The customer may return any item she is not satisfied with.

  ☺ You may return any item you are not satisfied with.

  ☺ If you are not satisfied with any item, you may return it.

- Use the plural.

  ☹ A contractor must renew his insurance every year.

  ☺ Contractors must renew their insurance every year.

- Turn a noun phrase into a verb phrase.

  ☹ A prospective student must turn in his or her application at least two weeks before classes start.

  ☺ A prospective student must apply at least two weeks before classes start.

  ☺ You must apply at least two weeks before classes start.

- Use "a," "an," or "the" instead of a pronoun.

  ☹ Your supervisor must explain her decision in writing.

  ☺ Your supervisor must explain the decision in writing.

Use appropriate gender for specific people

Of course, if you are talking about a specific person, it's fine to name the person and to use the appropriate gender-based pronoun to refer to that person. Figure 10-5 is the beginning of a news story about an unusual female athlete.

SAN FRANCISCO -- With tiny, shuffling steps, 98-year-old Keiko Fukuda took a seat in a director's chair on the mat of (her) dojo, a storefront studio in an old Victorian at the corner of Castro and 26th.

This 4-foot-10, 100-pound granddaughter of a 19th-century samurai is the most revered woman in the history of judo.

In August, (she) became the only woman ever to attain the 10th dan, or highest degree black belt.

Figure 10-5 If you are talking about a particular person, use the appropriate pronouns.
www.espn.go.com

Converse directly even for serious messages

You can convey serious and important messages – even legal rules and notices – using "you." In fact, people are much more likely to take in those messages if you write with "you" because they can see themselves in the text. Figure 10-6 is from a government regulation.

More on clear legal writing online –
Interlude 4 after Chapter 11

§123.100 **Am I eligible to apply for a home disaster loan?**
(a) You are eligible to apply for a home disaster loan if you:
   (1) Own and occupy your primary residence and have suffered a physical loss to your primary residence, personal property or both; or

Figure 10-6 Personal pronouns work well even in legal documents.
http://ecfr.gpoaccess.gov (Title 13, Part 123)

2. Use "I" and "we"

Did you notice the pronoun "I" in the question heading of Figure 10-6? That's the voice of the site visitor.

"I," "you," and "we" all work well in web writing.

Look back at Chapter 9, "Including Useful Headings," for more examples of headings with pronouns.

Be consistent in how you use "I," "you," and "we"

Web writers often ask me how to use these three pronouns when writing questions and answers. Whose voice should come where?

You can set your style in either of two ways:

- Picture the site visitor asking the question.
- Picture the site asking the question.

When the site visitor asks the question

I suggest using

- "I" and "my" in the question (the voice of the site visitor)
- "you" and "your" in the answer (the site is talking *to* the site visitor)
- "we" and "our" for the organization that is answering the question

The British charity, Shelter, uses this technique (Figure 10-7).

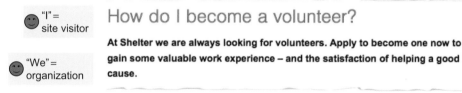

How do I become a volunteer?

At Shelter we are always looking for volunteers. Apply to become one now to gain some valuable work experience – and the satisfaction of helping a good cause.

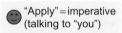

"Apply" = imperative (talking to "you")

"I" = site visitor

"We" = organization

Figure 10-7 You can picture the people conversing through this web content.
http://England.shelter.org.uk

When the site asks the question

This often happens in forms.

I suggest using

- "you" and "your" in the question (the site asking the site visitor)
- "I" and "my" in the answer (the voice of the site visitor)
- "we" and "our" for the organization that is asking the question

Amazon.com does this well (Figure 10-8).

Figure 10-8 In forms, the question might have "you" and the label might have "I" and "my."
www.amazon.com

In blogs and social media, "I" is fine

If you don't use "I" for the voice of the site visitor, you can use it for
yourself. When you use pronouns, you remind your site visitors that they
are conversing with a person.

Figure 10-9 is a Tunisian blogger's admiration for local craft work.

"I" is appropriate for a blogger talking about personal experiences or options.

Figure 10-9
www.subzeroblue.com

For your own work, "I" is fine

You may be the sole author of an article or opinion piece or a story, even
if it is not a blog. You may be an author or consultant with your own web
site. Make the story or site be your voice. Converse with your site visitors
as fantasy writer Allan Frewin Jones does (Figure 10-10).

Figure 10-10 "I" is appropriate for an author's site.
www.allanfrewinjones.com

For an organization, use "we"

"We," "us," "our" are best when you are writing on behalf of a group – your team, your division, your organization. It's what you would say in a conversation. Most web sites do this at least on the Contact Us page.

Sometimes, it's not about "I," "you," and "we"

You may be talking about objects, situations, or people other than your site visitors. In that case, it's okay to use the appropriate nouns. You can still keep the sentences short and active and follow the other guidelines in this chapter as in this example about butterflies.

This web article is facts about butterflies. So not using pronouns is okay.

Short, active sentences make this educational piece easy to read.

A list would work well for the three families in the last sentence.

Sound clips to hear the uncommon words would be a nice addition.

3. Write in the active voice (most of the time)

Sentences in the active voice (active sentences) describe "who does what to whom." In an active sentence, the person or thing doing the action (the actor) comes before the verb. That's the logical order for English sentences. Active sentences help people grab information quickly and easily.

Sentences in the passive voice (passive sentences) start with the object that is acted on instead of the actor. They either put the actor after the verb in a "by . . ." phrase or they leave the actor out entirely.

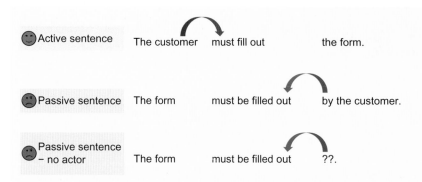

Sentences in the active voice put the actor (the "doer") before the verb.
In most situations, active sentences are easier to understand than passive sentences.

For this guideline, I've said "most of the time." Sometimes, the passive is appropriate. Sometimes, the focus belongs on the object. Sometimes, it really does not matter who is responsible for doing the action. You may need the passive to avoid blaming or scaring your site visitors.

However, an entire web page in the passive is boring and difficult to understand. It's not conversational. Eyes glaze over. People leave. Or they misinterpret the information.

A "think aloud" study showed this clearly: The study used sections of a government regulation. The people in the study were from the real audience for that regulation.

Flower, Hayes, and Swarts, "The Scenario Principle"

When these people tried to make sense of the regulation, they didn't just shorten sentences and shorten words. They told themselves stories! They turned the original writing (long, passive sentences with no pronouns) into active sentences with actors and action verbs.

That's a lot of mental work! No wonder people give up quickly on hard-to-read content. And, even worse, the readers misinterpreted many of the passive sentences. Their translations were wrong.

Don't risk people leaving. Don't risk people misunderstanding. Write active sentences with actors and action verbs.

Case study 10-2 shows how to make writing much clearer by turning passive sentences into active ones so that "you" the reader know what to do.

Case Study 10-2	Writing in the active voice

? Do you agree with my comments on this web content?

Laboratory Supplies

The ordering of laboratory supplies <u>is done</u> through the departmental buyer, in   . The general procedure for this is to fill out ̃ form. This is the order form. A number of important points **must** be <u>noted</u> for ordering and filling out this form. Generally supplies <u>must be ordered</u> at least one week

The description of the items needed must also be specific. An item number <u>should be looked up</u> in the catalogs in the office and <u>written</u> in the *ITEM* blank, along with a description. The *QUANTITY* and *UNIT/SIZE* items are very important. Some supplies comes in cases, thus only indicating *QUAN.* "*1*" could mean "one," or "one case." Thus, if the item comes in a case, this <u>should be indicated</u> in the *UNIT/SIZE* blank. The price <u>must also be indicated</u> in the appropriate blank. The order form <u>must be signed</u>, and the name <u>must be printed</u> as well. If the name <u>is not printed</u>, and the buyer cannot read the signature, he/she will not know whom to notify when the order arrives. To further simplify this, it would be very useful to not only write the daytime phone number, but also the e-mail address. E-mail is the easiest and most convenient method for notification. The completed order forms <u>should be returned</u> to the black container in the office.

 The writer only names one of the people in this conversation – the buyer.

But the conversation includes two people: buyer and person needing supplies.

The content is about actions, but it doesn't speak *to* the actor.

 I've put a red line under passive verbs.

Now, consider the planning questions for this web content:

- Purposes:
  - Get the right supplies to people who need them.
  - Not be bothered with questions or phone calls.
  - Have people fill out the form correctly.

- Persona: People in the organization who need supplies.
  - Very busy
  - Not my main job
  - Only do this occasionally
  - Want to get through this task quickly
  - Don't want to mess up; don't want the hassle of getting the wrong stuff

- Conversation:

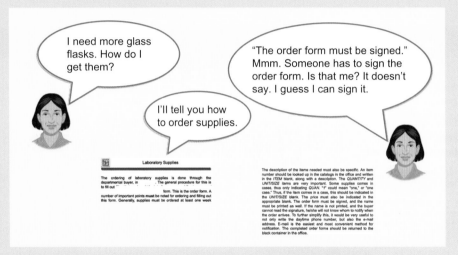

When we consider purposes, persona, and conversation, we can see that these instructions are likely to fail. People will call the buyer or disturb the buyer in person with questions. Or people will fill out the form incorrectly, and the buyer will have to converse again, in email or in person, before actually ordering the supplies.

In most situations, people get information from active sentences more quickly and more accurately than from passive sentences. And writing in the active voice pressures you to find out who is responsible for actions – information that your site visitors often need.

 Would this be better?

Ordering Laboratory Supplies

The departmental buyer in ……… handles all orders for laboratory supplies. If you need supplies, fill out the ……… form. You can get the form from the buyer in ……

1. Fill out the form

To assure that you get the correct supplies, you must fill out the form carefully and correctly. Please pay special attention to these parts of the form:

- ITEM: Look up the item in the catalogs in the office. Put in both the item number and a specific description.

- QUANTITY and UNIT/SIZE: Be sure to tell us both quantity and unit/size. If you write "1" for quantity but don't tell us the unit / size, we won't know if you want 1 piece or 1 case.

- PRICE: You must fill out the space for price. The catalog you are ordering from should tell you the price.

2. Sign and print your name on the form

We want to get the supplies to you; but if we can't read your name, we won't know to whom to deliver them.

3. Give us your phone number and email address

We need to know how to reach you. Please give us both a phone number and an email address. We find email is the easiest way to contact people.

4. Turn in the completed form

Put your completed order form in the black container in …… The buyer will handle your order and notify you when your supplies arrive.

My suggested revision

4. Write short, simple sentences

Your busy site visitors have no time to untangle your text. Try to keep your sentences to about 10 to 20 words. Cut the fluff. Say it once clearly. Keep each sentence to one thought – or two tightly connected thoughts.

If people have to read a sentence more than once to understand it, rewrite it.

Very short sentences are okay, too

Sentences do not need even 10 words to be meaningful and sharp. If you write in questions and answers, a short answer may be all that people need.

Writing very short messages in social media

Twitter limits us to 140 characters. SMS allows us only 20 more than that. Texting on a smart phone or other mobile device can stress our thumbs. And so we tend to abbreviate, write telegraphically, drop some grammar rules.

That's fine as long as you (the sender) and the people whom you want to get the message understand what you are writing and consider the style appropriate for the medium. Your content strategy should include decisions about abbreviations and telegraphic writing – when it's okay; when it isn't. You may decide that writing Thx c u soon is fine in tweets, SMS, Facebook, Google+, and other social media – but that it is not okay in regular web content for a general audience.

If you are part of an organization, remember your brand. The voice of the brand may change slightly in different media, but that may not be your individual decision. It's part of the organization's content strategy.

Fragments may also work

The personality, tone, and style of your site may make sentence fragments acceptable to your site visitors even in regular web content. Consider the description of a blog in Figure 10-11. The fragments work well here.

What's a blog?

A blog is a personal diary. A daily pulpit. A collaborative space. A political soapbox. A breaking-news outlet. A collection of links. Your own private thoughts. Memos to the world.

Your blog is whatever you want it to be. There are millions of them, in all shapes and sizes, and there are no real rules.

Fragments work well in the informal style of this site.

Figure 10-11 Blogger.com's explanation of a blog
www.blogger.com

Finding your voice and style

Clear, simple writing need not be monotonous. Writing can have character and flavor and still be clear. Part of your content strategy should be to understand the personality you want your site to portray: formal, informal, irreverent, funny, serious, and so on. Then match your writing style to that personality.

For example, the layout, design choices, typography, and writing style of the Dot's Diner site all show the down-home personality of these friendly Louisiana diners. Wouldn't you stop by next time you want a late-night meal?

On deciding the personality you want to come through your messages – Bloomstein, *Content Strategy at Work*, 2012

www.dotsdiner.com

We can all think of sites where the same choices would not be appropriate. But no matter how formal and technical your site's personality is, you can still write clearly – with personal pronouns, active voice, short sentences, words your site visitors know. You can still write conversationally!

Busy site visitors always need clear writing

The guidelines in this chapter apply to legal, scientific, and technical writing just as much as they do to personal sites, e-commerce, and nonprofits. In fact, the more complex the topic, the more you need to be sure that you are writing in a clear, coherent style so that your site visitors understand your key messages.

Figure 10-12 shows how the writers at the Mayo Clinic use short, active sentences with vivid word pictures to explain stress.

Figure 10-12 You can write clearly even about medical and technical topics.
www.mayoclinic.com

5. Cut unnecessary words

Sometimes, sentences are longer than necessary because the writer uses several words where one (or none) will do.

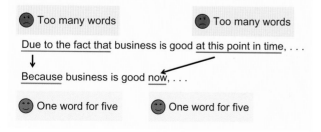

As I suggest in Chapter 14 on moving from first draft to final copy, don't let your first draft be your final draft. Read what you wrote and see where you can cut it. Let it rest – for a few minutes, an hour, a day. When you read it again, see what more you can cut while making your meaning clearer and sharper.

6. Give extra information its own place

In English, once we see the actor or object that starts the sentence, we look for the verb. We expect the grammatical subject and the verb to be near each other. If extra information takes us off on a tangent, we may lose track of what the sentence is about. When the extra information ends and we are back in the main sentence, we may get back on the main track – and then forget the extra information.

Don't put extra stuff between the grammatical subject and the verb. Don't put extra stuff between the verb and the grammatical object.

Case Study 10-3 shows you both how tangled a sentence can get and how to untangle it.

Case Study 10-3   Untangling a convoluted sentence

 Is the first sentence of this excerpt as easy as it could be?

Interested persons, on or before June 14, 2013, may submit to the Hearing Clerk, 1000 Pennsylvania Avenue, NW, Washington, DC 20000, written comments regarding this proposal. Faxed comments will be accepted at 202-555-1234. To submit comments electronically, go to this site:

The first sentence isn't too long (26 words), but the writer interrupts the main thought twice.

Finding the underlying sentence

Let's untangle the stuffed sentence by finding the subject, verb, and object of the main clause.

Now you can see that the writer has stuffed the date between the subject and the verb and the address between the verb and the object.

Revising the sentence

 Would your site visitors find this version easier to use?

We invite you to comment on this proposal.

Deadline: June 14, 2013

Submit written comments

      electronically at
                          www.....

      by mail to
                          Hearing Clerk
                          1000 Pennsylvania Avenue, NW
                          Washington, DC 20000

      by fax to
                          202-555-1234
                          Attn: John Jones

Thinking "personas, conversations"

The revised sentence also matches the order in which site visitors need the information: key message first, then answers to people's questions in the order they would ask them.

Learning from this case study

A sentence with many commas probably has extra information stuffed into it. To untangle sentences like this one:

- Think of your site visitors, the questions they would ask, and the order in which they would ask them.

- If people need different pieces of information at different times, separate those pieces.

- Keep the main parts of the sentence together (subject – verb – object).

- Put the key message first.

- Pull out extra information and make each piece its own sentence (or fragment).

- Consider using visuals, fragments, and lists where they convey the information quickly and accurately.

7. Keep paragraphs short

For school essays, reports, and stories, you probably had to write at least three sentences, and more likely five or six sentences, in each paragraph. That's too long for the web – and certainly for anything people are going to read on a mobile device.

A one-sentence paragraph is fine

Keep your web paragraphs very short. Look at how short most paragraphs are on news sites (Figure 10-13).

How to make the perfect cup of tea – be patient

Making the perfect cup of tea involves a secret ingredient – patience, claims a new study.

Scientists have discovered that the key to the best tasting brew is to let it sit for six minutes before drinking.

Not only does it avoid scolding but by then it has cooled to 60C, the optimum temperature to let the flavours flood out.

But leave it until after 17 minutes and 30 seconds and the tea will be past its best.

The team at the University of Northumbria's School of Life Sciences spent 180 hours of testing and a panel of volunteers consumed 285 cups of tea in the laboratory to come up with an equation for the perfect cuppa.

They concluded that the best method was to add boiling water to a tea bag in a mug and leave for two minutes.

Then remove the bag and add the milk and leave for six minutes until it reaches optimal temperature of 60C.

Leave too long and it drops below 45C and the flavours destroying the "all round sensory experience".

The research, which was commissioned by Cravendale Milk, also found that in Britain we drink a staggering 165 million cups of tea per day, or 60.2 billion a year.

It also revealed that the average Briton makes their first cup of tea at seven and a half years old.

Ian Brown, senior lecturer at the University of Northumbria said it was the

Figure 10-13 Online, paragraphs with one short sentence make a news article easy to read. www.telegraph.co.uk, **by Richard Alleyne, Science Correspondent**

Lists or tables may be even better

In many cases, you can take information out of sentences and make it more scannable through lists or tables. I'll show you how to do that in the next chapter. Before we get there, however, let's consider the last 3 of our 10 guidelines for tuning up your sentences.

8. Start with the context

Start each paragraph with a topic sentence – a sentence that sets the context, that tells readers what the paragraph is about.

Checking your topic sentences

You can use this technique to know if you have good topic sentences:

1. Leave the first sentence of each paragraph in regular black type.
2. Change the color of the rest of the paragraph to gray.
3. Read just the black type.
4. Ask yourself: Does the content make sense? Does it flow? Will my site visitors get the gist of the messages?

Even within a sentence, set the context first. Research shows that people jump to act as soon as they see something that tells them to act. They don't always read on to see if more information restricts the action.

For a fascinating study showing that people don't wait for the context, see Dixon, 1987.

Case Study 10-4 shows how the context is often in the wrong place.

Case Study 10-4   **Starting with the context – the topic**

 Is the following paragraph instantly clear?

> Approved fumigation with methyl bromide at normal atmospheric pressure, in accordance with the following procedure, upon arrival at the port of entry, is hereby prescribed as a condition of importation for shipments of yams.

Slightly simplified from a U.S. Department of Agriculture regulation

 If you were talking to someone and this was the information you had to tell them, what part of the sentence would you say first? What would come next? How would you break up the information?

Reversing the order

When telling this information to someone, you would probably reverse the order. You would start with the yams because that's the answer to "What are we talking about?"

The yams are the context, the topic, the connection to what the person you're in this conversation with came to find out about. The yams belong at the beginning – whether you are telling someone this out loud or in writing.

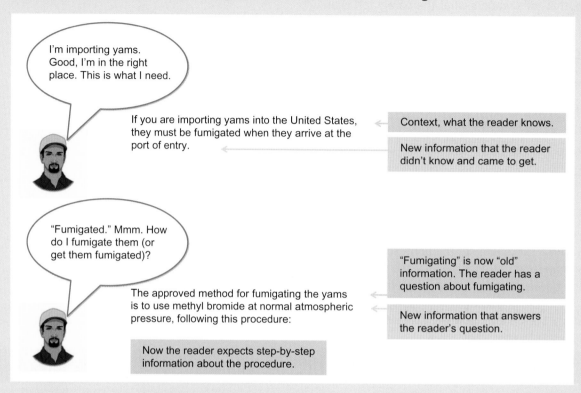

Simplifying even further

Once you've untangled a complex sentence, you will often see other problems to attend to.

In the "yams" example, the original only talked about "fumigation." It didn't say who was responsible for fumigating the yams. So, in my first try at writing more clearly, I put it in the passive.

But you know that active is better. Also, our importer is going to want to know *who* does the fumigating.

Sometimes, to write clearly, you have to find out more information than you originally had.

Also, we may not have to put all those technical words into the second sentence. If an "approved fumigator" has to do the procedure, that's the person who needs to know about "methyl bromide" at "normal atmospheric pressure." So, it might be better to wait and put that information into the procedure.

We might let go of more words and write this:

If you are importing yams, [*person*] must fumigate them when they arrive at the port of entry.

☺ Much simpler for the main persona – the importer.

To fumigate yams, [*person*] must use this procedure:

☹ As the writer/editor, I would have to find the subject matter specialist who knows what to put for [*person*]. Can it be "you"? Or is it "an approved contractor"?

Learning from this case study

Once again, we see how focusing on your site visitors helps you write well for the web.

- Think about what your site visitors do and do not know.
- Start with what they know. Then introduce new information.
- Consider using the pattern, "if, then." It follows the reader's logic and makes you put first things first, second things second. (You almost always need the "if" in the "if clause," but you don't actually need to write the word "then" in the "then clause." For example, write "If it's raining, take an umbrella.")
- Hear the conversation. You don't have to put in a heading for every question the site visitor would ask. But if you listen in your head for what someone would ask after reading each bit of what you write, you'll convey the content in logical order for your site visitors.

The principle of "context, topic, known" before "new" is sometimes also called "given-new." It's based on linguistic research about how people converse. (Clark and Haviland, "Comprehension and the Given-New Contract")

9. Put the action in the verb

Much of the web is about action. Verbs are action words.

If you bury the action in a noun, you often end up with just a form of "to be" (is, are, was, were) instead of an action verb. Weak. Boring. Uninteresting placeholder.

	noun hiding a verb		weak verb

☹ Weak sentence   The Commission's recommendations for changes were few in number.

strong verb

☺ Strong sentence   The Commission recommended few changes.

	noun hiding a verb		weak verb	noun hiding a verb

☹ Weak sentence   Retention of these records for seven years is a requirement for licensees.
requirement → require → must
retention → retain → keep

strong verb

☺ Strong sentence   Licensees must keep these records for seven years.
You must keep these records for seven years.

This table gives you the most common endings for nouns that hide verbs. Use the table to help you move the action out of nouns and put the action where it belongs – in the verb.

Look for this	As in this example	Which should be this verb
-al	deni**al**	deny
-ance	mainten**ance**	maintain, keep
-ence	concurr**ence**	concur, agree
-ment	assign**ment**	assign
-sion	transmis**sion**	transmit, send
-tion	recommenda**tion**	recommend
-ure	fail**ure**	fail, if you don't

After you find the verb that's hidden in the noun, see if you can replace it with a shorter, stronger, plainer verb. You can often do that, as in

- requirement → you are required to → you must
- Please see to the transmission of this message. → Please transmit this message. → Please send this message.

10. Use your site visitors' words

Remember you are conversing with your site visitors. Make that the heart of your content strategy on every level. Keep it in mind when you decide what topics to write about and what to say for each topic. Think conversation as you construct paragraphs, sentences, lists, and tables. And when you choose words.

Write for *your* site visitors

You may be saying, "We have special words that have specific meaning in our field. We have to use them." If everyone you are conversing with shares your special language, it's fine to use those words.

As Sarah Bauer asked when she used the example in Figure 10-14 from lululemon.com, "How many non-yoga participants know what 'downward-dog' means?"

Bauer, It Works For "You": A User-Centric Guideline To Product Pages, *Smashing Magazine,* **January 10, 2012**

why we made this

Scuba diving in the chilly waters of British Columbia taught us valuable lessons about the benefits of a deep hood and a well-fitted jacket. We designed this cozy hoodie to keep us toasty post-dive or pre-Downward-Dog.

Figure 10-14 Using special words your site visitors know can appeal to your market. www.lululemon.com

Lululemon makes clothes for yoga. It knows its site visitors. It appeals to them with their vocabulary (as well as with features of its clothes, like an emergency hair tie on the hoodie's zipper).

Know your site visitors

The examples Bauer used in her blog article were of companies that had done the research to understand their site visitors – to know the words their site visitors use when searching, when buying in other channels, when talking about the topics of the site.

I see the opposite happen: Writers greatly overestimating how much of their company's internal jargon others know.

Your site visitors may not know words that are commonplace to you. Research shows that people who know a special vocabulary overestimate others' knowledge of those words by about 25% to 30%.

Lydia Hooke showed this for a government regulation in the 1970s. More recently, see Hayes and Bayzek, 2008.

- A lawyer in one specialty may not know the words that are common in another specialty. And people coming to the web for information about wills or leases are probably not lawyers.
- A doctor in one specialty may not know the words that are common in another specialty. And many health care workers are not doctors. Most patients are not doctors.
- Your site visitors may come from all over the world. Many are not native speakers of the language of your site.
- Even in your country, your site visitors may include many people who are there temporarily or new to the country. They may not be fluent in your site's language.

You should offer your content in many languages and in culturally appropriate ways for your diverse site visitors. Localizing web sites and apps is an important topic, but it is beyond the scope of this book.

And always use plain language

Lots of words aren't technical terms or specific words that will help market to *your* site visitors. They're just big words that take everyone longer to read and understand.

You can often find a short, simple word that makes your content more conversational. Try it. Start with my list and add your own examples of long, less-common words that you can replace with short, simple words.

Instead of this	Try this
ascertain	find out
attempt	try
compensation	pay
component	part
inception	start
initiate	begin
inquire	ask

Instead of this	Try this
obtain	get
prior to	before
purchase	buy
request	ask for
subsequent	next
terminate	end
utilize	use

As I said at the beginning of the chapter, using these short, simple words is not "dumbing down" your content. It's respecting your busy site visitors' time.

And here's the research that supports this point: Plain language helps both low-literacy **and high-literacy** site visitors.

Kathryn Summers and her team worked on a web site for a medicine that millions of people take. They tested the web site with both low-literacy and high-literacy web users. They then revised the site to resolve the problems the low-literacy web users had.

(Those problems were not only the words. Summers and her team also used many of the other guidelines for good web writing. They reorganized into a clear, logical, flowing story. They shortened paragraphs and sentences. They turned paragraphs into bulleted lists. And they always used the shortest, simplest, plainest word that had the right meaning.)

Then they tested the new site with both low-literacy and high-literacy web users.

Conclusion: As you see in the tables in Figure 10-15, the plain language changes helped low-literacy site visitors get what they needed faster and more accurately. **And those same changes helped high-literacy site visitors even more!!**

Tasks completed successfully	% of tasks		Improvement
	Before	After	
Low-literacy web users	46%	82%	+77%
High-literacy web users	68%	93%	+37%
All users	59%	89%	+52%

Time spent on tasks	Time (minutes)		Improvement
	Before	After	
Low-literacy web users	22:16	9:30	+134%
High-literacy web users	14:19	5:05	+182%
All users	17:50	6:45	+164%

Figure 10-15 Revising by following plain language guidelines improved this web site for both low-literacy and high-literacy web users.
http://iat.ubalt.edu/summers/papers/Summers_ASIST2005.pdf

High-literacy readers are likely to be the busiest and least patient of your site visitors. Respect their time by using plain language.

Summarizing Chapter 10

Key messages from Chapter 10:

- Writing informally is not "dumbing down"!
- Talk *to* your site visitors – use "you."
  - Use the imperative in instructions.
  - Use "you" throughout.
  - Use "you" to be gender-neutral.

- – Use appropriate gender for specific people.
- – Converse directly even for serious messages.

- Use "I" and "we."
  - – In blogs and social media, "I" is fine.
  - – For your own articles, "I" is fine.
  - – When you write for an organization, use "we."
  - – Be consistent in how you use "I," "you," and "we."

- Write in the active voice (most of the time).

- Write simple, short, straightforward sentences.
  - – Very short sentences are okay, too.
  - – Fragments may also work.
  - – Busy site visitors always need clear writing.

- Cut unnecessary words.

- Give extra information its own place.

- Keep paragraphs short.
  - – A one-sentence paragraph is fine.
  - – Lists or tables may be even better.

- Start with the context.

- Put the action in the verbs.

- Use your site visitors' words.
  - – Write for *your* site visitors.
  - – Know your site visitors.
  - – And always use plain language.

- Research shows that using these guidelines for clear writing for the web helps both low-literacy and high-literacy site visitors.

Using Lists and Tables

A great way to let go of words without losing essential meaning is to use lists and tables. Lists put active space around each item. Tables take away redundant words. Both let people skim and scan.

Six guidelines for useful lists

Let's start with six guidelines for useful and usable lists.

1. Use bulleted lists for items or options.
2. Match bullets to your site's personality.
3. Use numbered lists for instructions.
4. Keep most lists short.
5. Try to start list items the same way.
6. Format lists well.

1. Use bulleted lists for items or options

A list is easy to skim and scan.

Madrid has many wonderful museums, including the world-famous <u>Prado</u> with its collection spanning many centuries; the <u>Reina Sofia</u>, featuring 20th century Spanish artists (Dali, Miró, Picasso, and more); and the <u>Thyssen-Bornemisza</u>, fabulous private collection of international art.	Madrid has many wonderful museums, including: • <u>Prado</u> – world famous collection spanning many centuries • <u>Reina Sofia</u> – 20th century Spanish artists (Dali, Miró, Picasso, and more) • <u>Thyssen-Bornemisza</u> – fabulous private collection of international art

 When you were reading the paragraph version, did you find yourself making a mental list?

Lists help people

• see how many items there are

• check off items (mentally, even if they can't write on the screen)

• find a specific item quickly

Think "list" whenever you have several options or items. Compare the presentation of the same information in Figures 11-1 and 11-2, on what to pack for camp.

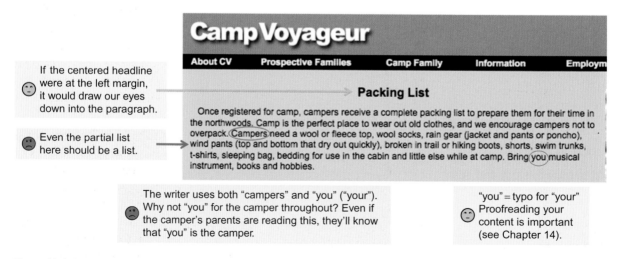

Figure 11-1 A list in paragraph form is difficult to use.

www.campvoyageur.com

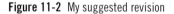

Pronouns help the conversation.

The list makes the page much easier to scan.

Camp Voyageur

About CV   Prospective Families   Camp Family   Information   Employn

Packing for camp

After you register for camp, we'll send a complete list of what to pack for your time in the northwoods.

Here are some ideas to get you started:
- Don't overpack.
- Bring old clothes.
- Be sure you have
  - a wool or fleece top
  - wool socks
  - rain gear (jacket and pants or poncho)
  - wind pants (top and bottom that dry quickly)
  - trail or hiking boots (broken in)
  - shorts
  - swim trunks
  - t-shirts
  - sleeping bag
  - bedding for use in the cabin

And, of course, bring your musical instruments, books, and hobbies.

Figure 11-2 My suggested revision

2. Match bullets to your site's personality

Round dark circles (ordinary bullets) are fine. However, if your site's personality and your content strategy allow something more innovative, you can show that personality visually in your bullets.

For example, the American Museum of Natural History uses different butterflies for each navigation option on the page about its butterfly exhibit (Figure 11-3).

Figure 11-3 Pictures of butterflies make good "bullets" for the links to web content about a butterfly exhibit.
www.amnh.org

More examples of graphics as bullets – Chapter 13 on illustrations

This should look familiar. I used the text of this page as an example in Chapter 10.

These butterflies "flutter" a bit within their white boxes as you mouse over them. That's okay because they move only slightly. They stay in their boxes and move only when you hover over them.

In the first edition of *Letting Go*, I complained that the home page of this exhibit had butterflies fluttering all around the page, interfering with what people would be trying to do. I'm glad to say that those roaming butterflies are gone. The home page of this exhibit now features an excellent short video.

Bullets should reflect the site's personality

As you work with content strategists, brand strategists, and other colleagues to establish the site's personality, think about the ways you and others in the organization will use bullets. The bullets don't have to be identical throughout the site, but they should always fit the personality that part of the site is expressing. Your style guide for the site should include what content owners may use as bullets. (More on style guides in Interlude 5 after Chapter 14.)

If you use different bullets, make sure their meaning is clear. For example, the different colors of the bullets at the ABC Teach site might (or might not) indicate groupings or different sections of the site – but it's not clear if they do or what each color represents (Figure 11-4).

How is this site using colors? Are the colored stars random? Or meaningful?

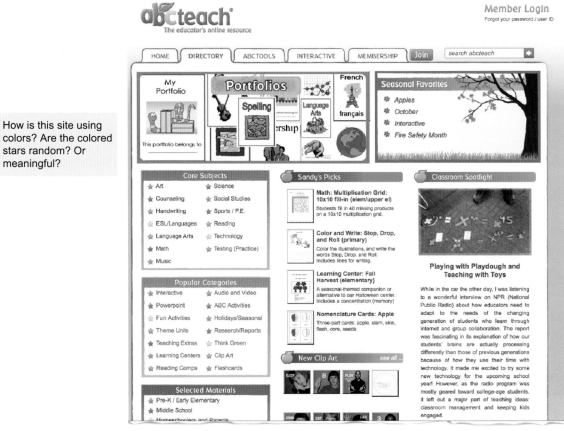

Figure 11-4 This colorful site looks like fun for teachers. But if people stop to wonder whether the colors indicate different sections or ages or something else, the site has caused them to take extra time.

www.abcteach.com

3. Use numbered lists for instructions

Many of the conversations people have with web sites are about how to do something: arrange travel, pay a bill, buy a product, and so on. Tasks sometimes require instructions. Instructions imply sequence. Sequence = numbered steps.

To delete one of your Twitter updates, log in to Twitter.com and visit your Profile page. Then locate the Tweet you want to delete, hover your mouse over the message, and click the "Delete" option that appears.

To delete one of your Twitter updates:
1. Log in to Twitter.com
2. Visit your Profile page.
3. Locate the Tweet you want to delete.
4. Hover your mouse over the message.
5. Click the "Delete" option that appears.

You'll see the actual Twitter page later in the chapter (Figure 11-9).

 Did you look at the paragraph at all? Did you go directly to the list? If you looked at the paragraph, did you find yourself turning it into a mental list, just as you did with the example in Guideline 1 about bullets?

Numbered lists help both site visitors and content authors.

With a numbered list, site visitors can

- see at a glance how many steps there are
- check off steps (mentally, even if they can't write on the screen)
- read one step, do it, and find the next step easily when they come back to the list
- do the steps in the correct order
- do all the steps (without inadvertently missing one)

With a numbered list, you as a content author can

- be sure you have not left out a step
- put the steps in the correct order (and save people from the potentially serious consequences of doing the steps in the wrong order)
- check that the procedure works well (by reviewing or trying out the steps)

Turn paragraphs into steps

Don't frustrate your site visitors. If your site visitors are asking "How do I …?" give them instructions in a numbered list.

In Figures 11-5 and 11-6, on how to prepare concrete for a particular type of bonding, notice how I've turned three dense paragraphs into sections on why, what, and how. My revision with headings and lists is slightly longer than the original, but it is likely to be much easier for people to use.

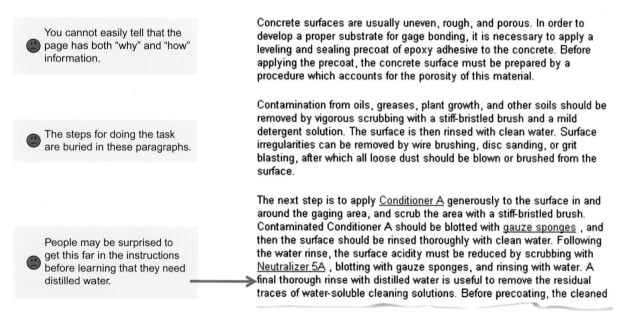

Surface Preparation for Strain Gage Bonding

Surfaces Requiring Special Treatment

Concrete

Concrete surfaces are usually uneven, rough, and porous. In order to develop a proper substrate for gage bonding, it is necessary to apply a leveling and sealing precoat of epoxy adhesive to the concrete. Before applying the precoat, the concrete surface must be prepared by a procedure which accounts for the porosity of this material.

Contamination from oils, greases, plant growth, and other soils should be removed by vigorous scrubbing with a stiff-bristled brush and a mild detergent solution. The surface is then rinsed with clean water. Surface irregularities can be removed by wire brushing, disc sanding, or grit blasting, after which all loose dust should be blown or brushed from the surface.

The next step is to apply Conditioner A generously to the surface in and around the gaging area, and scrub the area with a stiff-bristled brush. Contaminated Conditioner A should be blotted with gauze sponges , and then the surface should be rinsed thoroughly with clean water. Following the water rinse, the surface acidity must be reduced by scrubbing with Neutralizer 5A , blotting with gauze sponges, and rinsing with water. A final thorough rinse with distilled water is useful to remove the residual traces of water-soluble cleaning solutions. Before precoating, the cleaned

You cannot easily tell that the page has both "why" and "how" information.

The steps for doing the task are buried in these paragraphs.

People may be surprised to get this far in the instructions before learning that they need distilled water.

Figure 11-5 It's hard to find the steps in paragraphs like these.
www.vishay.com

If you write instructions as paragraphs, you may forget to put down a step and not notice. Your site visitors may lose their place in the paragraph and skip a step. When you write instructions in paragraphs, you may get steps out of order without realizing it, creating problems for people who are trying to do the task.

I broke the information into "why," "what," and "how."

 The bulleted list tells you what to have ready so that you aren't surprised while doing the steps.

 I broke the 12 steps into three logical groups. A 12-step list with no breaks is long.

 I reorganized sentences to put the action verb at the beginning of the step.

 Each step is one action.

Preparing Concrete for Strain Gage Bonding

Why must concrete be specially prepared?

Concrete surfaces are usually uneven, rough, and porous. To develop a proper substrate for gage bonding, the concrete must have a leveling and sealing precoat of epoxy adhesive. Before applying the precoat, you must first prepare the concrete surface with a procedure that accounts for the fact that it is porous.

What do I need to prepare concrete for precoating?

You need

- Conditioner A
- Neutralizer 5A
- gauze sponges
- a stiff-bristled brush
- a mild detergent solution
- distilled water
- a wire brush or a disc sander or a grit blaster

How do I prepare concrete for precoating?

Clean the surface

1. Remove contamination from oils, greases, plant growth, and other soils by scrubbing vigorously with a stiff-bristled brush and a mild detergent solution.
2. Rinse the surface with clean water.
3. Remove surface irregularities by wire brushing, disc sanding, or grit blasting.
4. Blow or brush all loose dirt from the surface.

Apply Conditioner A

5. Apply Conditioner A generously to the surface in and around the gaging area.
6. Scrub the area with a stiff-bristled brush.
7. Blot contaminated Conditioner A with gauze sponges.
8. Rinse the surface thoroughly with clean water.

Apply Neutralizer 5A

9. Scrub the surface with Neutralizer 5A to reduce the surface acidity.
10. Blot with gauze sponges.
11. Rinse with clean water.
12. Rinse again with distilled water to remove the residual traces of water-soluble cleaning solutions.

Figure 11-6 My suggested revision

For branching, consider a table under the step

Instructions are not always a simple list where everyone must do all the steps. Sometimes, the next step depends on which of two or more conditions are true – "If this…, do x," "If that…, do y."

You can still give clear instructions. Consider Figures 11-7 and 11-8, where I show how I would clarify instructions on removing wine stains from fabric.

If the process is very long and complex, think about it as a little web site rather than as one web topic. Create a pathway page where each link leads to part of the process. Look back at Chapter 6.

How to Remove Red Wine Stains From Fabric

Instructions

Difficulty: Easy

Big numbers in color help make these instructions stand out.

In Step 1, what does "do not pretreat" mean? Should I not blot the stain? Should I blot but not go on to step 2?

1 Blot the stain immediately with paper towels. If it is a dry clean only garment do not pretreat the stain and get it as fast as you can to the cleaners. Pretreatment of the stain can cause irreversible damage and the dry cleaner may not be able to remove the stain.

2 Combine 1 teaspoon laundry soap or pretreatment (or dish soap, like Dawn) and 1 cup hydrogen peroxide in a small bowl. Soak a clean sponge in the mixture, squeeze it halfway dry, then gently blot the stain.

3 Place a dry towel or washcloth between the front and back of the garment if the stain has not penetrated through to the back of the fabric. This will prevent staining on the back of the material.

4 Review the washing instructions on the label of the fabric. Heed any special care instructions.

5 Wash in cool water and air dry if the fabric is machine-washable.

6 Wash gently in the sink with a mild detergent if the fabric is hand-wash only.

Setting out "Things You'll Need" visually like this is excellent.

Things You'll Need

Landry detergent, laundry pretreatment or dish soap

Clean sponge

Washing machine

Paper towels

Hydrogen peroxide

Towel or washcloth

Steps 5 and 6 are alternatives. You do one or the other, not both. But they aren't formated to show that.

Figure 11-7 When instructions include "if" statements, hiding the "if" inside an instruction or putting two "ifs" in consecutive steps may confuse people.
www.eHow.com

I wrote Step 2 to make explicit the branching that was implicit in Step 1 of the original.

1. Blot the stain immediately with paper towels.

2. Check the label on the fabric. Dry clean only? Washable?

Dry clean only	Stop here. Get it as fast as you can to the cleaners. If you do more than gently blot the stain, the dry cleaner may not be able to remove it.
Washable	Follow the rest of these instructions.

3. Combine…

4. Place a dry towel…

The table in Step 5 makes the choice and resulting instruction easy to grab when skimming.

5. Review the washing instructions on the fabric. Machine-washable? Hand-wash only? Heed any special instructions.

Machine-washable	Wash in cool water; air dry
Hand-wash only	Wash gently in the sink with a mild detergent

Figure 11-8 My suggested revision to clarify the branching and alternative instructions

Follow "if, then" in instructions and tables

The original eHow instructions 5 and 6 use the structure "then, if": "Wash in cool water and air dry if the fabric is machine-washable." That's backwards. You have to read to the end, decide if that's true of your fabric, and then go back to the beginning to get the action.

Remember the concept of "given-new" – context before action – from Chapter 10, Guideline 8, Case Study 10-4. Always try to put the "if" part before the "then" part of a sentence.

However, the guideline to put context before action, if before then, conflicts with the guideline to start instructions with an action verb.

How do you do both? My solution: Make the decision point explicit with an action verb. (For example, Review the washing instructions…) Then put the "if, then" options in a table.

In the table, always put the "if" part in the first column. (More about that later in the chapter when we get to tables.)

Show as well as tell

Sometimes, a picture can help clarify a step. The Twitter example that started this section shows where to find the "delete" option (Figure 11-9).

To delete one of your Twitter updates:

1. Log in to Twitter.com
2. Visit your Profile page
3. Locate the Tweet you want to delete
4. Hover your mouse over the message (as shown below), and click the "Delete" option that appears

Voila! Gone forever... almost. Deleted updates sometimes hang out in Twitter search. They will clear with time.

Good conversation. The writer anticipates site visitors' question: "I followed your steps, but my message didn't disappear. Why not?"

Figure 11-9 Screen shots often help people use instructions.
https://support.twitter.com

Use numbered lists for noninstructions thoughtfully

Sometimes, you can use a numbered list when you are not giving steps. For example, blog articles like "10 Tips for ..." or "5 Keys to ..." are very popular. In many chapters of this book, I've numbered the guidelines. In these cases, it's clear that the numbered items are not steps.

But if the same blog post included a numbered list of instructions, the two different uses of a numbered list might confuse people. If you have both types of lists – a set of instructions where people should do each step and a set of options where people should choose only one – don't use numbers for both of those lists. Use numbers for the instructions and bullets for the options.

Case Study 11-1 shows how using both lists at once might confuse people.

Case Study 11-1	Using both bulleted and numbered lists

E-commerce sites have to explain when you can return an item and how to return it. They also want you to order something else, so they have to tell you how to reorder.

For how to reorder, Lands' End does a great job. A bulleted list is best here because the four items are options. You do only one.

Want to reorder?

Choose whichever method is most convenient:

- Send back the items you wish to return, then place a new order online
- Send back the items you wish to return along with your completed reorder
- Call us at **1-800-963-4816,** or
- Fax us your completed packing slip reorder section at **1-800-332-0103**.

www.landsend.com

But higher up on the same web page, Lands' End doesn't follow that same good pattern when telling people how to return the item. They use numbers for the options and bullets for the steps.

Use any of the following options to return Lands' End products purchased online or from one of our catalogs.

Numbers with action verbs makes this list look like instructions. ☹

1. Return Internet or catalog orders at a Sears store.

Just follow these guidelines

But the numbers are for options. The bullets are the steps. ☹

- Bring the Lands' End items you wish to return to any Sears® store.
- Make sure to bring the original packing slip for the items you wish to return.
- You will receive a return confirmation from Sears. Lands' End will then either credit your card, issue a refund check, or send you a Lands' End gift card, as you choose.

Please Note: Sears cannot accept exchanges or returns from Lands' End stores, Amazon.com®, or Lands' End Business Outfitters.

Notes at the end make some site visitors read instructions they can't use. ☹

2. Use our Easy Return label for a flat fee of $6.95.

Securely package the items you wish to return, fill out and include the Return Form, and affix the Easy Return shipping label found on your packing slip. Give the package to your mail carrier or drop it off at any U.S. Post Office or collection box. A flat fee of $6.95 will be deducted from the amount of your refund.

Please note: Not all orders are eligible for the Easy Return label service. If your packing slip does not have one, use return methods 1 or 3.

Option 2 also has steps, but they're buried in the paragraph. ☹

3. Send your return to us with the shipper of your choice.

Securely package your return including the Return Form, and send to:

Using bullets where this example has numbers and numbers where it has bullets would better match people's expectations and would be more consistent. My suggested revision would look like this:

How do I return an item?

Choose whichever method is best for you:

Bullets for the three options. ☺

- **Return catalog orders and some Internet orders at a Sears store.**
  Please note: If you bought the item from Amazon.com, a Lands' End store, or a Lands' End Business Outfitters, Sears cannot help with your exchange or refund. Use one of the other two ways to return the item.

Notes *before* the steps. Site visitors who can't use the option learn that before reading the steps. ☺

  To return an item at a Sears store:

  1. Make sure you have the original packing slip for the item(s) you want to return.
  2. Take the items and original packing slip to any Sears store.
  3. Choose how you want your refund: credit on your card, a check, or a Lands' End gift card.

Numbers for the steps. ☺

  Sears will confirm in writing that you have returned the items. Lands' End will refund your money in the way you chose.

  or

- **Use our Easy Return label for a flat fee of $6.95.**
  Please note: First check to see if the packing slip that came with your item has an Easy Return label. If it does not, you cannot use this method. Use one of the other two ways to return the item.

  To return an item with the Easy Return label:

  1. Fill out and include the Return Form with your item(s).
  2. Package the item(s) with the Return Form securely.

Numbers for steps in the second option, too ☺

  3. Affix the Easy Return shipping label from your packing slip on the outside of your package.
  4. Give the package to your mail carrier or drop it off at any U.S. Post Office or postal collection box.

  Lands' End will deduct the flat fee of $6.95 from the amount of your refund.

  or

- **Send your return to us with the shipper of your choice.**
  Securely package your item(s) with the Return Form and send to:

  Lands' End Returns

4. Keep most lists short

How long can a list be and still work well? It depends.

Short (5–10 items) is best for unfamiliar items

If people will not immediately recognize all the items in the list, break up long lists. If possible, group the items so that you can make several shorter lists each with its own heading.

Look back at Figure 11-6 about concrete to see how I broke up a list of 12 items.

Long may be okay for very familiar lists

Some lists can be long because your site visitors immediately understand the topic of the list and know how far down the list the item they want is likely to be.

For example, a list of U.S. states and territories has more than 50 items. However, if the list is in alphabetical order, the length is not a problem for most people. They find the right entry quickly, whether you use a dropdown (Figure 11-10) or an open list (Figure 11-11).

If some of your site visitors want to print the list, it's better in an open format like Figure 11-11 than in a dropdown like Figure 11-10.

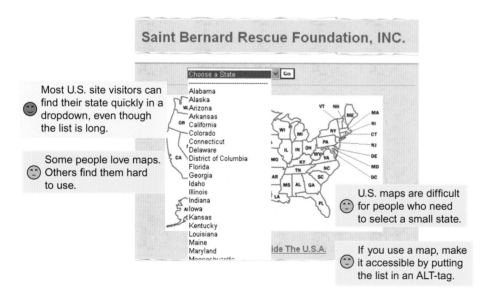

Most U.S. site visitors can find their state quickly in a dropdown, even though the list is long.

Some people love maps. Others find them hard to use.

U.S. maps are difficult for people who need to select a small state.

If you use a map, make it accessible by putting the list in an ALT-tag.

Figure 11-10 If your site visitors are familiar with the list, know which item in the list they want, and know how far down the list it will be, a long list may be okay.
www.saintrescue.org

😊 If you have room, setting out a long list like this makes it easy to use.

😊 Grouping items logically and showing that with headings helps.

A	G	N	R
Alabama	Georgia	Nebraska	Rhode Island
Alaska	Guam	Nevada	
American Samoa		New Hampshire	S
Arizona	H	New Jersey	South Carolina
Arkansas	Hawaii	New Mexico	South Dakota
		New York (except New	
C	I	York City)	T
California	Idaho	New York City	Tennessee
Canal Zone	Illinois	North Carolina	Texas
Colorado	Indiana	North Dakota	
Connecticut	Iowa	Northern Mariana	U
		Islands	Utah
D	K		
Delaware	Kansas	O	V
District of Columbia	Kentucky	Ohio	Vermont
		Oklahoma	Virginia
F	L	Oregon	Virgin Islands
Florida	Louisiana		
Foreign or high-seas		P	W
events	M	Pennsylvania	Washington
	Maine	Puerto Rico	West Virginia
	Maryland		Wisconsin
	Massachusetts		Wyoming
	Michigan		
	Minnesota		
	Mississippi		
	Missouri		
	Montana		

Figure 11-11 If you have room, setting out the list like this works well.
www.cdc.gov

5. Try to start list items the same way

People are very pattern-oriented. We find it faster and easier to read a list when all the entries are in the same sentence structure.

To delete one of your Twitter updates:	**To delete one of your Twitter updates:**
1. Log in to Twitter.com	1. Log in to Twitter.com
2. Visit your Profile page.	2. You must then visit your Profile page.
3. Locate the Tweet you want to delete.	3. The Tweet you want to delete must be found next.
4. Hover your mouse over the message.	4. Over the message, hover your mouse.
5. Click the "Delete" option that appears.	5. Click the "Delete" option that appears.

Which list worked best for you? Did you choose the one on the left where each item starts with a verb?

But did you first assume it would be the one on the right – because all my previous comparisons have had the "good" choice on the right?

If you did, that's how quickly you had built a pattern from the little tables like this in this chapter. I tripped you up (at least momentarily) by breaking the pattern I had created. (Sorry to do that. I did it to make a point.)

When you are writing web content, remember that if you set the patterns clearly and follow them well, your patterns can help people. Parallelism – starting each list item the same way – is an excellent pattern to create and follow.

6. Format lists well

Information design – the way you present information on the screen – can also help or hinder people from finding what they need easily. Information design applies to lists (and tables) as well as to all other features of typography and layout.

When designing lists, you want people to connect the list with its introduction, see at a glance that you are giving a list, and find each list item easily. Four keys to formatting lists well:

- Reduce space between the introduction and the list.
- Put a space between long list items.
- Wrap lines under each other, not under the bullet.
- Put what happens on a line by itself.

Reduce space between the introduction and the list

Plain vanilla HTML puts a line of space between the text before a list and the first item in the list. To help people visually group the introduction with the list, reduce that space through a cascading style sheet (CSS). In this book, we use 12 points between paragraphs but only 6 points between the introduction to a list and the first list item.

Put space between long list items

Single spacing works for lists with short items. However, you need more space between items for numbered lists (where each item is usually a full sentence) and for bulleted lists where each item is more than a line long.

Wrap lines under each other

To make your lists look and work as lists, the bullets or numbers have to stand out. If the text wraps back to the beginning of the line (under the bullet or number), each list item looks like a paragraph with a funny symbol at the beginning. It doesn't look like a list.

Compare the Lands, End example I used (and revised) in the first edition with the way Lands, End gives the same list now (Figure 11-12).

Return Internet or catalog orders at a Sears store.
Just follow these guidelines:
• Bring the Lands' End items you wish to return to any participating Sears store where Lands' End merchandise is sold.
• Make sure to bring the original packing slip for the items you wish to return.
• You will receive a return confirmation from Sears. Lands' End will then either credit your card, issue a refund check, or send you a Lands' End gift card, as you choose.

This 2007 list was hard to use because the
• text wrapped back to the margin
• bullets didn't stand out
• page had no space between the bulleted items

Return Internet or catalog orders at a Sears store.

The 2012 version had none of those problems.

Just follow these guidelines

• Bring the Lands' End items you wish to return to any Sears® store.
• Make sure to bring the original packing slip for the items you wish to return.
• You will receive a return confirmation from Sears. Lands' End will then either credit your card, issue a refund check, or send you a Lands' End gift card, as you choose.

Figure 11-12 Make sure the text wraps under itself — not back under the bullet.
www.landsend.com

Put what happens on a line by itself

When giving instructions, sometimes you want to tell people what happens after they do a step. A good way to show that is to put the result on a line by itself, under the step, and indented like the step. Figure 11-13 shows what I mean.

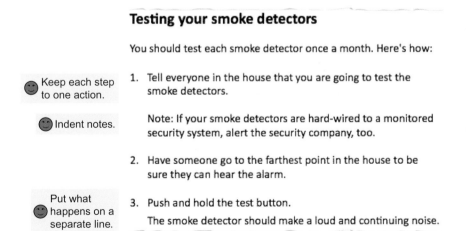

Testing your smoke detectors

You should test each smoke detector once a month. Here's how:

Keep each step to one action.

1. Tell everyone in the house that you are going to test the smoke detectors.

Indent notes.

Note: If your smoke detectors are hard-wired to a monitored security system, alert the security company, too.

2. Have someone go to the farthest point in the house to be sure they can hear the alarm.

Put what happens on a separate line.

3. Push and hold the test button.

The smoke detector should make a loud and continuing noise.

Figure 11-13 Keep the instructions easy to follow by putting extra information under the instruction and indented with the text.

Lists and tables: What's the difference?

Now that I have convinced you (I hope) of many good ways to use lists in your content, let's turn to tables. Tables, like lists, are a great way to let go of words so people can grab the essential information.

 Think about the difference? What is a list? What is a table? When would you use each?

How lists and tables differ

	Lists	Tables
Categories of information	1	At least 2
Number of columns	1 (even if it wraps to look like more than one)	At least 2
Shows relationship?	No	Yes

The list of states and territories in Figure 11-11 may look like a table because it is set in four columns. It's not. It's a list, wrapped on itself. It has only one category of information (names of states and territories).

A table is a set of "if, then" sentences. Read the first column as the "if" clause. Read the second column (and other columns) as the "then" clause(s). For example, "*If* we are comparing the number of categories for lists and tables, *then* lists have one and tables have at least two." "*If* we are comparing the number of columns..." and so on.

Six guidelines for useful tables

Use these guidelines to help your site visitors find the right information for their situation quickly and easily.

1. Use tables for a set of "if, then" sentences.

2. Use tables to compare numbers.

3. Think tables = answers to questions.

4. Think carefully about the first column.

5. Keep tables simple.

6. Format tables well.

1. Use tables for a set of "if, then" sentences

When you see the same words repeated in several sentences (as in Figure 11-14), think "table." Take the common words and make them the column headings. Remove the redundant words, as I've done for Figure 11-15.

The DME applicants are governed by the guidance in FAA Order 8610.4. "Aviation Mechanic Examiner Handbook."

The DPRE applicants are governed by the guidance in FAA Order 8610.5. "The Parachute Rigger Examiner Handbook."

The DAR-T applicants are governed by the guidance in FAA Order 8100.8. "Designee Management Handbook."

Figure 11-14 When you find yourself repeating words, as in this example, think "table."
www.faa.gov

If you are applying for	You are governed by
Designated Mechanic Examiner (DME)	Aviation Mechanic Examiner Handbook (FAA Order 8610.4)
Designated Parachute Rigger Examiner (DPRE)	The Parachute Rigger Examiner Handbook (FAA Order 8610.5)
Designated Airworthiness Representatives Maintenance (DAR-T)	Designee Management Handbook (FAA Order 8100.8)

 Each site visitor probably wants information from only one row of the table.

Tables save space and save site visitor's time by letting go of words.

Figure 11-15 My suggested revision

2. Use tables to compare numbers

When you have numbers that relate to each other, think "table." A table is a good choice for the comparisons in Figure 11-16, but we could improve the table in several ways.

Shading every other row is a great way to make tables easy to use.

The table allows quick comparisons of cost by season and vehicle size.

But when does each season start and end?

Model		Daily Rental Rates			
		Winter	Spring	Summer	Fall
24 ft Class C motor home	More Information	$129	$159	$179	$149
	Minimum Days	3	4	5	3
29 ft Class C motor home	More Information	$159	$179	$219	$169
	Minimum Days	3	4	5	3
31 ft Class C motor home	More Information	$179	$209	$259	$199
	Minimum Days	3	4	5	3
32 ft Class A motor home	More Information	$199	$229	$289	$219
	Minimum Days	3	4	5	3
36 ft Class A motor home	More Information	$239	$279	$349	$259
	Minimum Days	3	4	5	3

More information belongs under each model name, not where it is. Where it is should say Cost for Each Day.

The names make size differences obvious. But what makes Class C different from Class A?

A small picture or brief description would help show the differences among the vehicles.

Figure 11-16 Tables make numbers easy to compare, but this table could be even better.
www.unitedrvrentals.com/rental_rates.html

3. Think tables = answers to questions

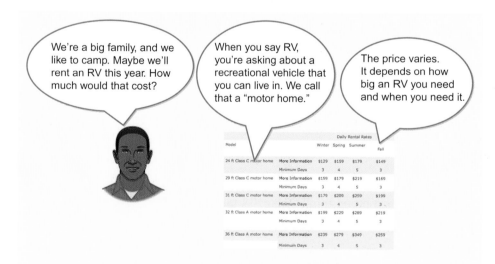

Tables are the answer to questions when the answer is "it depends."

Tables answer questions. You don't have to use the question as a heading. You don't have to have the question anywhere in your table. But thinking about the conversation site visitors come with and the question(s) that the table answers can help you set up the table.

4. Think carefully about the first column

Whenever the answer to a question is "it depends," think "table." What the answer depends on becomes the first column of the table. The answer to the question for each site visitor's situation becomes the second column.

This is another case where the principle of "given-new" applies. (Look back at Chapter 10, Guideline 8, Case Study 10-4, the "yams.")

We read sentences across the page (left to right in English and many other languages, right to left in Arabic and Hebrew). When we identify text as a list, however, we read *down* the page. When we see a table, we scan down the first column to find our situation and then we look across that row to get what we need.

What if the answer depends on many things?

If the answer to people's question is "it depends on many things," you may not want to create a table. The table might have to be too complex for most web users or too large to fit well on the web page – and certainly to fit well on a mobile.

For example, the answer to "How much does a new laptop cost?" may be "It depends on how much memory you want it to have, what size screen you want, how fast you want it to run, what weight you are willing to carry, and so on."

For complex situations, consider asking site visitors a series of questions or giving them filters to apply to their choices rather than putting all the information in one table.

Case Study 11-2, about shipping costs, is relevant to every e-commerce site. It's also a great case for letting go of words, for the difference between a bulleted list and a table, and for handling multiple situations at the same time.

Case Study 11-2   Knowing when to use a table

Consider the typical conversation about shipping costs for any e-commerce site.

 Consider the next example with a bulleted list. Is this the best way for the site to take the next turn in the conversation?

Shipping

For U.S. Shipping: Orders placed on our website will be shipped by UPS. Shipping charges for shipments in the contiguous U.S. will vary depending on the value of your order:

- $3.99 for orders valued at $0.00 to $25.00
- $5.99 for orders valued at $25.01 to $50.00
- $7.99 for orders valued at $50.01 to $75.00
- $9.99 for orders valued at $75.01 up to $100
- $11.99 for orders valued over $100

 Did you come up with the same critique that I did?

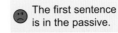 Will site visitors understand "contiguous U.S."?

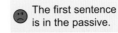 The first sentence is in the passive.

We don't need the second sentence. The information in the list sends the same message.

A list is not the best way to give this information. Each item is backwards.

You must read to the end of each item to see if it is the one for you.

Shipping

For U.S. Shipping: Orders placed on our website will be shipped by UPS. Shipping charges for shipments in the contiguous U.S. will vary depending on the value of your order:

- $3.99 for orders valued at $0.00 to $25.00
- $5.99 for orders valued at $25.01 to $50.00
- $7.99 for orders valued at $50.01 to $75.00
- $9.99 for orders valued at $75.01 up to $100
- $11.99 for orders valued over $100

Two clues that this list should be a table:
- Each line has 2 categories of information.
- The words "for orders valued" occur in each line.

 Now consider the example with a table. Would this be a better answer to our site visitor's question?

Shipping charges

For U.S. Shipping
(To all states, except Alaska, Hawaii, and territories)

A short active sentence conveys a key message. → We ship by UPS.

The table is much easier to scan than the list was.

Value of your order	Shipping charges
up to $25.00	$3.99
$25.01 to $50.00	$5.99
$50.01 to $75.00	$7.99
$75.01 to $100.00	$9.99
Over $100.00	$11.99

The link is clearer than "contiguous U.S." and helps people who need it get their information. (The original is ambiguous. Should this link also cover military APO, FPO? Should that be another link?)

The value of the order goes in the first column because that's what people know when they come to the table.

The shipping charges go in the second column. People look across the row from what they know to get the answer they need.

5. Keep tables simple

Two-column tables are best both for space and ease of use. Sometimes, however, you have more than two related pieces of information to give people for each row of a table. How large can a table be before it becomes too much for site visitors?

How many columns?

Use only as many columns as your site visitors will be able to see all at once on whatever screen they are using. If all your information pieces are small, you may be able to fit three or even four columns in your table and still have people see it even on their mobiles.

Consider web constraints

The web constrains us much more than paper did.

- **No fold-outs.** You can't create fold-out pages the way some old paper reports did.

- **No horizontal scrolling.** One of the strongest findings from usability testing is how few people notice a horizontal scroll bar.

- **Small screens.** You cannot assume that all your site visitors have large monitors with maximized windows. If your app or site is likely to be viewed on a mobile device, you know you need to keep your tables small. But even if all your site visitors are at desktop computers, they may still have smaller monitors than the one you are working on. They may magnify what they can see so they are not using your default resolution. They may keep many windows open and not use the entire screen for your site.

Consider breaking up large and complicated tables into a series of smaller, more specific tables. Or layer your tables – allowing your site visitors to drill down to more details through links in the table.

Consider site visitors' conversations

The example about renting an RV back in Figure 11-16 combines size of vehicle, cost, number of days, and season all in one table – a lot of information. Yet, it may work because people are primarily using it for comparison. They actually want all that information.

The example in the case study is different. When they come to the Shipping Charges table, site visitors know where they want the package to be sent. Information for any other geographic location is not relevant and would only get in the way of their finding what they need.

That's why I would use links to take people to the small table that is relevant to the location they want. Having small, specific tables for shipping is easier for most people than a large matrix with information for different people in different columns. People have difficulty jumping over columns that are not relevant to them.

 Research shows that older adults are less able to quickly suppress nonrelevant information than younger people are. As we age, our ability to sort relevant from nonrelevant seems to decrease.

Gazzaley, 2009

How many rows?

Although most site visitors scroll vertically today, a long table may be more difficult to use than a long list. A table shows relationships. Your site visitors must remember the column headings for a table to understand how the pieces of information in each row relate to each other.

Break very long tables into a series of smaller tables that allow you to keep the context-giving column headings close to the information.

 For information on how to construct and tag a table so that screen-readers can work with it: http://webaim.org/ techniques/tables/.

6. Format tables well

Information design applies to tables, too – as it does to all parts of all your web content.

Reduce lines: Help people focus on information

People use tables to see relationships along a row. Thick lines between columns stop people from moving easily along the row – just the opposite of what you want people to do.

Also, heavy lines draw people's eyes. You want your site visitors to focus on the essential information in the table, not on the lines between the pieces of information. Don't make each cell of a table into a box with thick, equal-weight borders all around it.

A few ways to format better tables:

- Eliminate outside lines around the whole table.
- Lighten the lines between columns.
- Use shading for alternate rows instead of lines.

The RV rental example in Figure 11-16 shows how effective shading can be to separate rows of a table.

Line up columns: Don't center text in a table

Aligning text on the left makes each column easy to scan. Centering interferes with scanning in tables just as it does in other parts of your content. In tables, set all column headings and columns with words flush left, ragged right. When you give numbers, line them up on a decimal tab.

 Which table is easier to use, Figure 11-17 or Figure 11-18?

Account type	Minimum deposit to open account	Minimum daily balance for Annual Percentage Yield (APY)	Interest rate	Annual Percentage Yield (APY)
Money Market	$250.	$1,000.	0.4987%	0.50%
Gold Money Market	$25,000.	Tier 1: $0 - $9,999.99	0.8957%	0.90%
		Tier 2: $10,000 - $49,999.99	1.09401%	1.10%
		Tier 3: $50,000 and above	1.19401%	1.20%
Platinum Money Market	$50,000.	Tier 1: $0 - $9,999.99	0.8957%	0.90%
		Tier 2: $10,000 - $49,999.99	1.09401%	1.10%
		Tier 3: $50,000 and above	1.19401%	1.20%

Figure 11-17 Centering makes tables look busy and hard to use.
Adapted from the web site of a bank

Account type	Minimum deposit to open account	Minimum daily balance for Annual Percentage Yield (APY)	Interest rate	Annual Percentage Yield (APY)
Money Market	$250.	$1,000.	0.4987%	0.50%
Gold Money Market	$25,000.	Tier 1: $0 - $9,999.99 Tier 2: $10,000 - $49,999.99 Tier 3: $50,000 and above	0.8957% 1.09401% 1.19401%	0.90% 1.10% 1.20%
Platinum Money Market	$50,000.	Tier 1: $0 - $9,999.99 Tier 2: $10,000 - $49,999.99 Tier 3: $50,000 and above	0.8957% 1.09401% 1.19401%	0.90% 1.10% 1.20%

Figure 11-18 My suggested reformatting – aligning text on the left margin of each column and aligning numbers on the decimal point

Summarizing Chapter 11

Key messages from Chapter 11:

Lists

- Use bulleted lists for items or options.
- Match bullets to your site's personality.
- Use numbered lists for instructions.
  - Turn paragraphs into steps.
  - For branching, consider a table under the step.
  - Show as well as tell.
  - Use numbered lists for noninstructions thoughtfully.
- Keep most lists short.
  - Short (5–10 items) is best for unfamiliar items.
  - Long may be okay for very familiar lists.
- Try to start list items the same way.
  - Format lists well.
  - Reduce space between the introduction and the list.
  - Put space between long list items.
  - Wrap lines under each other.
  - Put what happens on a line by itself.

Tables

- Understand the difference between lists and tables.
- Use tables for a set of "if, then" sentences.
- Use tables to compare numbers.
- Think tables = answers to questions.
- Think carefully about the first column.
- Keep tables simple.
- Format tables well.
  - Reduce lines: Help people focus on information.
  - Line up columns: Don't center text in a table.

Legal information abounds on the Internet: terms of use, privacy policies, accessibility policies, and more. Some web sites are all about legal issues; many provide access to legal documents.

Letting go of the words and writing in plain language are as applicable to legal information as to any other web content. Legal documents are conversations between your site visitors and your organization, just like everything else on your web site.

Accurate, sufficient, clear – You can have all three

A company's lawyers want information to be correct – accuracy. They want the information to cover the situations that might arise – sufficiency.

But, most of all, companies want people to follow the terms of use, to understand the company's policies, to not sue the company, and to not need to be sued by the company.

Clear writing makes that happen. Unclear writing contributes to problems. Clarity supports accuracy and sufficiency to achieve everyone's goals.

 Do you agree that the plain language version in this example is more likely to inspire trust and make site visitors comfortable?

 In the process of or following consultation of this web site, data pertaining to identified or identifiable persons may be processed.

 When you use this web site, we may collect data about you or people you tell us about – for example, people to whom you are sending a gift. We may use that data to...

The plain language version is just as legal as the less understandable version. In fact, I would argue that the plain language version explains more. Therefore, it serves its legal purpose better.

> In the United States, all new information from federal government agencies to the public must be in plain language: *Plain Language Act of 2010; Executive Order (for regulations), January 2011.* For requirements for plain language in other countries, see Asprey, 2010.

Avoid archaic legal language

Many words in legal information just shout, "This is legal stuff. You won't understand it." That's because they aren't part of regular English anymore.

"Heretofore," "the said example," "to wit," and many other words and phrases that we see only in legal documents were plain language hundreds of years ago. People actually talked that way, so reading those words was easy for people – then.

Language changes over time. Words come into the language. Words leave.

We don't talk with the words in Figure Interlude 4-1. Why use them? They don't make the information "more legal."

PRIVACY

Information provided pursuant to section 13 of Italian Legislative Decree No. 196 of 30 June 2003 (Personal Data Protection Code, hereinafter referred to as "P.C.")

 You don't need to use legal language to tell people about the law.

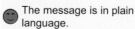 The acronym "P.C." appears only once, at the end of the page. Site visitors will likely forget what it means by then. Better to drop the "hereinafter referred to" here and just repeat the full name when it comes up again.

Figure Interlude 4-1 Words like "pursuant to" and "hereinafter" make legal information difficult for people to understand.
www.benetton.com

If the company must tell people which law requires the information, they might write that the way I show in Figure Interlude 4-2.

PRIVACY

The law says that we must give you this information. (Legislative Decree No. 196, *Personal Data Protection Code*, Section 13, 30 June 2003)

Separating the message from the citation helps make the message clear.

The message is in plain language.

Figure Interlude 4-2 My suggested revision

The list in Figure Interlude 4-3 from the U.S. Federal Register gives you a good start to writing with no archaic legal language.

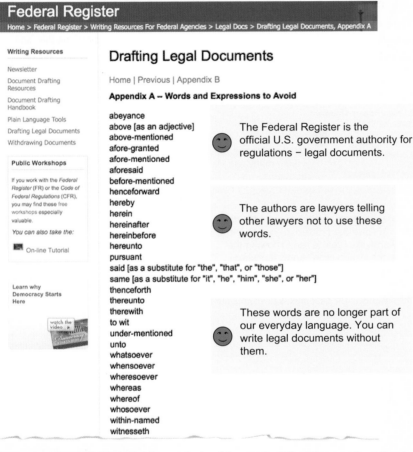

Figure Interlude 4-3 Words like these make legal documents difficult for your site visitors to understand.
www.archives.gov/federal-register/write/legal-docs/appendix-a.html

Avoid technical jargon

You can also explain technical information clearly in your legal notices.

 We collect information to analyze our traffic patterns.

 We gather information about how visitors navigate through our web site by using clickstream data.

 We collect information to understand how people use our web site.

Words like "traffic patterns," "navigate," and "clickstream data" may be everyday language to you. But they aren't to most of your site visitors. Think about your personas.

Use site visitors' words in headings

Headings help in legal information, just as they do in any content. All the guidelines from Chapter 9 on headings apply to your privacy policies, terms of use, and other legal information. Questions and statements are just as legal as noun-based headings. Figure Interlude 4-4 shows you the headings that American Express uses.

Thanks to Carolyn Boccella Bagin, the plain language specialist who worked with American Express on this. And thanks to others who answered my request for examples.

What's in this Online Privacy Statement:
How Do We Collect Information?
How Do We Use Information?
How Do We Share Information?
What Are Your Choices?
Other Information
Questions About this Statement?
Glossary

"collect," "use," "share," "choices" these words match many site visitors' concerns.

"Other information" is vague. It covers another set of questions, so a second tier of linked headings here under "Other information" would be more useful.

A glossary where words are linked in the text can solve the problem of needing to use words like "cookie" and knowing that some site visitors won't know the word in this meaning.

Figure Interlude 4-4 If you use your site visitors' words in the headings, site visitors are more likely to read your legal information.
www.americanexpress.com

Follow the rest of this book, too

All the guidelines for clear content apply to legal information.

You can use

- personal pronouns
- very short sections with a heading over each
- short, active sentences
- lists
- tables
- examples

For more on plain legal language, see the web sites of

- **Clarity** – www.clarity-international.net
- **Center for Plain Language** – www.centerforplainlanguage.org
- **Plain Language Action and Information Network (U.S.)** – www.plainlanguage.gov
- **PLAIN Network International** – www.plainlanguagenetwork.org

You may find this model privacy policy useful. With it, I show how you can have a successful conversation with your site visitors even about highly technical and legal matters.

Of course, you may need to modify the information based on the facts for your web site or app. You may need to add other information to cover situations that are special for your site or app. If you do, write in the same style – friendly, personal, clear, and also legal.

Our Privacy Policy

Updated: [date]

Be sure to let people know the date that the policy was last changed.

Does [...] collect personal information about me?

What does [...] do with my personal information?

Does [...] share my information?

Does [...] store information on my computer? ("cookies")

Does [...] collect information about children under 13?

What if I have other questions?

Put same-page links at the top to give site visitors a quick overview and let them get to specific questions easily.

Does [...] collect personal information about me?

If you are just browsing our web site, we do not collect any personal information about you.

We may ask you for and collect personal information, such as your name, email address, postal address, phone number, and possibly credit card information, when you

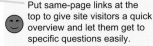

- order something on our web site, by phone, or in one of our stores
- open an account with us
- subscribe to an email newsletter
- participate in a survey, contest, or other event

Make it a conversation between "you" and "we." Many legal documents now use personal pronouns.

If you buy from us, we may also keep records of your purchases so that you can track your orders and so that we can serve you better by tailoring information for you.

What does [...] do with my personal information?

We use personal information related to an order to process the order. We may contact you by email, phone, or postal address to confirm the order or if we have questions.

"collect" "do with" "share" – use words that resonate with site visitors.

We may also use your personal information and information about your product interests to send you emails about products and promotions or to ask you questions about your preferences. If you do not want us to send you these emails, contact us.

Does [...] share my information?

We never tell anyone your email address or phone number. We may share your postal mailing information and your product interests with other carefully selected companies whose products may interest you. If you do not want us to share information about you, contact us.

Continued

Does [...] store information on my computer? ("cookies")

To recognize you as a returning customer and to show you information the way you want it, our computers put a small piece of information on your computer. This is called a "cookie."

A cookie tells us about your computer and lets our computers remember what you are currently doing or did in the past at our web site. For example, a cookie lets us track your shopping cart while you are on our web site.

A cookie does not give us any of your personal information, such as your name or email address.

Cookies also help us understand how people use our web site. They help us know which sections of the site are most popular and how people look for information on our site. We use this information to improve our web site and to serve you better.

Does [...] collect information about children under 13?

We never knowingly sell to or collect any personal information from children under 13. If you believe your child has given us personal information, please help us remove that information from our computers by contacting us.

What if I have other questions?

Please contact us. We are happy to answer your questions.

[contact information]

 Explain technical terms, like "cookies" in plain language.

Always give site visitors a way to continue the conversation.

Writing Meaningful Links

12

Links connect pages in your web site and they connect your site to other sites. You've seen many examples throughout the book, especially in Chapter 4 on home pages, Chapter 5 on pathway pages, Chapter 8 on headlines, and Chapter 9 on headings (in the section on same-page links). In this chapter, I add seven more guidelines to the ones you've already worked with earlier in the book.

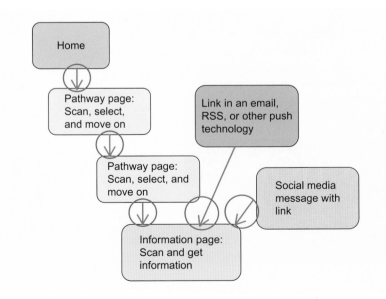

Seven guidelines for writing meaningful links

1. Don't make new program or product names links by themselves.
2. Think ahead: Launch and land on the same name.
3. For actions, start with a verb.
4. Make the link meaningful – not Click here or just More.
5. Don't embed links (for most content).
6. Make bullets with links active, too.
7. Make unvisited and visited links obvious.

1. Don't make new program or product names links by themselves

Many organizations create programs and products with cute names. Once people know the name, it may make sense. It may even be memorable. But until people know what it means, it's meaningless to them. Remember that your web site must serve new people, not just those already "in the know."

In the first edition, I showed two examples of sites that used Compass as a link with no further explanation. One was the British Museum, hiding lots of great information behind a link that most people didn't recognize. The other was the Colorado Historical Society, where the link is relevant only to a small group of site visitors.

I'm happy to say both of those sites have changed for the better. But Figure 12-1 shows a nonprofit organization that has a tab for Compass. The organization seems to do wonderful work, and their Compass

Compass is Action's name for its programs for youth, but you can't guess that from the name.

Any of these might be better:
Young Adults
For Teenagers
16 – 21 Year Olds

Figure 12-1 Does everyone who needs Compass know the name?
www.actioninc.org

program offers many resources and services for young people. But are some people missing out because they don't know the program name?

2. Think ahead: Launch and land on the same name

As people move through web sites, the first question they ask as a new page loads is "Did I get where I thought I was going?" They quickly check the page headline to see if it matches the link they clicked on.

When the two match, site visitors can feel confident in their choices and in the site. You build trust and credibility. If the two don't match, site visitors may have at least a moment of confusion and cognitive trouble – and you don't want to cause that.

This match may be even more important now that so many of your site visitors are on mobile devices. Page load times can be longer for mobile than for other types of connections. If people don't think they've gotten the content they expected, they may be even more frustrated on a mobile than they were on their laptops.

SEO | Launching and landing on the same name helps your SEO. Some algorithms may lower your SEO score if the headline as a link and the headline on the page don't match.

Plan in both directions and with other content:

- How well does your headline on the page work as a link?
- How well does your link work as a headline on the page?
- How does this headline work with others at the same level or in the same part of the site?

This last question can get a bit tricky because you have to think about these questions:

- Where will this link show up?
- What type of page is this on?
- What other pages make a consistent set with this one?
- What other links will go with this one?
- What style are we using for all those links?
- How does all this fit into our content strategy?

You can do this well, just as the Ministry of Tourism in India does on its web site (Figure 12-2).

Thanks to Caroline Jarrett for letting me use her "launch and land" phrase: http://www.editingthatworks.com/step8.htm

Best is an exact match. But considering your entire content, you may need to have small differences between headline as link and headline on the page. For example, you might have an –ing form in one and the imperative of the verb in the other. But both should have almost all the same words – certainly the same keywords.

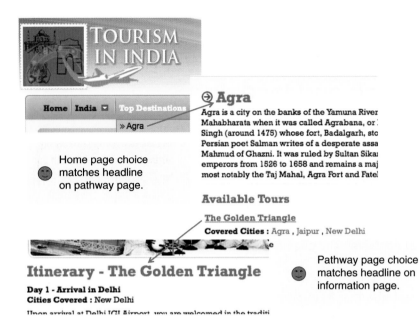

Figure 12-2 Matching the headline on the home page with the headline on the information page builds trust and credibility.
www.tourismicindia.com

3. For actions, start with a verb

In a study by Ann Chadwick-Dias and her colleagues at Fidelity Investments, web users, especially older adults, hesitated to click on single nouns as links, like <u>Accounts</u>. When the Fidelity team changed to action phrases, like <u>Go to Accounts</u>, site visitors of all ages were less hesitant to click.

Chadwick-Dias, McNulty, and Tullis, 2003

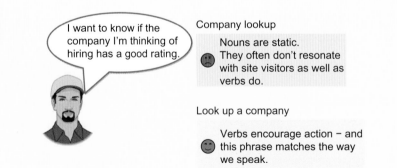

Remember: Write with strong verbs, not nouns that hide verbs (Chapter 10).

4. Make the link meaningful – Not <u>Click here</u> or just <u>More</u>

Most people scan web pages, first focusing on headings and links. Headings and links are colorful. They stand out. They draw our eyes.

Links that just say Click here, Here, More, Read More, See More, or Answer give no clue about what will appear if we click on them. When the page has many identical links, we can't see at a glance how they differ. And they draw our attention away from the meaningful information.

Blind web users scan with their ears, just as sighted people scan with their eyes. Screen-reading software helps them do this by allowing them to pull all the links on a web page into one list, as you can see in Figure 12-3. Imagine the frustration of hearing only Learn More, Learn More, Learn More, Learn More, or Click here, Click here, Click here.

More about how people listen to web sites: Theofanos and Redish, 2003

Thanks to Sarah Horton for capturing the JAWS links list.

Figure 12-3 A site visitor listening to this list of links won't get much useful information. JAWS from Freedom Scientific, reading links on a page at us.norton.com/products

Click here is not necessary

Most site visitors today assume that something that looks like a link is a link. You don't need to announce links with Click here. Just put what people will get by "clicking here" into your link format.

More or Learn More by itself isn't enough

In Figure 12-4, what do you notice first?

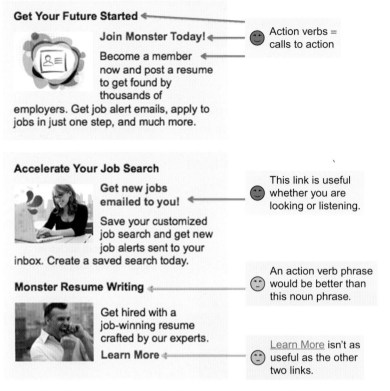

Figure 12-4 <u>More</u> or <u>Learn More</u> by itself isn't helpful even to sighted visitors who are quickly scanning the page. You don't need <u>Learn More</u> in any of these options. www.monster.com

Some people notice the pictures first, then the blue links, and only after that do they read the headlines and the text.

Looking at the links in Figure 12-4, you see that Monster.com did a great job with the first two of three calls to action. But then they didn't follow through on the third one. Figure 12-5 shows you how I might revise the third piece to be parallel to the other two.

Figure 12-5 My suggested revision

Say what it's "more" about

Be explicit and include the topic as T-Mobile's U.K. site does (Figure 12-6).

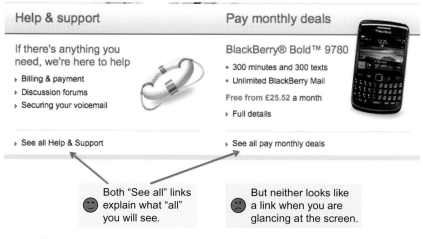

Figure 12-6 Add the section name to See all, More about, and similar links. www.t-mobile.co.uk

   Meaningless links don't help your SEO.

5. Don't embed links (for most content)

You use links not only to help people move down a path from home page → pathway page → information page. You also use links to help people move from an information page to related pages (more details, similar topics, "you might also be interested in," and so on).

A question that comes up regularly in my workshops is whether it is best to embed links in the text or always put them at the end of a segment of text or even separate them entirely from the text.

My answer, as with so many questions about creating great web conversations, is that it depends on your purposes, your site visitors, and why they are coming to your site. The point to remember is that an embedded link is always a distraction. If people choose to follow an embedded link, they leave your information in the middle of what you are saying. It's like switching conversational topics mid-sentence.

If you are listing articles where each article title is a link and then you have More or Read More after a very brief description, that may be okay. But I've seen sites where the article title is not a link — where More is the only link.

If people are browsing, embedding may be okay

Most Wikipedia articles are full of embedded links. The page in Figure 12-7 is just one of thousands of examples I could have selected. Does having many embedded links work for Wikipedia articles because people come to browse? Are they eager to see how a topic branches and connects to other topics?

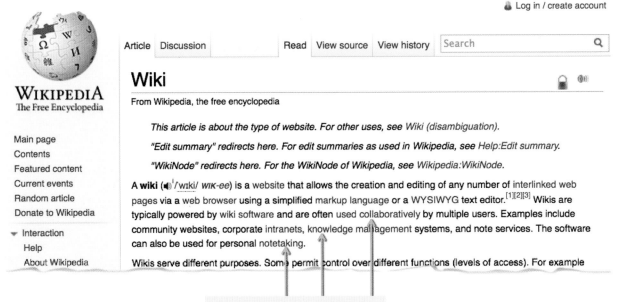

A typical article in Wikipedia has many embedded links.

Figure 12-7 Embedded links may work here because people come to browse.
http://en.wikipedia.org/wiki/Wiki

Put links at the end, below, or next to your text

If you want people to read your entire sentence, paragraph, or list, don't invite them to leave by embedding links. You would be giving your site visitors two tasks at the same time: reading and moving on. Site visitors often don't come back once they've been enticed away by a link.

In the first edition, I used an article from About.com on spas as an example. Figure 12-8 shows you part of what About.com had then, my suggested revision of that part, and what About.com has now. I'm pleased to say I think this writer is doing it right now.

Embedded definition links that open a small window and don't change the screen are okay. They clarify the ongoing conversation. They don't change the topic or take people to another page.

The most common is the <u>day spa</u>. This is for people who want to drop in for one or two treatments, or perhpe even indulge in a half-day, with lunch. <u>Spa treatments are not cheap</u>, so make sure you <u>choose the right day spa for you</u>. And when the day arrives, here's how to <u>make the most of your trip to the day spa</u>.

2007 – part of an About.com page with embedded links

Day Spas

The most common is the day spa. This is for people who want to drop in for one or two treatments, or perhaps even indulge in a half-day, with lunch.

<u>More about day spas</u>

<u>Spa treatments are not cheap</u>

<u>Make sure to choose the right spa for you</u>

<u>When the day arrives, make the most of your trip to the day spa</u>

2007 – the revision that I suggested for that content

Find The Perfect Day Spa

 Day spas come in a wide range of sizes, personalities and prices. It might be a small, homey spa with affordable prices, a medium-sized spa that's an expansion of a salon, or a huge resort spa that welcomes local vistiors. Here's what to look for in a quality day spa of any size, and how to find the perfect day spa for you -- whether you want to drop in for a quick massage or spend the day lounging by the – pool.

- Find Your Perfect Day Spa
- How To Spot A Quality Spa
- Make The Most Of Your Visit
- How Much Does A Day Spa Cost?
- How To Spot A Dirty Spa
- How To Pick Your Spa Treatment
- How To Find The Best Day Spa Deals

2012 – from the site with links after the text, not embedded

Figure 12-8 Three versions of similar information
www.about.com

6. Make bullets with links active, too

Let's end the chapter with two short sections on formatting.

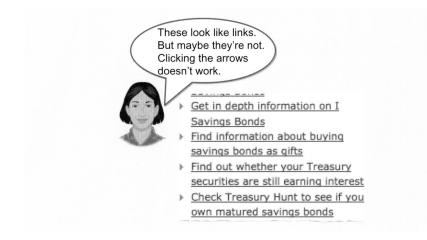

In usability test after usability test, I've watched frustrated web users try to click on bullets rather than the words next to the bullet. Whenever you use bullets next to links (circles, squares, arrows, numbers, thumbnail photos, icons, other small illustrations), include the bullets with the text in the clickable area.

I'm happy to say that both the examples I showed in Chapter 11 (the butterfly site, Figure 11-3, and the site for teachers, Figure 11-4) do this well. Unfortunately, other sites do not.

7. Make unvisited and visited links obvious

One of the basic principles of human behavior is that it is easier for people to recognize than to remember. Products should "afford themselves" – make it obvious how to use them. Your site visitors just want to satisfy the conversation they came for. They don't want to memorize your site. Help your site visitors by making links obvious and by indicating which links they've already been to.

Use your link colors only for links

Don't tease your site visitors by using the same color for links and nonlinks. Don't make people mouse around to discover what is and is not a link. Unfortunately, that's what you have to do at the Network Advertiser's page for opting out of cookies (Figure 12-9).

Opt-Out Status

			(Select all) (Clear) (Submit)
Member Company	**Status**		**Opt-Out**
aCerno More Information	**Active Cookie** You have not opted out and you have an active cookie from this network.		Opt-Out ☐
Adblade More Information	**Active Cookie** You have not opted out and you have an active cookie from this network.		Opt-Out ☐
AdBrite More Information	**Active Cookie** You have not opted out and you have an active cookie from this network.		Opt-Out ☐
AdChemy More Information	**No Cookie** You have not opted out and you have no cookie from this network.		Opt-Out ☐
Adconion	Active Cookie		Opt-Out ☐

☹ If listeners ask to hear only the links, this repetition of "More Information" won't be useful.

☹ Status information in blue looks like a link. But it's not.

Figure 12-9 The links and colors here may not help site visitors act effectively and efficiently.
www.networkadvertising.org

Show visited links by changing the color

Not changing the color of visited links is still on Jakob Nielsen's list of Top 10 Mistakes in Web Design. In Nielsen's 2011 update, it was #3!

www.useit.com/Alertbox/9605.html

When links don't change color, people have to remember where they've been – and they often don't remember. So they revisit the same link again (and again), wasting time and effort. Or they skip the right link, thinking they've already tried that one.

Of course, the problem is made worse by links that aren't clear. Write your links to help people choose appropriately in the first place. But mistakes happen. People go down a wrong path. Help people both with clear writing *and* by showing them where they've been and where they have not yet been.

Summarizing Chapter 12

Key messages from Chapter 12:

- Don't make program or product names links by themselves.
- Think ahead: Launch and land on the same name.
- For actions, start with a verb.
- Make the link meaningful – not Click here or just More.
  - Click here is not necessary.
  - More or Learn More isn't enough.
  - Say what it's "more" about.

- Don't embed links (for most content).
    - If people are browsing, embedding may be okay.
    - Put links at the end, below, or next to your text.

- Make bullets with links active, too.

- Make unvisited and visited links obvious.
    - Use your link colors only for links.
    - Show visited links by changing the color.

Using Illustrations Effectively

13

The web is a very visual medium, and illustrations are part of your web conversations. So let's take this chapter to talk about what makes illustrations work well – or not work well.

As with all web content, when planning illustrations, you must think about purposes, personas, and conversations. Ask yourself:

- What do I want to achieve by having an illustration here?
- Why type of illustration is best for my purpose?
- Who is this content for?
- Will this illustration speak well to those people? (For example, if you use a photo of people to represent site visitors, will your site visitors say, "ah, yes, those people are like me"?)
- Does the illustration add value to the conversation? What value? In what way?

What about video?

Video has become extremely popular as a medium for web content. Video is a great way to make stories come alive and to demonstrate how to do a task. But producing great videos is not my expertise, so I can only give you a few general guidelines and refer you to other resources.

- Remember that not everyone has fast download time – keep to 5 MBs or less per minute if you expect the video to stream seamlessly.

- Make it short (3–5 minutes) or break it into short segments.

- Keep it simple. If a picture is worth 1,000 words, you can say a lot with just a bit of video.

- Make it interesting. A "talking head" (someone lecturing) is boring. But don't go wild. Don't lose your important message in a distracting whirlwind of colors and motion.

- Give the video an informative headline. (Look back at Chapter 8 about headlines.)

 For accessibility, be sure to make a transcript of the video available for site visitors who can't see. And provide captioning for site visitors who can't hear.

SEO | Remember SEO for video, too. Search engines can't yet actually search the images, so you need to get keywords into places like the video's file name and description. Also if you put the video on a video-sharing site like YouTube and then embed it in your site, you'll get not only wider distribution but also the SEO benefit of the times people view it on the video-sharing site.

For more on creating great videos for your web site: www.utexas.edu/web/video.

I've broken this chapter into two main sections:

- Five purposes that illustrations can serve
- Seven guidelines for effective illustrations

Five purposes that illustrations can serve

Illustrations serve purposes from exact representation to emotion-evoking mood setting (Figure 13-1).

Let's briefly consider these five and how they fit into content as conversation.

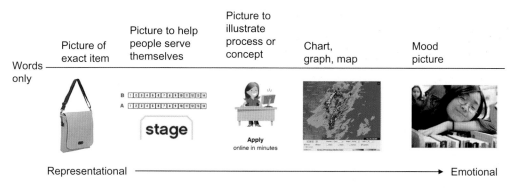

Figure 13-1 Your purposes in using a picture can range from showing the item someone might buy to setting the mood.

Exact item: What do customers want to see?

In e-commerce, of course, you typically show a picture of the item your site visitor might buy.

 Have you thought about how those pictures are part of the conversation with your customers?

Back in Chapter 1 (Case Study 1-2), you saw a page from eBags.com as an example of a conversation with few words. Figure 13-2 shows another example from the same site where you can see how eBags.com chooses pictures to respond to the most common questions site visitors have about their products.

Figure 13-2 Each picture responds to a question that potential buyers might ask.
www.ebags.com

What specifically do people want to know about what they might buy from your site?

If you aren't sure what people look at or ask about, talk to the people who speak directly with customers. Check what's being talked about in your company's – and your competitors' – social media. See what your competitors offer in pictures and ask yourself if those pictures are adding value to the conversation by answering a question customers probably have.

Self-service: What helps people help themselves?

In travel, theater, sports, and many other situations, pictures or diagrams help people serve themselves – and save you customer service calls. Think of showing, not just telling.

Showing options visually

Pictures can help people select appropriately from different options. For example, a theater's seating chart allows easy comparison all at once (Figure 13-3).

Connecting paper documents to online forms

If your company or client is getting calls because people can't find something on a paper document that they need for an online form, consider an illustration.

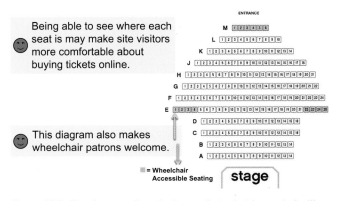

Being able to see where each seat is may make site visitors more comfortable about buying tickets online.

This diagram also makes wheelchair patrons welcome.

Figure 13-3 Showing a seating chart – or what a hotel room looks like – answers site visitors' questions and helps them serve themselves.
www.arenastage.org

- When e-commerce sites started requiring the security code from credit cards as well as the number and expiration date, many sites included a picture of the back of the card to show people where to find the code.

- The state of New Jersey sends car owners a paper document to remind them to renew their vehicle registration. The paper document includes a personal identification number (PIN) for renewing online. Many people didn't notice the PIN and, thus, couldn't do the task online. New Jersey's solution: Include a picture of the paper document on the web page, indicating where to find the PIN (Figure 13-4).

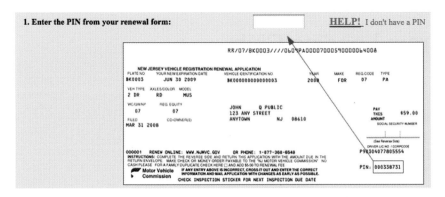

Figure 13-4 One good use of pictures is to clarify where to find something that people need so they can finish their online task.
www.nj.gov/mvc

Of course, an even better solution would be to revise the paper document to make the PIN more obvious. Consider the conversation going on here.

Always imagine the conversation as you write. Consider how illustrations would fit well into that conversation. But also think about whether you can do something elsewhere to make the process simpler for site visitors. You might be able to help them serve themselves better.

Process: Will pictures make words memorable?

Showing a process with pictures as well as words can be both eye-catching and informative (Figure 13-5).

Personal Loans from Lending Club

Apply
online in minutes

Get Funded
in a few days

Make
fixed monthly
payments

Figure 13-5 Pictures draw our eyes to the process and can make it more memorable.
www.lendingclub.com

As with all web content, keep your process pictures simple. Animate the process only if that adds useful information and won't annoy people. Instead of animation, consider providing a video as well as the simple pictures.

More about animation later in this chapter, including a lovely example of useful animation – teaching the process of tying knots

Charts, graphs, maps: Do they help site visitors get my message?

Visuals are particularly useful for showing data.

Let people decide how much to see

To keep maps, charts, and graphs simple, consider letting people choose how much data to see. Weatherzone does that (Figure 13-6).

Sydney, Australia, usually has wonderful weather. When rain comes, it's often a quick thunderstorm. I just happened to catch a rainy day.

You can keep the map simple or see many aspects, such as rivers and roads.

Figure 13-6 When possible, let your site visitors decide how much data to combine in one picture.
www.weatherzone.com.au

Show numbers in charts – with a key message title

Compare Figures 13-7 and 13-8. Which makes the key message stand out better?

Of course, you might want to have some text with the graph to elaborate on what the numbers mean. As the press release says, we may be looking at what's happening in two different segments of the population. You might also want to have another graph – with trend lines to show that sales of soda are decreasing while sales of bottled water are increasing.

And remember to always explain the chart in ALT-text so people who are listening to the screen can get the information, too.

Good bite: Headline = statement with the key message.

Good snack: Sentence under headline = a bit more of the key message.

When you are comparing numbers, tables or charts are better than text.

Figure 13-7 Comparing numbers in text is difficult. www.nacsonline.com

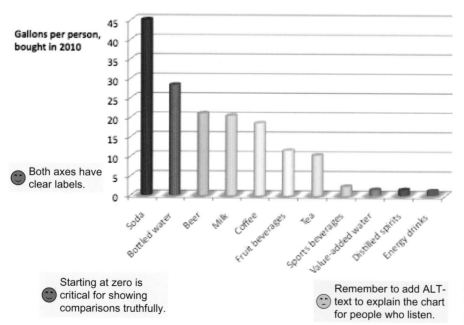

To compare numbers, charts, graphs, and tables can be much more helpful than text.

Good bite: Chart title has the key message.

Both axes have clear labels.

Starting at zero is critical for showing comparisons truthfully.

Remember to add ALT-text to explain the chart for people who listen.

Figure 13-8 My suggestion to make the comparison much clearer

Follow principles of good data reporting

Accuracy is as critical in web graphics as in any other medium, and it's just as easy to mislead with statistics on the web as on paper. Don't do it. A mistake that many people make, for example, is to show only partial data, starting where the data does instead of at zero. But that magnifies and exaggerates differences in the data.

Mood: Which pictures support the conversation?

And now we've reached the other end of the continuum – illustrations (almost always photos) that are primarily meant to evoke an emotional response. These photos are representational. They show real people or objects. But their purpose is not to say, "here's what this jacket that you might buy looks like" or "this is how many people will fit in a compact car." Their purpose is to engender good feelings about the brand and the site.

Match photos to your messages

Figures 13-9 and 13-10 show how you can express mood and send positive messages with people and with animals (in this case, birds).

Figure 13-9 This landing page for students shows diversity and a love of books. Does it make you feel you would be comfortable going there?
www.ccny.cuny.edu

Renew Today

You can feel confident your support is making a difference for nature. Renew now ▶

This picture doesn't take up much room while sending the message, "your money is helping this puffin couple kiss."

Figure 13-10 The Nature Conservancy, a nonprofit that buys and preserves land throughout the world, uses pictures like this to encourage people to join, renew, and donate.
www.nature.org; Photo © Suranjan Mukherjee, used with permission

Think about what the photo is saying

Even mood pictures are part of the conversation. They send messages. For example, pictures of people send messages about "you'll fit in here" or (often inadvertently) "you won't fit in here."

Mood pictures help set the tone of the conversation. Often, their role is to say "feel good about us" (sort of like asking people to "like this" on Facebook). They can support your brand adjectives and brand messages: "We're trustworthy; bank with us." "We're a cool place; shop here often."

Always ask yourself what messages different people are likely to take from your mood pictures. For example, compare the banner in Figure 13-11 from a different university with the one in Figure 13-9 that you just saw from City College of New York. Which picture makes you more interested in the university whose site they come from?

Figure 13-11 Is it clear what message this is sending? Does it entice you to that university? Pictures of buildings usually don't bring out the same warm and fuzzy feelings as pictures of people. www.unm.edu

Seven guidelines for using illustrations effectively

For all five types of illustrations, keep these guidelines in mind:

1. Don't make people wonder what or why.
2. Choose an appropriate size.
3. Show diversity.
4. Don't make content look like ads.
5. Don't annoy your site visitors with blinking, rolling, waving, or wandering text or pictures.
6. Use animation only where it helps.
7. Make illustrations accessible.

In the first edition, I also had the guideline, don't make people wait through splash or Flash. The guideline is still critical, but I'm happy to say that most people have learned it. The example I used in the first edition, www.freehearingtest.com, hasn't changed. But with that exception, I see almost no "you must wait through this" Flash introductions anymore.

1. Don't make people wonder what or why

If your site visitors have to stop to figure out what you are showing or why you are showing it, the illustration has lost its value. The picture in Figure 13-12 is from a museum's web site. I found it so distracting – and spent so much time and effort trying to figure out what it represents – that I gave up on the museum's information without delving further into the site.

Thanks to Caroline Jarrett who found this picture when we were planning a workshop together.

Figure 13-12 An obscure picture may be so distracting that people miss the important content on your web page.
www.kshs.org

2. Choose an appropriate size

Like the bears' beds in the Goldilocks story, illustrations may not work if they are too small or too large.

Don't let large pictures push content down too far

Photos on many web pages take up so much room that the critical content is pushed below the fold. Yes, people scroll – but not always and only if they see something above the fold that lets them know that what they need is further down on their screen.

Look back at Case Study 5-2 and notice how the site visitor didn't spend any time on the picture.

If you use large pictures on your pages, be sure that critical content is still near the top. Make sure the navigation and nonpicture content are easy to find and easy to read (legible). Remember that people may be on smaller screens and at lower resolutions than you are. Test! Test! Test! with representative web users for your site, with the size monitor or screens they typically use, and at typical resolutions.

Make sure small pictures are clear

Small pictures (thumbnails) sometimes violate the guideline to not make people wonder what or why. If you are reducing photos to serve as icons or bullets, avoid using ones with lots of detail.

In Figure 13-13 from the Lonely Planet's online pages for India, which pictures are instantly clear? Which are not?

Looks like wine bottles. Clear picture. Clear connection to the story. →

Classic Indian drinks: from wine to liqueurs

30 August 2011

Thirsty travellers take note: a chilled pint of Kingfisher beer alone does not an Indian evening make. Traipse through this...
> Read more

Is this part of the Taj Mahal? Is the Taj Mahal in the back of the picture? Hard to tell. →

Side trips from the Taj Mahal

27 August 2011

What? You mean there's other stuff to do in Agra apart from seeing the Taj Mahal? You bet there is.Agra's...
> Read more

Film posters? Films = crowds? Not clear from the small picture. →

5 great ways to join the crowds in India

26 August 2011

Lonely Planet editorial intern Soumya Rao hails from Hyderabad, India. So we asked her to write an article about how...
> Read more

Figure 13-13 Thumbnail pictures should be instantly clear.

www.lonelyplanet.com

3. Show diversity

Pictures of people make web sites vivid, attractive, and conversational. They remind visitors that you are talking with them through the web site.

But that works only if your site visitors identify with the people in the pictures. Pictures of people send very strong messages. In many usability tests, I have seen participants choose not to click on a link because the photo with the link made them think the information was for a different group – not for them.

To represent your site visitors, think broadly

Think cross-culturally even within your country. Think of diversity in ethnicity, gender, and age – while, of course, being appropriate for your site and for the specific content. Think globally. Choose photos that are appropriate for different versions of your site in different locations, while thinking about appropriate diversity in each of those locations.

Show your internal diversity, but be truthful

If your organization includes a diverse group of people, show that.

For example, the Boys & Girls Club of America (BGCA) has a mission "to enable all young people, especially those who need us most, to reach their full potential...." And they show that with real alumni in Figure 13-14.

Figure 13-14 Diversity is obvious from this picture of people who really participated in the Boys & Girls Club of America.
www.bgca.org

Test! Test! Test!

You may be surprised by the messages people take from your pictures.

Tom Brinck shared a story with me of his experience trying to develop the visual strategy for an organization:

> The organization wanted to recruit more minorities and women than it had. So it showed a diverse group as employees. But that was their hope for the future, not their present reality. And potential hires knew that. In usability testing, when the photos had half or more women in the group, women laughed and said something was wrong. They knew there weren't that many women in the organization. In an effort to show equality, the web designers had created a mismatch with current reality that seemed misleading to the very people the organization was trying to recruit.

Tom's story shows the value of usability testing. For all mood pictures, especially pictures of people, it's very difficult to predict site visitors' reactions.

Another story, this time from my own work:
> I was doing a usability test of a site for a group that does medical research. The home page had two pictures of scientists, a young woman concentrating as she looked into a modern microscope and a man with a white coat and a

stethoscope. Participants said the people in the photos were serious researchers and made them feel the site would have credible research information. That was just the mood and brand that the agency wanted to project. "Serious" worked here.

But "serious" doesn't always work. A colleague told me that his team found it impossible to include a photo with a serious expression on a health care site. With every "serious expression" picture that they tested, some people thought the person looked unhappy or even angry. The team ended up showing only smiles.

Even the grouping that you use may evoke emotions and explanations that surprise you. A site for people concerned with cancer tried a photo of a man with two children. One test participant's reaction was, "Oh, poor family. Did the Mom die?"

Putting your prototype web pages in front of people whom you want as site visitors is the only way to know what messages people will take from the pictures. Don't ask, "Do you like it?" Ask, "What are these pictures saying to you?" "What adjectives come to mind when you look at these pictures?"

And, always show the photos in context. Show the whole web page with the rest of the page's web content. Context matters.

4. Don't make content look like ads

 What is your reaction to the home page in Figure 13-15 on the next page? It was the home page of a U.S. county's site in 2011.

Many people expect colorful small boxes to be ads – especially on the right side of a web page. Ads often appear there, and ads try to attract attention with color and graphics. If your site visitors are looking for information from your site – and aren't interested in an ad that they think will take them away from your site – they are very likely to ignore those colorful boxes. So don't put content from your site – or links to that content – into ad-like boxes.

5. Don't annoy people with blinking, rolling, waving, or wandering text or pictures

Movement is eye-catching. Paying attention to movement in our peripheral vision was a key survival skill when we shared space with lions on the savannah. On the screen, however, movement is just plain annoying. It takes our eyes from the task we are trying to do.

Figure 13-15 I doubt if this site conversed well with residents or business owners.
www.douglas.co.us

Figure 13-16 has moving text in three places on the screen.

$\mathbf{AAa}$
ACCESS   Think of slow readers. Think of your older site visitors. Think of people who must magnify text. Rolling text frustrates people rather than satisfying their need.

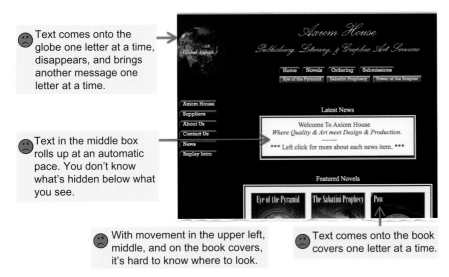

Figure 13-16 This web site may be much harder for many people to use than the designers realize.
www.axiomhouse.com

6. Use animation only where it helps

The only good reason to animate graphics is if it helps explain the content. For example, animation can be very useful to walk someone through a process.

Today, video is the most common technique for animation. But situations still exist where a nonvideo animation works best. For example, Animated Knots by Grog uses motion and text together very well to show how to tie many different knots (Figure 13-17).

The web site also offers a video. Both mobile app and web site use clear and colorful icons with words for navigation.

Figure 13-17 The first four of seven steps in tying a square knot. You can watch the animation all at once, or you can move through it step by step. Each step also makes a bit more of the text dark — so you can follow the steps in text as well as pictures. www.animatedknots.com (animated knots mobile app)

7. Make illustrations accessible

For people who use screen-readers, you must annotate illustrations so the assistive software can describe them. You do that by writing "alternative" text with the ALT attribute to an image <IMG> tag. I'm going to call that ALT-text.

Make ALT-text meaningful

If the illustration is meant to convey substantive information, be sure to convey that information in the ALT-text, too. If the illustration is a mood picture, your ALT-text should describe what is in the picture — focusing on the elements that create the emotional response you expect.

To write good ALT-text, you must know *why* you are using the illustration. I hope that working through the different purposes for illustrations in this chapter has helped you think about what you are putting on your site.

To test whether you have a good description for each illustration, the World Wide Web Consortium accessibility guidelines suggest that you imagine reading the web page aloud over the telephone. What would you say about the image to make your listeners understand it?

Summarizing Chapter 13

Key messages from Chapter 13:

- Illustrations can serve many purposes.
  - Exact item: What do customers want to see?
  - Self-service: What helps people help themselves?
  - Process: Will pictures make words memorable?
  - Charts, graphs, maps: Do they help site visitors get my message?
  - Mood: Which pictures support the conversation?

- Don't make people wonder what or why.

- Choose an appropriate size.
  - Don't let large pictures push content down too far.
  - Make sure small pictures are clear.

- Show diversity.
  - To represent your site visitors, think broadly.
  - Show your internal diversity, but be truthful.
  - Test, test, test.

- Don't make content look like ads.

- Don't annoy people with blinking, rolling, waving, or wandering text or pictures.

- Use animation only where it helps.

- Make illustrations accessible.

Getting from Draft to Final

14

Writing is a process that goes beyond a first draft. You may do it all yourself, but it's better if you include other people.

First draft ≠ final draft

The best writing comes from revising.

- Think of writing as revising with yourself as your own first editor. Read as you write. Read before you send or post. If you can, let your writing rest. Then, read it again. Read it out loud. Use the spell checker, dictionaries, handbooks, and style guides. Edit, revise, and proofread. Also, check your links. Check your facts.

- If you have colleagues, share drafts and help each other. You can also use a spouse, partner, in-law, or friend as your colleague. Two sets of eyes are always better than one.

- By yourself, with your colleagues, or with a usability specialist, walk your personas through their conversations.

- You may be lucky enough to have an expert editor to help you, especially for blog posts or longer pieces of content.

- Technical, legal, or policy specialists may have to review your content before it gets posted. You may have to negotiate what you may say and how you may say it. You can make those reviews positive experiences.

This chapter has guidelines and tips for all five of these situations.

Read, edit, revise, proofread your own work

Let's explore these guidelines for helping yourself:

- Think of writing as revising.

- Read what you wrote.
- Check your links.
- Check your facts.
- Let it rest.
- Read it out loud.
- Use dictionaries, handbooks, and your style guide.
- Run the spell checker, but don't rely on it.
- Proofread.

Think of writing as revising drafts

 Do you ever get writer's block? Find it hard to sit down to write? Procrastinate as long as possible?

Some people find it hard to start writing because they think that whatever they put down has to be perfect on the first try. Not so!

Your first draft should not be your final draft. A good way to get over writer's block is to remember that you can fix it later. Perfection is never achievable, but you'll get closer to it with each revision. (And you must at some point stop revising and meet the deadline to publish!)

When you look at a book like this one, you see only the final result. You don't see the many, many drafts it went through. If you watched me for half an hour, you would see lots of backspacing; deleting; cutting, adding, and moving text; rewriting; starting over; staring into space; trying something and rejecting it; and so on. Writing is a very messy activity.

Successful writers read their own work. They read it – and revise it – many times. Even with social media (and email!), you can – and should – read what you wrote before you send or post it.

You may find writing even the first draft easier if you follow the method of this book: Think conversation. Have a persona. Imagine the persona's conversation. Write a clear headline. Outline with good headings. Write the conversation that goes with each heading.

Look back at Checklists 7-1 and 7-2 to remind yourself of a way to put together good web content.

Read what you wrote

If you've ever been embarrassed by a message you sent or posted without reading what you wrote, you know how little things slip by. Your fingers may not have typed what you thought they did. You may have left out a word – or put in an extra one. You may have thought you were making sense but, on reading it, realize that others may not understand what you mean.

As you read what you wrote, ask yourself:

- Does it really say what I want to say?

- Would someone else take the same meaning from it that I do?

- Does it fit with my other writing? Does it fit with other content on the web site?

- Is my tone right for the situation?

- Is it as clear and concise as I can say it?

- Will my readers know all the words I am using? (If not, must I use words that will be new to my readers? Have I explained new words and concepts clearly?)

- Are the sentences grammatical? Are the words spelled correctly? (If you are writing for social media where telegraphic words are okay, you still need to ask: Am I using spelling that is going to make sense to my readers?)

Check your links

If your content includes links, click on each one. Make sure the link leads to a page with the same words you used in the link – or at least something similar enough to reassure your site visitors.

And remember not to rely only on Click here for your links.

Check your facts

Make sure what you say is accurate. How do you know the sources you used are credible?

For example, Wikipedia and other "pedias" are great resources – but open community writing and editing doesn't guarantee accuracy. Search engines may give preference to sites that other sites link to, but that measure of "success" or "trust" doesn't guarantee accuracy. Even reading the same information over and over on different sites does not make that information true. The sites could all be copying each other or the same original site.

When considering the credibility of what you read online, ask questions like these:

- Do the facts make a consistent whole, or does information in one place contradict information in another place?

- Is the source a respected authority on the topic?
  - Government: Are they an impartial, research-based, data-gathering, and data-delivering group, or are they politically biased?

- Nonprofit: Are they nonpartisan and nonpartial, or are they pushing an agenda?
- Commercial: Are they being even-handed, or are they slanting information to market their product?

- Does the article name the author? What can you learn about that author?

- Does the content have a date so that you can tell when the information was written?

Many sites now include dates and authorship or ownership – information they can publish from their content management system. For example, Figure 14-1 shows this information from a typical page at the web site of the U.S. Centers for Disease Control and Prevention (CDC).

Email   Print   Share   Syndicate   Updates   Subscribe

Page last reviewed: July 18, 2011
Page last updated: February 1, 2012
Content source: National Center for Immunization and Respiratory Diseases, Office of the Director
Page maintained by: Office of the Associate Director for Communication, Division of News and Electronic Media
URL for this page: http://www.cdc.gov/Features/PreteenVaccines/

Figure 14-1 You can increase people's sense of trust by showing how up-to-date the information is and who is responsible for the information.
www.cdc.gov

Remember also that you can still check facts offline. Find a person who knows and check the facts with that person. Use books. But keep in mind that just because it is in print (offline or online) doesn't make it true. Books – even textbooks – sometimes copy errors from each other.

Let it rest

Many good recipes require rest time for the food. So does good writing.

You don't have to post anything immediately – even a blog entry, a tweet, or a comment. I know bloggers who write at lunchtime and post in the evening. I often schedule a tweet for a few hours from when I write it so I can review it after I've been away from it for a bit.

For web content that is going to last a long time, you should be able to put your draft away for a day or two as part of your writing process.

Why let it rest?

When you are too close to what you have written, you are likely to miss problems.

- You may not notice flaws in the logic or gaps in the information. You know what you want to say, so you don't see where your readers may not follow your points.

- You don't notice typos. You read the words you intended to write instead of the ones that are there. You skip over words that shouldn't be there.

You can, of course, fix and repost after publishing – even for social media entries. That's a tremendous advantage that online media have over paper. But sending a second tweet to say "sorry, this is what I meant," or having people on your RSS feed see each slightly updated blog entry, can annoy them and embarrass you. Get it right before you send it.

What should you do after your draft has rested?

When you go back to your draft after a few minutes, hours, or days; you'll read it with fresh eyes. Ask yourself:

- Is this really what I want to say?
- Can I say it more clearly? More concisely?
- Do I need to add anything to make it clearer?
- What can I cut?
- Does it have the right tone?
- Will the headline work well where it will appear on the site?
- Are there headings? Enough headings? In the right places? In the right words?
- Did I catch all the typos?

Read it out loud

Reading your content out loud may seem like a strange thing to do, but good writing sounds good when spoken. When you read out loud, you'll know if your sentences, paragraphs, and list items are short enough. If you hesitate, stumble, or have to take too many breaths in one sentence, rewrite!

Use dictionaries, handbooks, style guides

Don't mislead, misinform, or annoy your readers by misspelling words or using words incorrectly. Lots of help is available online. Use it.

Read this sentence:

I LOVE PARIS IN THE THE SPRING.

Read it again carefully. Do you see the problem? Did you see it when you first read the sentence?

Part of your content strategy is choosing or writing a style guide. Follow it.

Style guides – Interlude 5 right after this chapter

Run the spell checker but don't rely on it

You know that the spell checker is only checking each word against the program's internal dictionaries.

- If the word is in the dictionary, the spell checker will accept it, even if it's not the right word in the right place. (If you've ever typed "now" for "not" or "our" for "out," you know what I mean.)

- If the word is not in the dictionary, the spell checker will reject it, even if it is the right word in the right place. (On my own computer, of course, I've added my name to the dictionary. But if you try it on yours, the spell checker will probably want to turn Redish into "reddish" or "radish.")

Read this sentence out loud:

Eye kin knot sea ewe.

Spell checkers would say it is fine; but, of course, it is not.

Proofread

Because the spell checker isn't perfect, you should also proofread what you wrote. A good way to do that is to go through what you have written *line by line* from the *end* of your copy back up to the beginning. That helps you look at each word separately and not get caught up in reading for meaning.

Share drafts with colleagues

Successful writers share their work in draft, try their writing out with relevant audiences, and revise based on what they learn from their early readers. Let's explore these guidelines for sharing drafts:

- Accept and learn from the process.
- Work with colleagues to fit the content strategy.
- Share partial drafts.
- Have someone read it out loud.
- Ask what your key message is.
- Pay attention to comments.
- Put your ego in the drawer, cheerfully. ☺

Accept and learn from the process

Your attitude about sharing drafts is critical. Make it fun. Make it a learning experience. I love the way Tom Brinck, creative director and usability specialist, puts it:

> You should delight in feedback and getting your content just right. You should enjoy the surprises and discovery when people come from a

Check out Tom's book: Brinck, Gergle, and Wood, *Usability for the Web: Designing Web Sites that Work* different perspective and want something you totally didn't expect. If you're brewing in resentment over having to suppress your supposedly good ideas, you're going to die young of stomach ulcers. Take the opposite perspective: Share your ideas and love what you learn, not as your ideas are "shot down," but as your ideas compete in an ecology of good ideas and improve as a result.

Work with colleagues to fit the content strategy

If you are part of an organization, you should also be working with other web team members to be sure your content fits the content strategy. Fits = appropriate tone, message, style. Fits = good length for the design and the medium.

Remember that the web site represents the organization and not you – or others – as individual writers. That's part of what content strategy is all about: making the site the "voice of the organization." The content strategy may allow you your own voice, especially for blog posts or articles that you sign. But for most web content, most of the time, in a large organization, site visitors should not be able to tell who wrote what.

Share partial drafts

Share one piece or part of a piece to see if you are on the right track with message, level of detail, tone, organization, writing style, and so on. That could save you lots of time and grief. The earlier you learn what to change, the less effort it takes to make the changes. The Internet has many options now for sharing drafts.

Have someone read it out loud

Find a few people who are part of the audience you want to reach. Ask them to read your web content. Ask them to read out loud. Where they hesitate, stumble, or reread: rewrite!

Ask what your key message is

When they have read your content, don't ask for their reaction. Ask them what message they get.

Pay attention to comments

Use what you hear from sharing early drafts.

Also pay attention to what you hear *after* you have published or posted. With social media and responder technology now so prevalent on the web, you get to hear what others think about your content *after* as well as before you put it up. Learn from the feedback you get. Use it to converse even better in the next content you write.

Put your ego in the drawer, cheerfully ☺

If you are writing poetry or fiction, your own blog, or your own site, your voice as author is a large part of what you are projecting though your web content. That's fine.

But if you are part of an organization, it's not about you as author. It's about communicating so clearly that your site visitors can satisfy their own conversations with the site.

Of course, you should take pride in your work. That pride can be in working as a team with colleagues to have a web site that has a consistent writing style, tone, vocabulary, and message.

Don't get into arguments about what "I" like or what another "I" likes. Put your "I" away. Make everyone else put their "I" away. Get out your personas. Talk about the conversations your site visitors come to have with your content.

Also put your ego in the drawer when you get feedback. Listen with an open mind. Don't get defensive about your writing.

When you start to bristle at comments, read the quote from Tom Brinck again.

You don't have to act on every suggestion, but consider each with respect.

Walk your personas through their conversations

Throughout this book, I've urged you to write every piece of content with a specific persona in mind – to imagine the conversation that person wants to have with your content. You can also use personas and conversations to assess how well the site is doing.

When I do a persona-based, conversation-based review, I work with the web team to understand

- the business goals for the site or app
- the site visitors they hope will use the site or app (personas)

- the scenarios that will bring those visitors to the site or app (conversations)

Then I try to carry through those conversations as if I were the personas. When the persona would run into trouble, I turn on my hat as a user experience expert and identify the reasons the web site is likely to cause problems for people like the persona.

You can do this for your own content. You can ask a colleague to do it with or for you. If you have usability colleagues, get them to do it with or for you.

Let editors help you

If you can, take advantage of help from a copy editor ("details" person) and a developmental editor ("big picture" person). You may want different people as copy editor and developmental editor. Although some people can do both well, the tasks require different skills. If your organization doesn't have editors, you and your colleagues might take on these roles for each other.

Get help with the details

Copy editing is looking at the "little picture" – the details of grammar, spelling, and punctuation. The best copy editors are very detail-oriented. They read your words very carefully.

Great copy editors are good spellers. They know the conventions of grammar and punctuation. If they are part of an organization, they know the organization's style guide.

It's almost impossible to catch all the typos in your own work. If at all possible, always have someone else copy edit your content.

Get help with the big picture

A developmental editor starts by going over the three planning questions from Chapter 2 with you:

- What are you trying to achieve through this content?
- Who are you conversing with through this content?
- How will those people use what you are writing? What are their scenarios, their conversations?

http://redish.net/blog/review-your-web-site-through-personas-and-conversations

Also do usability testing – Chapter 15. Walking personas through conversations is a great technique to use even before you do usability testing.

With the answers to those questions, a developmental editor helps you

- select the content your site visitors need
- make your key messages obvious
- write a good headline
- organize the content logically for your readers
- break up your content with clear headings
- write so your content is easy to scan, read, and use
- write with words your site visitors know

Negotiate successful reviews (and edits)

Everything in this section applies to working with editors as well as with reviewers. So add "and editors" in your mind as you go through these guidelines.

Your web content may have to go through review with

- managers
- policy analysts
- lawyers
- technical staff
- editorial staff
- web publication staff

Of course, not all content goes through all those reviews. But if your content goes through any of these reviews or if you are one of these reviewers, the hints in this section may help make reviewing a good experience. Let's talk about reviewing in three stages:

- setting up good reviews
- getting useful information from reviewers
- using reviews well

Setting up good reviews

Good reviews start at the beginning of a project – not at the end. When you first get an assignment, find out who will review what you write.

Meet with reviewers at the beginning

Discuss and agree on

- roles and responsibilities
- the schedule for drafts and reviews
- your plans for the content

Practice the doctrine of no surprise

The surest way to get a negative reaction is to shock your reviewers (or your editors) by showing them something that they do not expect and to which they can exclaim, "That's not the way we write here!"

Never shock. Always work with people *before* you deliver a draft so they know what to expect. Deal with any concerns they have about style or content *before* you give them content to review.

Doctrine of no surprise: Work with reviewers *before* giving them a draft so they'll know what to expect.

Help your reviewers understand good web writing

When I said just now, "discuss and agree on your plans for the content," I meant making sure your reviewers agree from the beginning on

- purposes: what you want to achieve through this web content
- personas: who the content is for
- scenarios, conversations: what will bring people to your content
- content: what you plan to cover (if you have an outline, share it with them)

If your reviewers don't think in terms of personas and conversations, this might be a great time to introduce both the concepts and your specific personas and their conversations.

If the conversational style that you have worked on throughout this book is different from what your reviewers expect, spend the time and effort to convince them of how important and useful it is. You are welcome to use examples from the book (with credit, please). Even better, of course, give them a copy of the book with relevant pages marked.

You might create a "before" and "after" example for even a small piece of your web content to show reviewers what you will be doing. Get them to express their concerns early so you can discuss the concerns and allay their fears.

Getting useful information from reviewers

Stay in touch with reviewers, but don't overdo it.

Tell reviewers when the schedule changes

Schedules change. If a change affects when you will get your content to reviewers, let them know. Negotiate new dates. Don't just assume they can accommodate every slip in your schedule.

Give reviewers a "heads up" a few days in advance

Everyone is overly busy, including your reviewers. Remind them when you are about to send a draft.

Make your expectations clear

It's frustrating to expect a technical review and then get your draft back with nothing more than a few commas changed. Improve your chances of getting what you need by making your expectations clear.

Deliver your draft for review with individual cover emails. Tell each reviewer

- what stage the draft is at
- what specific help you need from that reviewer
- when you must have the review back
- to call or write if he or she has questions or needs to renegotiate dates

And remind reviewers politely that you expect them to comment and suggest, not to rewrite. Writing the content is your job.

If you have specific needs, let reviewers know

In your cover email, remind each reviewer of that reviewer's role (policy, technical, legal, etc.). In addition, you may have specific questions for a reviewer. Develop a way of asking that makes it obvious you have a question and who that question is for. I often use square brackets [ ], put the reviewer's name in bold, and use a color so that it stands out on the screen, as in this example:

> [**Jim**: Please tell me who is responsible for approving travel requests. I want to turn the passive sentence in the original into an active sentence here. Please fill in the blank for me at the beginning of my sentence. Thanks.]

If you use a different color for each reviewer, they can each quickly find what they should answer.

Thanks to Ahava Leibtag for the suggestion of different colors for different reviewers.

Using reviews well

When you get reviews back, read them carefully and with an open mind.

Don't get defensive

Reading reviews is another good time to put your ego in the drawer. Be open to reviewers' comments. You don't have to agree with all of them. You may not have to – or be able to – make all the changes every reviewer wants. But you must consider them all respectfully.

Don't automatically accept changes

If you get conflicting comments on facts, find out what the real story is. If you are not sure that a change is correct, do the research to find out. If you get conflicting comments on style, work to resolve the differences – or to convince reviewers that your style is best for your site visitors.

Rewrite to avoid misunderstandings

If a reviewer misunderstood something you wrote, you may not have stated it as clearly as you could. Try again. And run that piece by the reviewer again.

Persuade

If the reviews that trouble you are based on different perceptions of purpose, personas, conversations, or appropriate style, you may need to evangelize clear writing. Within the constraints of your organization's culture, push for clear web writing even for legal and technical information. Your site visitors need you to do this for them. I hope the guidelines, explanations, and examples in this book not only persuade and mentor you, but also prove useful to you in persuading and mentoring others.

Negotiate

The teamwork that creates successful web sites often involves compromise. Work with reviewers to put accurate, reliable, and clear information on your web site. Remember that even legal information can be accurate, sufficient, and also clear and easy to understand.

Clear legal writing – Interlude 4 after Chapter 11

Communicate

Reviewers who feel that you ignored their comments are less likely to give your content a thorough review on the next round. Keep a summary of the changes you make and do not make, especially for legal, policy, and technical reviewers. If you have several rounds of review, include the summary from the previous round. Your reviewers need clear communication just as your site visitors do. And your explanations can help educate your reviewers about clear writing.

Summarizing Chapter 14

Key messages from Chapter 14:

- Read, edit, revise, proofread your own work.
  - Think of writing as revising drafts.
  - Read what you wrote.
  - Check your links.
  - Check your facts.
  - Let it rest.
  - Read it out loud.
  - Use dictionaries, handbooks, style guides.
  - Run the spell checker but don't rely on it.
  - Proofread.

- Share drafts with colleagues.
  - Accept and learn from the process.
  - Work with colleagues to fit the content strategy.
  - Share partial drafts.
  - Have someone read it out loud.
  - Ask what your key message is.
  - Pay attention to comments.
  - Put your ego in the drawer, cheerfully. ☻

- Let editors help you.
  - Get help with the details.
  - Get help with the big picture.

- Negotiate successful reviews (and edits).
  - Meet with reviewers at the beginning.
  - Practice the doctrine of no surprise.
  - Help your reviewers understand good web writing.
  - Tell reviewers when the schedule changes.
  - Give reviewers a "heads up" a few days in advance.
  - Make your expectations clear.
  - If you have specific needs, let reviewers know.
  - Don't get defensive.
  - Don't automatically accept changes.
  - Rewrite to avoid misunderstandings.
  - Persuade.
  - Negotiate.
  - Communicate.

As you create your web content, you and your colleagues may have questions about grammar, spelling, punctuation, and writing style.

Organic = Don't spend a year writing a book. Start with whatever decisions you already have. Set it up as a mini web site with an index card for each topic. Add to it over time. Let it grow from authors' and editors' questions.

> Mmm. Are we writing "data base" or "database"? "email" or "e-mail"? "web" or "Web"?

> How are we doing lists? When do we start each item with a capital letter and when don't we?

> What style are we using for headings on our intranet?

Use a style guide for consistency

All groups – businesses, government agencies, nonprofits, online communities, social media groups, universities – have personalities and cultures. Language choices are an important part of culture: How formal or colloquial should the style be ("cannot" or "can't")? What is acceptable usage ("each person … they")? Which way do we spell words that are new to the language ("website" or "web site")?

A style guide helps everyone keep content consistent within and across sites, apps, and social media. The style guide is part of your content strategy.

Even if you are the only contributor to your web site (your blog, your site as a consultant or author) a short "cheat sheet" style guide is useful. I've created one for this book, so I don't have to look back at other chapters to remind myself that, for this book, at least, it's "web site," "web," "Internet," and "intranet."

One reason for a style guide: Words in transition

At any given time, some aspects of every language are in transition. For example, many words come into English with a hyphen, like "e-mail," and over time lose the hyphen.

But different people and different organizations are at different places in the transition. Some still use the hyphen; others don't. To have consistent content, you have to decide where your organization is in that transition.

Use a style guide to remind people

A style guide is also useful for people to check on grammar, spelling, and usage that they aren't sure about: "affect" versus "effect," "that" versus "which," "its" versus "it's" (Figures Interlude 5-1 and 5-2).

Figure Interlude 5-1 Part of the table of contents (pathway page on the intranet) for one company's style guide. (ATD is a made-up name, but the screen is based on a real example that I developed with a client's web team.)

Style Guide for the ATD Web Site

Affect and Effect

What is the difference?

Most of the time, "affect" is a verb and "effect" is a noun.

Examples of "affect" and "effect"

This policy affects only new customers.

This policy takes effect on January 1.

The effect of this change will be to reduce the time it takes to prepare web pages.

Note: You can often write a better, shorter sentence without "effect."

Possible revisions of the examples, without "effect"

This policy starts on January 1.

This change will reduce the time it takes to prepare web pages.

- Policy Template
- Procedure Template
- Suggest a change to the Style Guide
- Contact Us

Figure Interlude 5-2 One topic in the style guide

Don't reinvent

If you work in an organization, first find out if other groups already have a style guide. If the organization has adopted a particular general guide or has its own style guide, consider how applicable it is for online writing.

Don't just ignore what is already being used elsewhere in the organization. Work with whomever owns the style guide to turn it into the guide for online writing that you need. If the organization's choice of a general style guide is too formal, too old, not appropriate for the new content strategy, find the right way in your organization's culture to get it changed.

Don't repeat the entire universe in your style guide. Many excellent general style guides exist. Pick one and have all the content contributors use it. In your specific style guide, focus instead on what the content contributors aren't sure about or what they argue about.

Appoint an owner

As with any content, the style guide needs an "owner." Someone must be responsible and accountable for writing and maintaining it. The owner might convene a committee that represents different groups within the organization so that good conversations occur among content contributors, editors, and the style guide owner.

Get management support

The style guide also needs a champion, a sponsor. This should be someone with the interest to endorse it fervently and the clout to make people follow it.

Make it easy to create, to find, and to use

Here are several tips for creating a usable and useful style guide:

- Put it online where people can find it easily.
- Start small. Don't try to write it all before you get it out there.
- Make it organic. Let it grow from authors' and editors' needs.
- Keep it small. Include only what people need.
- Allow different styles for different media and situations if that makes sense in your organization's culture. (For example, the style guide might allow "Thx" in a tweet or a Facebook post, but require "Thank you" in an email.)
- Use the database model that we discussed in Chapter 6. Make each topic its own small index card. Don't write a book!
- Make it easy to find topics – both by searching and through links.
- Write it clearly, using all the guidelines for clear web writing.
- Show as well as tell. Give examples.
- Do usability testing to make sure that authors and editors can find and use it.
- Have an easy-to-use feedback mechanism that allows and encourages people to ask questions and suggest new topics.

Test! Test! Test!

15

I urge you to adopt the mantra: "Test! Test! Test!" Usability testing is that important.

Any time you have someone try to *use* what you've developed you are doing usability testing. If you ask someone to read your web content out loud and tell you what it means, you are doing a usability test. If you have someone try to find information on your web site and have them think out loud while doing it, you are doing a usability test.

Why do usability testing?

Almost all usability testing that web teams do now is "formative" testing – having site visitors (or people you would like to be site visitors) try out the web site or app *before* you launch it. The purpose is *diagnostic*. You want to see what is working well and what is not working well, so you can fix what is not working well before you launch.

You must do usability testing because

- you are almost certainly not typical of your site visitors
- what matters is what works for the site visitors – not what different members of the web team want or think is best
- by watching a few people struggle, you save many people from pain, frustration, and failure
- the earlier you find what's not working, the easier and less expensive it is to fix

Usability testing is an incredibly important part of the toolkit of every user experience (UX) specialist – but it's not the only one. We've already discussed

- predesign user research, personas, scenarios – Chapter 2
- content strategy, including inventory and analysis of content – Interlude 1 after Chapter 2
- card sorting – Chapter 5
- persona-based, conversation-based review – Chapter 14
- style guide – Interlude 5 just before this chapter

Don't assume; test! Don't argue; test! Don't risk failure after launch; test!

A few words about words

The people who come to help you in a usability test are "participants." Don't call them "subjects." You're not doing a psychology experiment or a medical study.

Be careful how you talk about "test." You are not doing "user testing" – that would be testing the users. You are doing "usability testing" where the participants test the site or app.

Don't say, "We want to test how well people can use the site." That blames problems on the users. Say, "We want to know how the site works for people like you." That puts the burden on the site.

What you learn in a usability test can help you change the site or app. You cannot change the users.

Although I use the words "usability testing" when I'm talking to colleagues, I never say "testing" or even "evaluation" to participants. I ask people to come "try out the site." When they are with me, I tell them that they'll be "working with" a particular site. That's much better than trying to convince them that you are not testing them after you've used the words "usability testing."

What's needed for usability testing

Usability testing has many variations, but all usability tests share these six attributes:

- **Real issues.** You have thought about what you want to learn and planned the test to give you answers to your questions.
- **Real people.** Participants represent (at least some of) the site visitors or app users you want.
- **Real tasks.** The stories (scenarios, conversations) you have them try out with the web site or app are ones that they really want to do or that are realistic to them.
- **Real data.** You watch, listen, ask neutral questions, and take notes as they work. (In remote unmoderated tests, you may get only what they did – clickstream data – without hearing why or being able to ask questions.)

- **Real insights.** You put away your assumptions and biases as you review the data. You see what is working well and what is not.

- **Real changes.** You use what you learned. You keep what is working well and improve what could be better.

What's not needed for usability testing

You don't need:

- **Finished product.** Don't wait until your product is finished. Test early. Test often. Test your current site or app before you revise it. Test with paper prototypes. Be informal. Just do it.

- **Special space.** If you have a usability lab, great! But it's not necessary. Test in someone's cubicle, workers' break room, participants' homes, at a conference where the people you want to work with gather, or in a conference room – as in Figure 15-1.

Figure 15-1 An informal usability test of a web site, using a paper prototype. Whitney Quesenbery is taking notes at the far table. Caroline Jarrett facilitated the session and took the photo. Used with permission of The Open University, the photographer, and the people in the photo.

- **Special software.** It's great if you have it. Several excellent programs are available to capture what is happening and to allow you to take notes. But they are *not necessary*. When I'm sitting next to a participant, I still use paper and pencil – even if I have a note-taker using software in another room.

- **Videotape.** The most common use of videotape is to convince people who don't yet believe in usability testing or who think that only stupid users have problems. Seeing is believing. If you can't get people to come observe the test in person (which they should!) – or if you don't have space and have too many observers – then, yes, videotape the sessions. But don't assume you'll do detailed data analysis from the tapes. In most schedules, there's no time for that.

- **A formal test report (maybe).** What you need as a report depends on the type of usability testing you are doing and on your organization's or client's culture and process. You may only need a quick list of findings and recommendations that everyone agrees on.

- **Participants to come to you.** You save time and can schedule more sessions if participants all come to the same place, but it's not necessary. You can test remotely with you in one place, the participant in another, and observers each at their own location. If you go to people's work places or their homes, you also get to see their web setups as well as their physical and social environments. So, don't let "people don't have time to come to do a usability test with us" stop you.

How do we do a usability test?

No matter what variation you use, every usability test – like other user research projects – goes through five phases:

- planning
- conducting
- analyzing
- reporting
- using the results

In the following sections, I summarize several ways to do usability testing.

What most people do

Formative testing. Small-scale. Five to 15 people, one at a time. Each session is about one hour. The participant works with the site or app while an experienced facilitator sits with the person (or in an adjacent room).

If you have not yet done usability testing, learn how from these excellent resources: Barnum, 2011; Krug, 2010; Rubin and Chisnell, 2008;

www.usability.gov

Here's what typically happens in a usability test session:

- The facilitator starts with a few questions to learn more about the participant and to make the participant comfortable.

- Then the participant tries to complete tasks (conversations, scenarios) with the site or app while thinking out loud.

- At the end, the facilitator asks a few more questions to get the participant's reaction to the site and to cover any specific issues (such as understanding of specific words on the site).

- Some groups use a formal rating-scale questionnaire at the end.

You can do this with or without video- and audiotaping. Someone should definitely take notes, but it can be with a specialized software program, word processing, or even on paper. Everyone connected to the project should observe either in person or remotely.

The level of analysis, reporting, and recommendations vary widely.

Even quicker: "A morning a month"

Formative testing. Three people. An hour each. One morning during the month. Teams should commit to doing testing this way every month on a regular schedule. Each month, the team selects specific issues to focus on and promises to act right away on the top insights from that month's testing. Each session follows the same pattern as in the previous description of "what most people do." Team members should observe the testing because everyone who observed (and only those who did) come together immediately after the three sessions to review insights and agree on changes. Brief write-up on agreement about insights and fixes. No formal report.

AAA
ACCESS Include people with special needs in your usability test to be sure that the site or app works for them.

What variations might we consider?

You can test

- remotely, with a facilitator
- remotely, without a facilitator
- around the globe
- in a group setting
- by fielding alternatives (A/B testing)

An interesting look at what different groups do for reports from formative usability testing: Theofanos and Quesenbery, 2005 (Although this paper dates from several years ago, the information in it is still what people do.)

"A morning a month" is the method in Krug, 2010.

Information on recruiting and working with seniors in usability testing – resources at http://redish.net/articles-slides/articles-slides-older-adults

Remotely, with a facilitator

You can do remote, facilitated tests with either method that I just described. The only difference is that people are not all in the same physical place. You use collaboration software to pass control of the screen from facilitator to participant and back again. You listen and talk either through the computer program or through a telephone connection. Observers can join from anywhere.

Working remotely greatly expands the reach of your testing. You can recruit the best participants no matter where they are. You can gain diversity among your participants without travel expenses.

Remotely, without a facilitator

With unmoderated testing, you trade the richness of think aloud for quantitative results from many people. Unmoderated testing may work well to know if people can *find* a specific piece of information. It's not the best technique for testing content when you want to know if the site has the content people need or if they understand the content (beyond finding a specific fact).

Many vendors now offer tools for unmoderated usability testing. For a good article on the pros and cons of unmoderated testing with a list of vendors – Soucy, 2010

Testing around the globe

Context matters. Culture matters. Language matters. If your web site is global, you should be sensitive to cultural differences. If you can, do usability testing in many contexts, cultures, and languages. You can do that either with local facilitators in different countries or remotely from one country to another.

Before you do any user-centered activities outside your own culture, educate yourself about working globally.

Barnum, 2010, has a running case study of testing the Chinese version of a hotel web site.

Other resources:

Quesenbery and Szuc, 2011, on how UX practitioners work globally

Dray and Siegel, 2005, on many aspects and cautions for international UX work

Testing in a group setting

In a typical usability test, the same facilitator holds individual sessions one after the other. And there's value in the continuity and consistency of having the same person interact with all the participants. But if you can't afford the time, you might do simultaneous sessions.

Hal Shubin of Interaction Design, Inc. (www.user.com) shared this story:

> The client needed quick feedback. Hal got four laptops, four participants, and four facilitators (himself and three quickly-trained people from the client's web team). They did four one-on-one sessions at the same time around the dining room table of one of the facilitators. Then, all eight

people – participants and facilitators – gathered in the living room to discuss what happened during the test sessions. Hal says the client learned a lot about how their customers use the web site and got good ideas about what needed to be done – all in one evening. It helped, of course, that the participants they selected were comfortable working in the same room and being together in the discussion afterwards.

Fielding alternatives (A/B testing)

Today, a common way to find out what works best with actual users is to launch different versions of content and see which does best in the marketplace. This is called A/B testing; although, of course, you could compare A, B, C, D, or more versions.

In A/B testing, "best" is the version that achieves a measurable goal: more sales, more completed forms, more pages looked at, and so on. Because conversion rates (getting people to click on an ad and then to complete a transaction) is so important to e-commerce companies, most now routinely use A/B testing.

A/B testing gives you real-world data. If you change only very specific aspects of the site, you know *what* made the difference. However, with A/B testing, you don't know *why*. Without listening to people, you don't know what about the change made it work (or not work). It may be hard to generalize from the results.

> **Check out** http://whichtestwon .com. **Each week, you get to see the results of a different real A/B test – and you get to match your guess about what happened in the test against other people's guesses and the actual results.**

Why not just do focus groups?

If your web team is part of a marketing department or you are in an agency that works primarily with marketing departments, you may hear, "we do usability testing; we get people together in a focus group."

A focus group is **not** the same as usability testing. They are different techniques that get you different information. Table 15-1 shows several points of difference.

What does a focus group need?

A well-run focus group is

- planned carefully with a prepared script and questions to ask
- facilitated by a trained person who can draw out the shy people and keep the overeager people from dominating the discussion
- allowed to stray from the script along interesting and relevant lines but kept within bounds so you get the information you need

Table 15-1 A focus group is different from a usability test

	Focus Group	Usability Test
People	8–10 at a time	1 at a time
Time	usually 2 hours	1 hour or less
Activity	talk; a group discussion where people react to what they are shown or asked	behavior, people actually use the site; usually also a brief individual interview without the influence of other group members
Good for	getting people's opinions, attitudes, desires, self-report	seeing how people actually do tasks; watching people interact with the site or app
Best time to do	only very early in the design process	iteratively, throughout the process from testing old site or app before revising, to paper prototypes, to working prototypes, to final site

Why isn't a focus group the best technique?

Focus groups are not the best technique for understanding how a web site or mobile app works for site visitors for two major reasons:

- **Group dynamics.** One person can trigger others agreeing to something they might not otherwise say. Even with a great facilitator, some people may not express their true feelings in the group setting.

- **Difference between talk and action.** What people say they do is often not what they actually do. People are not very good at imagining their own behavior. They have to actually put their hands on and "do" to realize when and how something will or won't work for them.

Can we combine usability testing and focus groups?

If you need to, you can combine aspects of usability testing with a focus group:

- First part of the time: Have people use the product either with a person watching and listening to each participant or letting the participants work on their own and take their own notes on where they succeed and where they have problems.

- Second part of the time: Bring them together to talk about the experience.

Hal Shubin's story would be an example. I've done this, calling it a task-based focus group.

A final point: Test the content!!

Lots of companies now do usability testing, but too many still focus only on the information architecture – on whether people can *find* what they need. That's necessary. But it's not enough. If your site visitors get to the right place, but the content doesn't work for them, they'll be frustrated and leave.

Don't stop when site visitors get to the right web page. Have them actually find the information on the page to satisfy their conversation or your test scenario.

If they are doing a transactional task (buying something, booking a ticket), watch them complete the task.

If they are looking up information, ask them to tell you what the content says. Don't just assume they have absorbed the message because they looked at the page.

Watch what they do on content pages. Do they skim? Do they read carefully? What parts do they read? Listen to what they say about the content.

Do usability testing to learn:

* Does the site have the content your site visitors want and need?
* Is the content presented with good information design – legible typography, good spacing, visible and useful headings?
* Is the content organized and broken up in a way that works for your site visitors?
* Does the writing help site visitors skim easily and read quickly?
* Are you using words that your site visitors understand immediately?
* Do site visitors interpret images to have the messages you meant?

Yes, you might ask them what they think of what they found. But also ask them to tell you what messages they got from the content. Test *understand* and *use* as well as *find*.

I hope this book has helped you create great content so that usability testing shows you are meeting your business goals by satisfying your site visitors' conversations.

Some useful articles, blog posts, and books

Adlin, T. and Pruitt, J., 2010, *The Essential Persona Lifecycle*, Morgan Kaufmann.

Ash, T., 2008, *Landing Page Optimization*, Sybex.

Asprey, M., 2010, *Plain Language for Lawyers*, 4th edition, Australia: Federation Press.

Barnum, C. M., 2011, *Usability Testing Essentials – Ready, Set…Test!*, Morgan Kaufmann.

Bauer, S., 2012 (January 10), It Works for "You": A User-Centric Guideline to Product Pages, *Smashing Magazine*, http://uxdesign .smashingmagazine.com/2012/01/10/it-works-for-you-a-user-centric-guideline-to-product-pages/

Bloomstein, M., 2012, *Content Strategy at Work*, Morgan Kaufmann.

Brinck, T., Gergle, D., and Wood, S., 2002, *Usability for the Web*, Morgan Kaufmann.

Chadwick-Dias, A., McNulty, and Tullis, T., 2003, Web usability and age: How design changes can improve performance, *ACM Conference on Universal Usability*, November, 30–37.

Coney, M. and Steehouder, M., 2000, Role playing on the web: Guidelines for designing and evaluating personas online, *Technical Communication*, 47, *3*, August, 327–340.

Cooper, A., Reimann, R., and Cronin, D., 2007, *About Face 3 – The Essentials of Interaction Design*, Wiley.

Courage, C. and Baxter, K., 2005, *Understanding Your Users*, Morgan Kaufmann.

Dillman, D., Smyth, J, and Christian, L, 2008, *Internet, Mail, and Mixed-Mode Surveys: The Tailored Design Method,* Wiley.

Dray, S. and Siegel, D., 2005, Sunday in Shanghai, Monday in Madrid?!, In N. Aykin (Ed.), *Usability and Internationalization of Information Technology*, Erlbaum, 189–212.

Druin, A., 2009, *Mobile Technology for Children*, Morgan Kaufmann.

Dumas, J. and Loring, B., 2008, *Moderating Usability Tests*, Morgan Kaufmann.

Dumas, J. and Redish, J., 1999, *A Practical Guide to Usability Testing*, revised edition, Intellect.

Gazzaley, A., 2009, The aging brain, *User Experience*, 8, *1*, 10–13, www.usabilityprofessionals.org/upa_publications/user_experience/past_issues/2009-1.html

Hackos, J. and Redish, J., 1998, *User and Task Analysis for Interface Design*, Wiley.

Halligan, B. and Shah, D., 2009, *Inbound Marking – Getting Found Using Google, Social Media, and Blogs*, Wiley.

Halvorson, K. and Rach, M., 2012, *Content Strategy*, 2nd edition, New Riders.

Handley, A. and Chapman, C., 2011, *Content Rules*, Wiley.

Hayes, J. R. and Bayzek, D., 2008, Understanding and Reducing the Knowledge Effect: Implications for Writers, *Written Communication*, 25, 104–118.

Henry, Shawn Lawton, 2007, *Just Ask! Integrating Accessibility Throughout Design*, http://uiaccess.com

Hinman, R., 2012, *The Mobile Frontier*, Rosenfeld Media.

Holtzblatt, K., Wendell, J., and Wood, S., 2004, *Rapid Contextual Design*, Morgan Kaufmann.

Jarrett, C. and Gaffney, G., 2009, *Forms that Work – Designing Web Forms for Usability*, Morgan Kaufmann.

Jarrett, C. and Minott, C., 2004, Making a better web form, *Proceedings of the Usability Professionals' Association Annual Conference*, http://www.editingthatworks.com/making%20a%20better%20web%20form.pdf

Johnson, J., 2010, *Designing with the Mind in Mind*, Morgan Kaufmann.

Jones, C., 2011, *Clout – The Art and Science of Influential Web Content*, New Riders.

Kaushik, A., 2009, *Web Analytics 2.0: The Art of Online Accountability and Science of Customer Centricity*, Sybex.

Kissane, E., 2011, *The Elements of Content Strategy*, A Book Apart.

Koyani, S., Bailey, R., and Nall, J., 2006, *Research-Based Web Design & Usability Guidelines*, 2nd edition, U.S. Department of Health & Human Services, www.usability.gov

Krug, S., 2010, *Rocket Surgery Made Easy*, New Riders.

Krug, S., 2005, *Don't Make Me Think!*, 2nd edition, New Riders.

Larson, K., 2004, The Science of Word Recognition, www.microsoft.com/typography/ctfonts/WordRecognition.aspx

Lindgaard, G., Fernandes, G., Dudek, C., and Brown, J., 2006, Attention web designers: You have 50 milliseconds to make a good first impression!, *Behaviour & Information Technology*, 25, *2*, March–April, 115–126.

Lupton, E., 2010, *Thinking with Type*, 2nd edition, Princeton Architectural Press.

Mathewson, J., Donatone, F., Fishel, C., 2010, *Audience, Relevance, and Search*, IBM Press.

Morville, P. and Rosenfeld, L., 2006, *Information Architecture for the World Wide Web: Designing Large-Scale Web Sites*, 3rd edition, O'Reilly.

Mulder, S. with Z. Yaar, 2007, *The User Is Always Right – A Practical Guide to Creating and Using Personas on the Web*, New Riders.

Nielsen, J., 2000, *Designing Web Usability*, New Riders.

Nielsen, J. and Loranger, H., 2006, *Prioritizing Web Usability*, New Riders.

Nielsen, J. and Pernice, K., 2010, *Eyetracking Web Usability*, New Riders, www.useit.com/eyetracking

O'Flahavan, L., 2011, The Bite, The Snack, And The Meal: How To Feed Content-Hungry Site Visitors, http://ewriteonline.com/articles/2011/11/bite-snack-and-meal-how-to-feed-content-hungry-site-visitors/

O'Grady, J. and O'Grady, K., 2008, *The Information Design Handbook*, F+W Media.

Pirolli, P., 2003, Exploring and finding information, In J. Carroll (Ed.), *HCI Models, Theories, and Frameworks: Toward a Multidisciplinary Science*, Morgan Kaufmann, 157–192. (Pirolli's work is also at www.parc.com)

Pruitt, J. and Adlin, T., 2006, *The Persona Lifecycle: A Field Guide for Interaction Designers*, Morgan Kaufmann.

Pulizzi, J. and Barrett, N., 2009, *Get Content, Get Customers*, McGraw Hill.

Quesenbery, W. and Brooks, K., 2010, *Storytelling for User Experience – Crafting Stories for Better Design*, Rosenfeld Media.

Quesenbery, W. and Szuc, D., 2012, *Global UX – Design and Research in a Connected World*, Morgan Kaufmann.

Rockley, A., 2012, *Managing Enterprise Content: A Unified Content Strategy*, 2nd edition, New Riders.

Rosenfeld, L., 2011, *Search Analytics for Your Site*, Rosenfeld Media.

Rubin, J. and Chisnell, D., 2008, *Handbook of Usability Testing*, 2nd edition, Wiley.

Scanlan, Chip, 2011 (March 2), Writing from the top down: Pros and cons of the inverted pyramid, Poynter.org, www.poynter.org/how-tos/newsgathering-storytelling/chip-on-your-shoulder/12754/writing-from-the-top-down-pros-and-cons-of-the-inverted-pyramid/

Soucy, K., 2010 (January 18), Unmoderated, remote usability testing: Good or evil?, *UX Matters*, www.uxmatters.com/mt/archives/2010/01/unmoderated-remote-usability-testing-good-or-evil.php

Spencer, D., 2009, *Card Sorting*, Rosenfeld Media.

Spool, J., 2005, Galleries: The hardest working page on your site, www.uie.com/articles/galleries

Spool, J., Perfetti, C., and Brittan, D., 2004, *Designing for the Scent of Information*, North Andover, MA: User Interface Engineering, www.uie.com

Stone, D., Jarrett, C., Woodroffe, M., and Minocha, S., 2005, *User Interface Design and Evaluation*, Morgan Kaufmann.

Summers, K. and Summers, M., 2005, Reading and navigational strategies of web users with lower literacy skills. *Proceedings from ASIS&T 2005*. http://iat.ubalt.edu/summers/papers/Summers_ASIST2005.pdf

Theofanos, M. F. and Quesenbery, W., 2005, Towards the design of effective formative test reports, *Journal of Usability Studies*, 1, *1*, November, 28–46. www.usabilityprofessionals.org/upa_publications/jus/2005_november/formative.html

Theofanos, M. F. and Redish, J. C., 2005, Helping low-vision and other users with web sites that meet their needs: Is one site for all feasible, *Technical Communication*, 52, *1*, February, 9–20. (Available at http://www.ingentaconnect.com/content/stc/tc)

Theofanos, M. F. and Redish, J. C., 2003, Guidelines for accessible and usable web sites: Observing users who work with screen readers, *Interactions*, X, *6*, November–December, 38–51. (This paper is also available at http://www.redish.net/content/papers.html)

Tidwell, J., 2010, *Designing Interfaces*, 2nd edition, O'Reilly.

Walter, A., 2011, *Designing for Emotion*, A Book Apart.

Walter, A., 2008, *Building Findable Websites – Web Standards, SEO, and Beyond*, New Riders.

Wroblewski, L., 2011, *Mobile First*, A Book Apart.

Wroblewski, L., 2008, *Web Form Design*, Rosenfeld Media.

A few of many useful web sites

A/B testing and conversion rates: www.whichtestwon.com

Accessibility: www.w3.org/WAI; www.section508.com; for links to information on accessibility for specific countries: www.w3.org/wai/policy

Nielsen, J., many important columns dating from 1996 to the present: www.useit.com

Older adults as web users: www.redish.net/articles-slides/articles-slides-older-adults

Plain language: www.plainlanguage.gov; www.centerforplainlanguage.org

SEO: www.searchengineland.com

Spool, J., many useful articles at www.uie.com

Usability: www.usability.gov; www.usabilitybok.org/methods

Usability Professionals' Association: www.upassoc.org

Some older research that's still valuable

Clark, H., and Haviland S., 1975, Comprehension and the given-new contract, In R. Freedle (Ed.), *Discourse production and comprehension*, Erlbaum, 1–40.

Dixon, P., 1987, The processing of organizational and component step information in written directions, *Journal of Memory and Language*, 26, 24–35.

Flower, L., Hayes, J. R., and Swarts, H., 1983, Revising function documents: The scenario principle, In P. Anderson, J. Brockmann, and C. Miller, (Eds.), *New Essays in Technical and Scientific Communication: Research, Theory, and Practice*, Baywood, 41–58.

Simon, H., 1997, *Administrative Behavior*, 4th edition, Free Press.

Subject Index

Index of Web Sites Shown as Examples

About Ginny Redish

Janice (Ginny) Redish is passionate about creating products that work for the people who use them.

As president of Redish & Associates, Inc., Ginny works with colleagues and clients on content strategy, information design, plain language, and especially on content as conversation.

Ginny always works closely with her clients' project teams and other consultants. She mentors and helps by reviewing current sites and apps, conducting usability studies, developing personas, setting and carrying out content strategy, and revising content to meet both the organization's goals and site visitors' needs.

Ginny is also sought after as a speaker and workshop leader. She is a dynamic instructor who has trained thousands of content contributors, copy writers, designers, developers, editors, writers, and others around the globe. She has keynoted conferences in eight countries.

To name just a few of the many clients Ginny has helped: AARP, the American Academy of Pediatrics, American Airlines, Hewlett-Packard, IBM, Nokia, SAP, Sony, Xerox. Ginny has also worked with many local, state, and federal government agencies.

Ginny is well known for her two earlier books, on usability testing and on user and task analysis. She has published numerous papers and book chapters on various aspects of user experience (UX), accessibility, plain language, and writing for the web.

Ginny's work has brought her many awards, including the President's Award from both the Usability Professionals' Association and the Society for Technical Communication (STC), the status of Fellow and the Rainey Award for Excellence in Research from STC, and awards for a lifetime of contributions to the field of clear writing from the ACM Special Interest Group on the Design of Communication, the IEEE Professional Communication Society, and the Center for Plain Language.

Ginny is a graduate of Bryn Mawr College and holds a Ph.D. in Linguistics from Harvard University.

Visit Ginny's web site at www.redish.net